P9-DMX-711

DATE DUE

STUDENT'S GUIDE TO LANDMARK CONGRESSIONAL LAWS ON THE FIRST AMENDMENT

STUDENT'S GUIDE TO LANDMARK CONGRESSIONAL LAWS

ON THE FIRST AMENDMENT

CLYDE E. WILLIS

STUDENT'S GUIDE TO
LANDMARK CONGRESSIONAL LAWS
John R. Vile, Series Editor

Greenwood Press
Westport, Connecticut • London

Library of Congress Cataloging-in-Publication Data

Willis, Clyde E.
    Student's guide to landmark congressional laws on the First Amendment / Clyde E. Willis.
       p. cm.—(Student's guide to landmark congressional laws, ISSN 1537–3150)
    Includes bibliographical references and index.
    ISBN 0–313–31416–0 (alk. paper)
    1. Freedom of speech—United States—History—Sources. 2. Freedom of religion—
United States—History—Sources. I. Title: Landmark congressional laws on the first
amendment. II. Title. III. Series.
    KF4770.W55   2002
    342.73'085—dc21   2001050137

British Library Cataloguing in Publication Data is available.

Library of Congress Catalog Card Number: 2001050137
ISBN: 0–313–31416–0
ISSN: 1537–3150

First published in 2002

Greenwood Press, 88 Post Road West, Westport, CT 06881
An imprint of Greenwood Publishing Group, Inc.
www.greenwood.com

Printed in the United States of America

The paper used in this book complies with the
Permanent Paper Standard issued by the National
Information Standards Organization (Z39.48–1984).

10 9 8 7 6 5 4 3 2 1

Contents

Series Foreword

Most of the Founding Fathers who met at the Constitutional Convention in Philadelphia in the summer of 1787 probably anticipated that the legislative branch would be the most powerful of the three branches of the national government that they created. For all practical purposes, this was the only branch of government with which the onetime colonists had experience under the Articles of Confederation. Moreover, the delegates discussed this branch first and at greatest length at the convention, the dispute over representation in this body was one of the convention's most contentious issues, and the Founding Fathers made it the subject of the first and longest article of the new Constitution.

With the president elected indirectly through an electoral college and the members of the Supreme Court appointed by the president with the advice and consent of the Senate and serving for life terms, the framers of the Constitution had little doubt that Congress—and especially the House of Representatives, whose members were directly elected by the people for short two-year terms—would be closest to the people. As a consequence, they invested Congress with the awesome "power of the purse" that had been at issue in the revolutionary dispute with Great Britain, where the colonists' position had been encapsulated in the phrase "no taxation without representation." The framers also entrusted Congress with the more general right to adopt laws to carry out a variety of enumerated powers and other laws "necessary and proper" to the implementation of these powers—the basis for the doctrine of implied powers.

Wars and the threats of wars have sometimes tilted the modern balance of power toward the president, who has gained in a media age from his position as a single individual. Still, Congress has arguably been the most powerful branch of government over the long haul, and one might expect its power to increase with the demise of the Cold War. Especially in the aftermath of President Franklin D. Roosevelt's New Deal and President Lyndon B. Johnson's Great Society program, the number and complexity of laws have increased with the complexity of modern society and the multitude of demands that citizens have placed on modern governments. Courts have upheld expansive interpretations of federal powers under the commerce clause, the war-powers provisions, and the power to tax and spend for the general welfare, and in recent elections Democratic and Republican candidates alike have often called for expansive new federal programs.

It has been noted that there are 297 words in the Ten Commandments, 463 in the Bill of Rights, 266 in the Gettysburg Address, and more than 26,000 in a federal directive regulating the price of cabbage. Although the U.S. Constitution can be carried in one's pocket, the compilation of federal laws in the *U.S. Code* and the *U.S. Code Annotated* requires many volumes, not generally available in high-school and public libraries. Perhaps because of this modern prolixity and complexity, students often consider the analysis of laws to be the arcane domain of lawyers and law reviewers. Ironically, scholars, like this author, who focus on law, and especially constitutional law, tend to devote more attention to the language of judicial decisions interpreting laws than to the laws themselves.

Because knowledge of laws and their impact needs to be made more widely accessible, this series on Landmark Congressional Laws presents and examines laws relating to a number of important topics. These currently include education, First Amendment rights, civil rights, the environment, the rights of young people, women's rights, and health and social security. Each subject is a matter of importance that should be of key interest to high-school and college students. A college professor experienced in communicating ideas to undergraduates has compiled each of these volumes. Each author has selected major laws in his or her subject area and has described the politics of these laws, considering such aspects as their adoption, their interpretation, and their impact.

The laws in each volume are arranged chronologically. The entry on each law features an introduction that explains the law, its significance, and its place within the larger tapestry of legislation on the issues. A selection from the actual text of the law itself follows the introduction. This arrangement thus provides ready access to texts that are often difficult for students to find while highlighting major provisions, often taken from literally hundreds of pages, that students and scholars might spend hours to distill on their own.

These volumes are designed to be profitable to high-school and college students who are examining various public policy issues. They should also help interested citizens, scholars, and legal practitioners needing a quick, but thorough and accurate, introduction to a specific area of public policy-making. Although each book is designed to cover highlights of the entire history of federal legislation within a given subject area, the authors of these volumes have also designed them so that individuals who simply need to know the background and major provisions of a single law (the Civil Rights Act of 1964, for example) can quickly do so.

The Founding Fathers of the United States devised a system of federalism dividing power between the state and national governments. Thus, in many areas of legislation, even a complete overview of national laws will prove inadequate unless it is supplemented with knowledge of state and even local laws. This is duly noted in entries on laws where national legislation is necessarily incomplete and where powers are shared among the three layers of government. The U.S. system utilizes a system of separation of powers that divides authority among three branches of the national government. Thus, while these volumes keep the focus on legislation, they also note major judicial decisions and presidential initiatives relating to the laws covered.

Although the subjects of this series are worthy objects of study in their own right, they are especially appropriate topics for students and scholars in a system of representative democracy like the United States, where citizens who are at least eighteen years of age have the right to choose those who will represent them in public office. In government, those individuals, like James Madison, Abraham Lincoln, and Woodrow Wilson, who have acquired the longest and clearest view of the past are frequently those who can also see the farthest into the future. This series is presented in the hope that it will help students both to understand the past and to equip themselves for future lives of good citizenship.

This editor wishes to thank his friends at Greenwood Press, his colleagues both at his own university and at other institutions of higher learning who have done such an able job of highlighting and explaining the laws that are the focus of this series, and those students, scholars, and citizens who have responded by reading and utilizing these volumes. When the Founding Fathers drew up a constitution, they depended not only on a set of structures and rights but also on the public-spiritedness and education of future citizens. When Benjamin Franklin was asked what form of government the Founding Fathers had created, he reportedly responded, "A republic, if you can keep it." When we inform ourselves and think deeply about the government's role in major areas of public policy, we honor the faith and foresight of those who bequeathed this government to us.

John R. Vile
Middle Tennessee State University

Preface

We have enshrined some of the most cherished rights of Americans in the First Amendment to the United States Constitution, including freedom of religion, speech, press, the right to assemble, and petition the government for a redress of grievances. Yet a recent survey of the American public by The Freedom Forum's First Amendment Center concluded that "Americans respect the First Amendment as an ideal but are ambivalent when it protects offensive ideas or troubling speech."[1] For example, although 74 percent of those surveyed believe that the First Amendment does not go too far in the rights it guarantees, 51 percent believe that the American press has too much freedom to do what it wants. Even though 95 percent of Americans believe that people should be allowed to express unpopular opinions, 74 percent do not believe that Americans should be permitted to burn or deface the American flag as a political statement, and 61 percent believe that it is presently prohibited by law. While 29 percent believe Americans have too little freedom of religion, almost 20 percent believe that the First Amendment was never intended to (and presumably should not) apply to religious groups that most people consider being extreme or on the fringe. Despite the fact that 65 percent of Americans consider monetary contributions to a political candidate to be an expression of free speech, 57 percent believe that restrictions should be placed on how much money an individual can contribute to someone else's election campaign, and 53 percent even believe that the government should place restrictions on how much money political candidates can contribute to their own election campaigns.

This paradoxical attitude toward First Amendment freedoms is explained by what one observer calls "a right not to be offended," by which he means the right to protect oneself from the rights of others.[2] Thus, while people are concerned with the rights they can exercise, they are also concerned with how they are affected when others exercise those same rights.

The First Amendment can also create tensions in other circumstances. Take, for instance, situations in which the First Amendment specifically prohibits Congress from enacting laws, but Congress is nonetheless obligated to secure other rights that can run counter to those First Amendment freedoms. One such situation involves national security. Although the government is obviously and legitimately concerned with protecting the security of the country, many laws deemed necessary to achieve that end can easily conflict with freedom of expression. Likewise, we see similar conflicts in congressional efforts to regulate pornography on the Internet for the benefit of children without endangering freedom of expression for adults.

As life becomes increasingly more complex and interrelated, the paradoxical nature of the First Amendment becomes more troublesome. Moreover, considering the social and legal complexities caused by this situation, Congress is assuming a broader and increasingly important role as the arbiter of First Amendment rights and other conflicting rights that are implicit in a democratic society. It is therefore a concern that warrants a closer look at the relationship of Congress to the First Amendment by examining the congressional landmarks in this significant field.

NOTES

1. See Kenneth A. Paulson, "State of the First Amendment 2000," First Amendment Center, Nashville. The survey can be accessed at http://www.freedomforum.org.

2. Robert O. Wyatt, *Free Expression and the American Public: A Survey Commemorating the 200th Anniversary of the First Amendment*, The American Society of Newspaper Editors Foundation, Reston, Virginia, 1991, p. 10.

Timeline of Events Related to Congress and the First Amendment

1620	Puritan separatists arrive at Plymouth Harbor on the Mayflower.
1621	Puritans of Plymouth Colony join native Wampanoag Indians in a Thanksgiving ceremony.
1634	Maryland is founded as a Catholic colony with religious tolerance.
1641	Massachusetts General Court drafts the first broad statement of liberties.
1663	Rhode Island grants religious freedom.
1708	Connecticut enacts a dissenter statute allowing full liberty of worship.
1710	The English Statute of Queen Anne institutes modern copyright law.
1712	Massachusetts Bay Colony enacts the first American anti-obscenity law.
1735	German-born colonial printer and journalist John Peter Zenger was acquitted of libel charges in New York City, establishing a legal precedent for freedom of the press.
1771	Virginia jails Baptist worshipers for preaching contrary to Anglican tenets.
1774	Massachusetts jails Baptists for refusing to pay religious tax.
1776	Continental Congress adopts the Declaration of Independence.

	Virginia's House of Burgesses passes the Virginia Declaration of Rights.
1786	The Virginia legislature adopts the Ordinance of Religious Freedom, which disestablishes the Anglican Church as the official church and prohibits harassment based on religious differences.
1787	Congress enacts the Northwest Ordinance, which deals with how the territories are to be governed, and the Constitutional Convention opens.
1789	The United States Constitution is adopted.
1790	Congress enacts the Copyright Act, the first intellectual property law.
1791	The Federal Bill of Rights is adopted.
1792	Thomas Paine publishes *The Rights of Man*.
1794	The Whiskey Rebellion breaks out in western Pennsylvania in protest of new taxes.
1795	President George Washington grants amnesty to the participants in the Whiskey Rebellion.
1796	Andrew Jackson opposes the inclusion of the word *God* in Tennessee's constitution.
1797–1798	French efforts to bribe American diplomats in the XYZ Affair embitter U.S. relations with France.
1798	Congress enacts the Alien and Sedition Acts, restricting aliens and curtailing freedom of the press, in anticipation of an expected war with France. These consist of the Alien Act, the Alien Enemies Act, and the Sedition Act.
	James Madison and Thomas Jefferson write the Kentucky & Virginia Resolutions in resistance to the Alien and Sedition Acts.
1801	Thomas Jefferson is selected as president and pardons those convicted under the Alien and Sedition Acts.
1803	The Supreme Court, in *Marbury v. Madison*, establishes the doctrine of judicial review, whereby the courts can decide statutes to be unconstitutional.
1836	Congress adopts a "gag rule" preventing debate on antislavery proposals.
1862	Congress enacts the Morrill Anti-Bigamy Law, which prohibits the practice of polygamy.

1864	Congress authorizes "In God We Trust" to be imprinted on U.S. coins.
	The first million-dollar presidential campaign occurs.
1868	The Fourteenth Amendment is ratified, which eventually extends the federal Bill of Rights to the states.
1873	Congress enacts the Comstock Act, which criminalizes the publication, distribution, and possession of obscene materials.
1879	The Supreme Court, in *Reynolds v. United States*, upholds the 1862 Morrill Anti-Bigamy Law.
1882	President James A. Garfield is assassinated, which leads to the 1883 Pendleton Act.
1895, 1896	Congress enacts two Indian Appropriations Acts, lowering the federal funding level and making U.S. government policy for no further appropriations for education in Christian missionary schools.
1901	President William McKinley is assassinated, which leads to laws deporting aliens.
1907	Congress enacts the Tillman Act, which for the first time bans some contributions to political election campaigns.
1910	Congress enacts the Publicity Act, which for the first time requires disclosure of federal campaign finances.
1917	Congress enacts the Espionage Act, which curtails freedom of expression during World War I.
	Congress declares war against Germany.
1918	Congress enacts the Sedition Act, strengthening and broadening the provisions of the Espionage Act of 1917.
1919	The Third Communist International (COMINTERN) is established by the Soviet Union to promote world communism by revolutionary means.
	The Supreme Court upholds the 1917 Espionage Act and introduces the "clear and present danger test" in *Schenck v. United States*.
	The Supreme Court, in *Debs v. United States*, upholds the 1918 Sedition Act.
1919–1920	U.S. Attorney General A. Mitchell Palmer and J. Edgar Hoover conduct massive raids, rounding up and deporting alien residents.

1920   The American Civil Liberties Union is organized to champion constitutional liberties in the United States.

1921   The Teapot Dome Scandal, involving illegal political contributions, occurs and leads to campaign finance reform.

President Warren G. Harding grants pardon to Eugene V. Debs, a presidential candidate who was convicted under the 1917 Espionage Act as amended in the 1918 Sedition Act.

The Supreme Court, in *Newberry v. United States*, denies congressional authority to regulate primary elections.

1925   High school teacher John T. Scopes is convicted in the "Scopes Monkey Trial" in Dayton, Tennessee, for teaching the theory of evolution in a biology class.

Congress enacts the Corrupt Practices Act in response to the Teapot Dome Scandal, establishing for the first time a broad-based regulatory system for election campaigns.

1926   Congress enacts the Railway Labor Act, which extends the right of association to unionized rail workers.

H.L. Mencken is arrested for distributing copies of *American Mercury* in violation of obscenity laws.

1930   A Boston bookseller is convicted for violating obscenity law by selling Theodore Dreiser's *An American Tragedy*.

1933   President Roosevelt pardons those convicted under the espionage acts of 1917–1919.

1934   The Supreme Court, in *Burroughs v. United States*, upholds the 1925 Corrupt Practices Act.

1935   Congress enacts the National Labor Relations Act, which extends freedom of expression and association to industrial workers.

1939   Congress enacts the Hatch Act, prohibiting federal employees from participating in political campaigns.

Georgia, Massachusetts, and Virginia symbolically ratify the Bill of Rights.

1940   Congress enacts the Alien Registration (Smith) Act, which criminalizes advocating the violent overthrow of the government or belonging to any group devoted to such advocacy.

Congress enacts the Hatch Act Amendments, limiting for the first time the amount of contribution that individuals may contribute to political campaigns.

1941	Congress authorizes the president to establish an Office of Censorship.
	Congress declares war against Japan after the Japanese bomb Pearl Harbor.
1942	President Roosevelt issues Executive Order 9066, authorizing the internment of Japanese Americans.
1943	The Supreme Court, in *National Broadcasting Co. v. United States*, holds that no one has a First Amendment right to a radio license or to monopolization of a radio frequency.
1945	World War II ends in the Pacific after the United States drops two atomic bombs on Japan.
1946	Winston Churchill makes his famous "Iron Curtain" speech, warning of Soviet aggression.
1947	The Communist Information Bureau (COMINFORM) is established to publish propaganda to encourage the international communist movement.
	The House Committee on Un-American Activities investigates suspected communist activities within the U.S. motion picture industry.
	The Supreme Court, in *United Public Workers of America (C.I.O.) et al. v. Mitchell et al.*, upholds the 1940 Hatch Act.
1948	Congress enacts the Universal Military Training and Service Act.
1949	Communist insurgents led by Mao Zedong capture China.
1950	The Korean conflict begins with the invasion of South Korea.
	Senator Joseph McCarthy launches a vigorous anticommunist campaign.
	Congress enacts the Internal Security (McCarran) Act, requiring, among other things, that communist organizations divulge information about themselves. This includes the Subversive Activities Control Act and the Emergency Detention Act.
1951	The Supreme Court, in *Dennis v. United States*, upholds convictions under the Smith Act.
1953	Ethel and Julius Rosenberg are executed for violating the 1917 Espionage Act by passing U.S. atomic bomb secrets to the Soviet Union.
1954	The Vietnam conflict begins.

Congress enacts the Communist Control Act of 1954, completely banning the Communist Party from political activity in the United States.

1956   Congress establishes the national motto: "In God We Trust," which had appeared on U.S. coins since 1864.

The Supreme Court, in *Railway Employees' Dept. v. Hanson*, upholds the 1926 Railway Labor Act's union shop provision.

1957   The Supreme Court, in *Roth v. United States*, holds that obscenity is not constitutionally protected speech or press.

The Supreme Court, in *Yates v. United States*, overturns convictions that were obtained under the Smith Act.

1961   The Supreme Court, in *Communist Party v. Subversives Activities Control Board*, upholds part of the 1950 Subversive Activities Control Act (part of the McCarran Act).

The Supreme Court, in *Scales v. United States*, upholds the Smith Act's registration requirement.

The Supreme Court, in *Noto v. United States*, overturns a conviction under the Smith Act.

1964   The student-led Free Speech Movement begins at the University of California–Berkeley.

The Supreme Court, in *Aptheker v. Secretary of State* and *Albertson v. Subversive Activities Control Board*, invalidates part of the 1950 Subversive Activities Control Act.

1965   Congress enacts the Draft Card Mutilation Act, criminalizing the destruction of draft registration cards.

Congress enacts Title I of the Elementary and Secondary Education Act, making public funds available to students and parents of students who attend sectarian schools.

1968   Congress enacts the Flag Protection Act, making it a crime to mutilate, deface, defile, or burn the U.S. flag.

The Supreme Court, in *United States v. O'Brien*, upholds the 1965 Draft Card Mutilation Act.

1970   Congress enacts the Family Planning Services and Population Research Act, which prohibits funding to organizations that use abortion.

The United States begins a military incursion into Cambodia.

1971   Congress enacts the Federal Election Campaign Act, which constitutes the first major overhaul of election campaign laws since the Corrupt Practices Act of 1925.

1974   Congress amends the Federal Election Campaign Act in the wake of the Watergate Scandal.

1976   Congress enacts the Tax Reform Act, restricting tax benefits to lobbyists.

            Congress enacts the Copyright Act, which contains provisions that protect the public's freedom of expression.

            The Supreme Court, in *Buckley v. Valeo*, upholds and invalidates parts of the Federal Election Campaign Act of 1971 as amended in 1974.

1977   President Jimmy Carter grants amnesty to those who evaded the draft during the Vietnam War.

1978   Congress enacts the American Indian Religious Freedom Act granting Native Americans rights of freedom to believe, express, and exercise the traditional religions of the American Indian, Eskimo, Aleut, and Native Hawaiians, including but not limited to access to sites, use and possession of sacred objects, and the freedom to worship through ceremonials and traditional rites.

1984   Congress enacts the Equal Access Act, which grants equality of opportunity to religiously oriented student groups in high school activities.

1985   The Supreme Court, in *Aguilar v. Felton*, invalidates the use of federal funds for education under Title I of the 1965 Elementary and Secondary Education Act.

1989   The Supreme Court, in *Texas v. Johnson*, extends First Amendment protection to flag burning as political protest, thereby overturning a provision of Texas's penal code.

            The *Conseil Europeen pour la Recherche Nucleaire* (CERN) begins the World Wide Web.

            Congress enacts the Anti-Dial-a-Porn Act, restricting a minor's access to pornographic material delivered by telephone.

1990   The Supreme Court, in *Board of Education of the Westside Community Schools v. Mergens*, upholds the 1984 Equal Access Act.

Congress enacts the National Foundation for the Arts and Humanities Act, restricting use of federal funds for cultural programs considered obscene.

The Supreme Court, in *United States v. Eichman*, invalidates the 1989 Flag Protection Act.

1991   The Supreme Court, in *Employment Division (Oregon) v. Smith*, upholds the denial of unemployment benefits to persons fired for using peyote in religious ceremonies.

The Supreme Court, in *Rust v. Sullivan*, upholds the 1970 Family Planning and Population Research Act.

1993   Congress enacts the Religious Freedom Restoration Act, placing heavier standards for governments to meet when their actions restrict religious freedom.

1994   Congress amends the American Indian Religious Freedom Act of 1978, shielding the use of peyote by members of the Native American Church from criminal prosecution.

1996   Congress enacts the Personal Responsibility and Work Opportunity Reconciliation Act, requiring states to contract with faith-based organizations on an equal basis with secular organizations.

1997   The Supreme Court, in *Boerne v. Flores*, invalidates the 1993 Religious Freedom Restoration Act.

The Supreme Court, in *Agostini v. Felton*, overturns its 1985 ruling in *Aguilar v. Felton*, approving the use of federal funds for education under Title I of the 1965 Elementary and Secondary Education Act.

1998   Congress enacts the Child Online Protection Act, restricting indecent material on the Internet.

2000   Congress enacts the Religious Land Use and Institutionalized Persons Act, reinstating some of the provisions in the 1993 Religious Freedom Protection Act.

2001   The Supreme Court, in *Legal Services Corporation v. Velazquez*, invalidates the limit on expression contained in the 1974 Legal Services Corporation Act.

Introduction

All legislative powers herein granted shall be vested in a Congress of
the United States, which shall consist of a Senate and House of Representatives.
                —Article I, Section 1 of the United States Constitution

Congress shall make no law respecting an establishment of religion,
or prohibiting the free exercise thereof; or abridging the freedom of
speech, or of the press; or the right of the people peaceably to assemble, and to petition the government for a redress of grievances.
                —Amendment I to the United States Constitution

In the past two centuries, Congress and the First Amendment have
had a varied and meaningful relationship. As we examine landmark
congressional laws that affect and are affected by the First Amendment, we will see that they involve internal security and symbolic
speech that were responses to great issues in world politics. The
presentation of the selected landmark statutes will place them
within the political and historical environment that produced them,
followed by an examination of the constitutional or legal issues that
surround them, ending with a verbatim presentment of relevant
portions of the law. We will see how changes in technology have
caused congressional reaction in fields as disparate as campaign
financing and obscenity on the World Wide Web. By looking at
laws regulating labor relations and intellectual property, we will see
how an effort to enhance certain First Amendment rights can have
the opposite effect. We will also examine the means by which Congress has used public financing to influence certain political ex-

pression. Finally, we will look at several issues in the field of religious freedom and observe how Congress has attempted to skirt the abyss between the individual's right to practice religion and the government establishment of a religious preference.

CONGRESS AND THE CONSTITUTION

There have been three types of congressional bodies in the history of the United States: the two Continental Congresses, the Congress under the Articles of Confederation, and the Congress that we know today. The First and Second Continental Congresses met in 1774 and 1775–1781, respectively. At the First, delegates from the thirteen colonies met and agreed to petition King George III to redress their grievances. The Second began meeting on May 10, 1775, and adopted the Declaration of Independence thirteen months later. Other accomplishments of the Second Continental Congress included the adoption of a constitution for a more permanent government. Members of this Congress adopted the Articles of Confederation on November 15, 1777, and submitted them to the states for ratification. A new government came into existence in March 1781, when the last state—Maryland—ratified this constitution.

The confederation was a very weak and ineffective government. In the words of its constitution, it was essentially a "league of friendship" among the states, with each state retaining its sovereignty and independence. There were many features of the confederation that contributed to the weakness. The powers of Congress under the Articles of Confederation were limited and, furthermore, there was no executive or enforcement mechanism to carry out what Congress did manage to command.[1] In May 1785, a congressional committee recommended changes to the Articles of Confederation, but nothing came directly of it. The following year a group of states led by Virginia began an independent movement to create a convention that would revise and amend the Articles of Confederation. On February 21, 1787, the confederation Congress adopted a resolution that supported such a move, and on May 25, fifty-five delegates led by George Washington began meeting in Philadelphia, which led to the federal Constitution of 1789. The constitutional convention sent its proposal for a new federal constitution to the confederation Congress on September 17, 1787, which, in turn, submitted it on September 28 to the conventions of each state for ratification. On June 21, 1788, New Hampshire became the ninth state to accept the new constitution, thereby creating a new federal government among the ratifying states.[2] The new federal government with the current Congress was scheduled to begin operating on March 4, 1979, under the 1789 Constitution.[3]

THE ORIGIN OF THE FIRST AMENDMENT

Article I, Section 1 of the 1789 Constitution of the United States provides that "All legislative powers herein granted shall be vested in a Congress of the United States, which shall consist of a Senate and House of Representatives."[4] The main task for the first federal Congress was to establish a government.[5] It had to organize itself and the other two branches of government. The executive branch had to be established, which included the presidency and all executive departments, including the military. The judicial branch was established through the Judiciary Act of 1789, which continues to form the basic structure of the federal court system. Other important items of business for the first federal Congress, as it met in New York City, included the creation of a system of public revenue, an arrangement for governing the territorial lands in the west—this included relations with the Native Americans—and a foreign relations policy.

Yet, with all of the pressing business of the day on so many extremely important structural matters, the issues of protecting individual liberty and states' rights by placing restrictions on the power of the federal government were not to be ignored.[6] On June 8, 1789, even before the last three states had approved the new Constitution, Representative James Madison of Virginia, who had originally opposed a bill of rights, introduced a series of amendments designed to protect individual rights by incorporating them into various parts of the Constitution's text. The amendments became a separate, self-contained Bill of Rights when Representative Roger Sherman of Connecticut insisted that they be tacked onto the Constitution to maintain the language and format of the Constitution as adopted. Although there were many members of Congress who wanted some form of protection of individual liberties, the sentiment was far from unanimous. Opposition to Madison's amendments came from Anti-Federalists, who were more concerned about protecting states' rights than individual rights, and Federalists, who considered them unnecessary and undesirable. Some, like the Federalist Representative James Jackson of Georgia, believed that establishing the structure of government took precedence. Comparing the Constitution to a new ship, Representative Jackson declared:

> Our constitution, sir, is like a vessel just launched, and lying at the wharf, she is untried, you can hardly discover any one of her properties; it is not known how she will answer her helm, or lay her course; whether she will bear in safety the precious freight to be deposited in her hold. But, in this state, will the prudent merchant attempt alterations? Will he employ two thousand workmen to rear off the planking and take asunder the frame? He certainly will not. Let us gentlemen, fit out our vessel, set up her masts, and expand her sails, and be guided by the experiment in our alterations. If she sails upon an uneven keel, let us right her by adding weight where it is wanting. In this way, we may remedy her defects to the satisfaction of all concerned; but if we proceed now to make alterations, we may deface a beauty; or deform a well proportioned piece of workmanship.[7]

The debate on Madison's proposals was somewhat bitter and sometimes quibbling, as illustrated by comments made concerning the freedom of religion amendment. Madison had suggested that "no national religion shall be established by law," to which a member of Congress objected to the use of the word *national*. Massachusetts Representative Elbridge Gerry, at times a Federalist and at other times an Anti-Federalist, protested because the word *nationalist* had been, to his mind, dishonorably applied to the Anti-Federalists in the battle over ratification. Gerry was so upset by the term that he declared that the contending groups "ought not to have been distinguished by federalists and anti-federalists, but rats and anti-rats."[8] Senator William Grayson of Virginia summed up the opponents' position as "playing the after-game," or, as we would put it today, "Monday morning quarterbacking."[9] In short, as Representative Jackson put it, many wanted to "let the constitution have a fair trial, let it be examined by experience, discover by that test what its errors are, and then talk of amending."

In spite of the opposition and bickering, Congress approved and submitted twelve amendments to the states on September 28, 1789. On December 15, ten of the twelve became part of the United States Constitution upon ratification by Virginia, which was the tenth state to do so. The first two proposed amendments failed; thus the third proposal became the First Amendment, and the grant of legislative authority set forth in Article I became limited in very significant ways. The First Amendment provided that "Congress shall make no law respecting an establishment of religion, or prohibiting the free exercise thereof; or abridging the freedom of speech, or of the press; or the right of the people peaceably to assemble, and to petition the government for a redress of grievances."

THE FIRST AMENDMENT AND THE ROLE OF CONGRESS

Congress is not most likely the first governmental institution that comes to mind when the First Amendment is mentioned. Most likely, the first thing to come to mind is the Supreme Court. After all, ever since Chief Justice John Marshall declared in *Marbury v. Madison* (1803) that "it is emphatically the province and duty of the judicial department to say what the [constitution] is," the judiciary has been just that—the last, authoritative interpreter of the Constitution (p. 177).[10] Whereas a Supreme Court decision is always the culmination of an important legal battle and is issued by the panel of nine black-robed Justices as one of a few long-awaited opinions each May and June, congressional enactments exist in a much different world. Congressional enactments occur at the beginning, almost before the battle has begun, and although they can be equally influential in our lives, there are so many issues and events simultaneously transpiring in Congress every work day of the year that even high-profile legislation can get lost in the bustle.

The second governmental institution most likely to come to mind when the First Amendment is mentioned is still not the Congress, but state governments. The reason for this is simple though perhaps surprising. By far, most laws and governmental actions that affect our lives come from state and local governments.[11] With so much media attention given to the federal government, it is easy to forget that it is limited to the powers that are derived from the Constitution. State governments, on the contrary, are unlimited—except for the powers given to the federal government by the U.S. Constitution. A list of some legal categories that are primarily concerns of state and local governments will illustrate how much state and local governments pervade our daily lives: torts (personal injury) and compensation systems, like workers' compensation programs; contracts, including all kinds of commercial and business transactions, property ownership and land use, criminal laws, and business organizations. Moreover, states are not precluded from acting in many areas that are concerns of the federal government. Thus, as we will see, the areas that are most likely to impact First Amendment freedoms come from state regulations such as laws affecting property use and educational programs.[12]

However important the Supreme Court and state governments are, Congress is a major participant in issues that concern First Amendment rights. First of all, Congress has been actively engaged in enacting laws that have a direct and significant bearing on First Amendment rights since the beginning of the nation. For example, the first intellectual property law was enacted with the Copyright Act of 1790. In 1798, Congress created a First Amendment furor with the passage of the Alien and Sedition Acts. Congress acknowledged an involvement with religious issues as early as the Northwest Ordinance of 1787, and during the first half of the nineteenth century it financed Christian education for Native Americans in a systematic way.

Second, Congress is becoming an extremely important "player" each year as the "playing field" changes. For example, whereas some years ago obscenity would have been more of a local concern regarding what books were sold at the local newsstand or what motion picture played at the local cinema, technology has brought everyone from Podunk to Manhattan into a common community that is so far removed from state boundaries that only Congress can aspire to regulate obscenity, as it is attempting to do with laws such as the Anti-Dial-a-Porn Act of 1989 and the Child Online Protection Act of 1998. Another example is that the federal government is becoming ever more involved in financing both public and sectarian schools; it is also using faith-based organizations to provide social services, through the Personal Responsibility and Work Opportunity Reconciliation Act of 1996.

THE STRUCTURE OF THIS BOOK

This work is not intended to be a comprehensive survey of First Amendment law. For one thing, its scope—congressional legislation and the relatively small amount of interaction between Congress and the courts—is insufficient to present a comprehensive treatment of First Amendment law. Furthermore, there already exists an abundance of general surveys to consult on First Amendment law. Nonetheless, there is a need for a work that focuses on the role of Congress by examining and presenting the landmark statutes that it has enacted in the field. A statute may be classified as "landmark" for several reasons:

1. It represents an important stage of development or a turning point in the history of the field concerned, such as the Comstock Act of 1873, which initiated federal involvement in the war against obscenity, or the Indian Appropriations Act of 1895, which ended an era of federal funding of Christian missionary schools for Native Americans, while ushering in an era of public school funding.

2. It establishes a significant legal concept or constitutional doctrine, as the Sedition Act of 1798 did by changing the common law of seditious libel in significant ways, or as the National Labor Relations Act of 1935 did by extending the right of association to workers in an industrial setting by allowing them to organize and bargain collectively.

3. It is a response to a particularly significant historical situation, such as the American Indian Religious Freedom Act Amendment of 1994, which exempted members of the Native American Church from prosecution under the antidrug laws for their ceremonial use of peyote.

4. It illuminates the rivalry that exists between Congress and the judiciary, such as the Religious Freedom Restoration Act of 1993 and the Religious Land Use and Institutionalized Persons Act of 2000.

In this book, the statutes are presented in a format that combines chronological order with a topical or categorical arrangement. The statutes are initially placed in topical categories—such as internal security, election campaign activities, and religion—and then examined in chronological order. The First Amendment affects each category differently because each category is imbedded in separate historical and policy situations. Moreover, congressional and judicial attitudes toward the different categories vary with different topics at different times.

Each chapter begins with a general overview of the subject matter addressed by the statutes covered in that chapter and a brief summary of how the statutes relate to each other within the chapter's context. Examination of the specific statute begins with the historical background of each statute, followed by a brief narrative summary of the statute's provision, then an examination of its application. This necessarily involves court cases that considered First Amendment claims presented to contest either the statute or some governmental action taken pursuant to the statute. Finally, each chapter concludes with pertinent excerpts of the statute, carefully edited for ease of use by students and other interested readers. The Appendices contain tables of the statutes and cases listed in the text with complete citations that may be useful to the reader for further inquiry.

After this introductory section, Chapter 1 covers statutes involving internal security. This issue not only extends to the very beginning of the nation, it has perhaps caused more antagonism among different people than any other issue has. Though never tested in a Supreme Court battle, the Alien and Sedition Acts of 1798 caused a tremendous First Amendment battle between the Federalists and the Republicans. Nonetheless, the Sedition Act did inaugurate a basic change in the law of sedition by recognizing truth as a defense to a charge of making statements that incited rebellion against the authority of a state. The Espionage Act of 1917 and the Sedition Act of 1918, as well as the Alien Registration (Smith) Act of 1940, were reactions to the great wars of the twentieth century and, along with the Communist Control Act of 1954, to the perceived threat of communism, especially during the Cold War. The constitutionality of internal security laws involves a spectrum with speech at one end and action at the other, with speech generally being protected by the First Amendment and actions not. However, as we will see in the field of internal security, words can become so mingled with actions in certain situations (e.g., during wartime) that expression can be restricted.

Chapter 2 covers symbolic speech. The First Amendment is applied to symbolic speech by using the same continuum, except the analysis goes in the opposite direction. Symbolic speech, such as using the flag in unpopular ways to make a political statement, can receive First Amendment protection if the act becomes so mingled with speech as to take on the attributes of speech. We examine two statutes that apply to symbolic speech: the Flag Protection Act of 1968, which was found to violate the First Amendment, and the Draft Card Mutilation Act of 1965, which was found to comply with the amendment.

Chapter 3 covers the struggle over the use of money in election campaigns. As the use of mass media and money in political campaigns grows at breakneck speed, the task of regulation is becoming ever more difficult. As Congress seeks to limit improper influence on candidates, prevent corruption, and broaden the opportunity for political participation by restricting the use of money, it runs headlong into the First Amendment's freedoms of expression and association. Several landmark laws illustrate this tension. The Tillman Act of 1907 was the first ban on campaign contributions, in this case prohibiting corporate contributions in a federal election. The Publicity Act of 1910 and its 1911 amendment marked the first time that Congress required candidates to disclose their sources of campaign contributions. The 1911 amendment also imposed spending limits for the first time. The Hatch Act of 1939 and its amendments have regulated the political activities of federal employees, and the Federal Election Campaign Act of 1971, especially after its 1974 amendments, was a comprehensive and drastic election campaign reform arrangement that was filled with First Amendment problems. The most significant legal issue regarding campaign financing involves a contribution-expenditure distinction, with the First Amendment protecting expenditures much more than contributions. Restrictions on campaign financing, especially limitations on how much candidates and individuals can spend on their own, affect not only freedom of expression but freedom of association, which the courts have held is an implicit component of First Amendment liberties.

Chapter 4 covers statutes that regulate obscene, pornographic, and indecent expressions, which has been going on in earnest since the Comstock Act of 1873. These laws present special problems. First, defining obscenity and its related terms has proven to be an all but impossible task for legislators and judges alike. Second, and related to the first, is the fact that the technology that transmits permissible pornography to adults is accessible to young people as well. The main constitutional barrier for Congress then is to structure a law that does not restrict adults while it protects children. Several statutes illustrate this technologically related problem. To navigate successfully the legal and technological maze, the Anti-Dial-a-Porn Acts spent nearly a decade going through three statutory versions, three different agency regulations, and five judicial proceedings before they were determined to be acceptable. The Child Online Protection Act of 1998 is confronting similar problems concerning computer technology and the World Wide Web.

Chapters 5 and 6 cover intellectual property and labor-management relations, which present very different substantive categories but share a similar legal component. In both cases, Congress has sought to enhance the ability of some people to express themselves, and in doing so has adversely affected the same right in others. For example, just as the copyright laws enhance creative expression by granting exclusive and monopoly rights to that expression, it also restricts the ability of others to express themselves with the same material. Using an expression-idea distinction generally solves this dilemma, with the First Amendment protecting everyone's right to use the idea as long as they do not use the author's particular form of expression.

Nevertheless, as we will see with the Copyright Act of 1976, working with this distinction is not very simple. Labor-management laws present similar problems. While the Railway Labor Act of 1926 and the National Labor Relations (Wagner) Act of 1935 granted certain free speech and associational rights to workers, they had the unintended effect of restricting the rights of others. For example, many workers insisted on the same free speech and associational rights *not* to have to join a union, and entrepreneurs insisted that they too have First Amendment rights.

Chapter 7 covers statutory restrictions associated with federally funded programs, illustrating how Congress can use purse strings to prevent or encourage various forms of expression. For example, the Family Planning Services and Population Research Act of 1970 prohibited the use of funds distributed under the act by any program that advocated abortion. The Tax Reform Act of 1976 encourages people to contribute to nonprofit organizations by exempting the organization from income tax liability and giving their donors an income tax deduction, while denying the same income tax deduction to donors of organizations that lobby Congress. The National Foundation for the Arts and Humanities Act of 1990 prohibited any National Endowment for the Arts money to be used by any project that fails to take into consideration "standards of decency." The permissibility of these funding restrictions has turned on two different propositions. The court in one case found a distinction between restrictions placed on "projects" and restrictions placed on "grantees," with the government able to restrict grantees' right of expression regarding the use of the public project, but not their rights overall. In another situation, the courts used a distinction between a funding program designed to facilitate private speech and one that seeks to promote a governmental message, holding that the former could not be restricted but the latter could.

Chapter 8 concludes the book, with an examination of statutes relating to religious freedom. These statutes illustrate the dual aspect of freedom of religion: the freedom to exercise religion as one pleases, and the restriction on Congress establishing or sponsoring a religion. These statutes illustrate how at times Congress strives to enhance the free exercise of religion and at others to avoid establishing a religion. For example, the Religious Land Use and Institutionalized Persons Act of 2000 seeks to enable religious organizations to have more leeway in complying with land use regulations, and it extends religious privileges to inmates at public hospitals and prisons. The Personal Responsibility and Work Opportunity Reconciliation Act of 1996 also seeks to facilitate the free exercise of religion by permitting faith-based organizations to receive federal funding for social service programs. An example of the possibility of running afoul of the Establishment Clause is the 1994 American Indian Religious Freedom Act Amendment, which protected the ceremonial use of peyote by members of the Native American Church. Another successful example is the legislation that established the national motto "In God We Trust" and revised the pledge of allegiance to the flag to include the words "one nation, under God." The section on freedom of religion will also reveal the extreme tension that can exist between Congress and the judiciary regarding the meaning and applicability of First Amendment language and concepts.

NOTES

1. It is interesting to note that the Articles of Confederation mention both religion and speech. Article III obligates the states to "assist each other, against all force offered to, or attacks made upon them, or any of them, on account of [among other things] religion," and Article V provides that "Freedom of speech and debate in Congress shall not be impeached or questioned in any court or out of Congress."

2. The other states that ratified the Constitution by this date were: Delaware, December 7, 1787; Pennsylvania, December 12, 1787; New Jersey, December 18, 1787; Georgia, January 2, 1788; Connecticut, January 9, 1788; Massachusetts, February 6, 1788; Maryland, April 28, 1788; and South Carolina, May 23, 1788.

3. Eventually, all of the original thirteen states ratified the Constitution and joined the union. The new federal government differed from the former confederation government in that while all states in the confederation government re-

tained their sovereignty, or autonomy and independence, they recognized the sovereignty of a central (federal) government in certain areas while retaining certain powers of government for themselves in other areas. There are three basic forms of government: a unitary government, in which political and legal sovereignty is possessed by a single national government; a confederation government, in which the states possess all of the sovereignty, and the national government is merely an association; and a federal system, in which sovereignty is shared by the national and state governments in different areas.

4. It is not within the scope of this work to examine the structure of Congress, but it is worth noting that the makeup and authority of this congress would be much different than those under the First and Second Continental Congresses (1774 and 1775–1781) and the Articles of Confederation (March 1, 1781–March 4, 1789). One major difference would be that legislation enacted by the new Congress in furtherance of the Constitution would—according to Article VI—be "the supreme law of the Land." The national Constitution provided that no state law could supersede congressional enactments, and state judges were required to uphold them.

5. The confederation Congress issued a call on September 13, 1788, for the election of members to the new federal Congress to be held on the first Wednesday in January 1789.

6. The state ratifying conventions had proposed more than two hundred amendments during the ratifying process. Although most of them concerned either the structure of the federal government or its relationship with the state, many related to individual liberties.

7. Gales, Joseph, Jr. and William W. Seaton, *The Congressional Register*, vol. I, page 416, 1824.

8. Debate in the House of Representatives, August 15–22, 1789, in "Birth of the Nation: *The First Federal Congress 1789–1791*," First Federal Congress Project of The George Washington University, Washington, DC (http://www.gwu.edu/~ffcp/exhibit/index.html) [accessed March 26, 2001].

9. Letter to Patrick Henry, September 29, 1789. See "Birth of the Nation: *The First Federal Congress 1789–1791*."

10. The Madison who was involved in *Marbury v. Madison* as secretary of state is the same Representative Madison who introduced and sponsored the First Amendment and served two terms as the nation's fourth president from 1809 to 1817, during which time he vetoed several congressional enactments on the grounds that they violated the First Amendment.

11. The term *local government* typically encompasses county or parish governments, which can be considered as branch offices of the state government, and municipal governments, which are public corporations formed by and through state law.

12. Although the First Amendment was only applicable to congressional actions, it was later extended to the states when the Supreme Court, in *Gitlow v. New York* (1925), began to incorporate various provisions of the Bill of Rights into the Fourteenth Amendment's prohibition that "No state shall . . . deprive any person of life, liberty, or property, without due process of law."

STUDENT'S GUIDE TO LANDMARK CONGRESSIONAL LAWS ON THE FIRST AMENDMENT

1

Internal Security

Internal security comprises the various means and efforts by a nation to combat subversive acts that could destroy the existing government. Subversive acts include treason, espionage, sedition, sabotage, terrorism, and insurrection. Three major categories of subversion implicate the First Amendment's protective umbrella regarding freedom of expression. In the order of the increasing applicability of the three terms to freedom of expression, they are treason, espionage, and sedition. Acts of treason and espionage are less likely to involve First Amendment considerations because they are more likely to embody actions rather than expression. Seditious acts, on the contrary, usually involve the First Amendment, for they are likely to be entirely composed of expression in speech or writing. We may briefly define these categories of subversion as follows. *Treason* is levying (declaring and waging) war against one's nation or helping those who do. *Espionage* is gathering and sharing confidential information about national security matters with unauthorized persons. *Sedition* is engaging in conduct or, more specifically, using language that incites others to rebellion or insurrection against the authority of the government.

Although it may be obvious that the First Amendment will not generally protect overt actions, it is not so obvious that spoken and written words can lose the amendment's protection by effectively becoming actions themselves in certain situations. The U.S. Supreme Court stated the applicable rule as follows: the view cannot be accepted that an apparently limitless variety of conduct can be labeled "speech" [merely because] the person engaging in the conduct intends thereby to express an idea . . . [W]hen "speech" and "nonspeech" elements are combined in the same course of conduct, a sufficiently important governmental interest in regulating the nonspeech element can justify incidental limitations on [speech] . . . [A] government regulation is sufficiently justified if it is within the constitutional power of the Government; if it furthers an important or substantial governmental interest; if the governmental interest is unrelated to the suppression of free expression; and if the incidental restriction on alleged First Amendment freedoms is no greater than is essential to the furtherance of that interest. (*United States v. O'Brien*, 1968, pp. 376–377)

The First Amendment is not only inapplicable in certain situations where words and actions are combined, it is also inapplicable when pure expression presents what has been called a "clear and present danger." Justice Oliver Wendell Holmes Jr. introduced the "clear and present danger" expression into First Amendment law in the famous case of *Schenck v. United States* (1919). The "clear and present danger" test is of paramount importance in understanding the relationship between congressional enactments in the field of internal security and the First Amendment, for it is the basic criterion by which the legislation must be judged. Thus, a more recent expression of the "clear and present danger" rule by Second Circuit Court of Appeals Judge Learned Hand is worth repeating. In order

to deprive an utterance of the protection of the [First] Amendment it is not always enough that the purpose of the utterer may include stirring up his hearers to illegal conduct—at least, when the utterance is political. The same utterance may be unprotected, if it be a *bare appeal to action* [emphasis added] . . . In each case [courts] must ask whether the gravity of the "evil," discounted by its improbability, justifies such invasion of free speech as is necessary to avoid the danger [that the statute seeks to prevent]. (*United States v. Dennis*, 1950)

It should be borne in mind that all statutory attempts to combat subversion, like any that affect the First Amendment, are subject to the "strict scrutiny" examination that courts use to examine congressional enactments that curtail freedom of expression.

Sedition (conduct or words that incite people to rebel against authority) grew out of the law of defamation. Defamation is the general term that is applied to harmful and often untrue statements by one that exposes another's reputation and standing in the community to damage. The two basic forms of defamation are libel and slander. Libel is committed in writing, slander by oral statements. The distinction is important because people are held to a higher standard of care when writing about others than when speaking about them.

Exploring the tension between freedom of expression and safeguarding the security of the government is the crux of this chapter. This examination will consider five congressional landmarks in the field of protecting the nation's security: the Sedition Act of 1798, the Espionage Act of 1917, the Sedition Act of 1918, the Alien Registration (Smith) Act of 1940, the Internal Security (McCarran) Act of 1950—which contains the Subversive Activities Control Act and the Emergency Detention Act[1]—and the Communist Control Act of 1954.

The Sedition Act of July 14, 1798, was part of a series of enactments made by the Federalist-dominated Congress, ostensibly to thwart a perceived threat of subversion by French sympathizers when the United States was teetering at the edge of war with France. These enactments were subject to extreme political criticism by the Republicans (later called Democrats), led by Thomas Jefferson and James Madison. The Espionage Act of 1917 was passed by Congress just two months after it had voted on April 6, 1917, to enter World War I. This act and its amendment, the Sedition Act of 1918, related to (among other things) obtaining and using national defense information and interfering with the war effort in a variety of ways, including causing disobedience and disloyalty in the armed forces.

The Smith Act of 1940 provided, among other things, for the punishment of anyone who "advocates, abets, advises, or teaches" the violent overthrow of the government. It was used against members of the Socialist Party before World War II and members of the Communist Party afterward. The Internal Security Act of 1950, often called the McCarran Act, was the major legislative vehicle for the well-known activities of Senator Joseph McCarthy, Representative Richard Nixon, and J. Edgar Hoover during the Cold War. Title I of the McCarran Act created the Subversive Activities Control Board and gave it authority to require registration by communist-dominated organizations. Title II authorized the president to declare internal security emergencies under certain conditions, and the attorney general power to detain people in some situations without due process of law.

NOTE

1. This act repealed the legal authority that followed other statutes and the Executive Order that detained Americans of Japanese ancestry.

THE SEDITION ACT OF 1798

Ten days after celebrating the twenty-second anniversary of the signing of the Declaration of Independence, President Adams signed a set of antisedition laws that have been variously called "the mischievous acts of the Federalists," "a First Amendment muzzle," and an act so bad that it "is not law, but is altogether void, and of no force."[1] These descriptions refer to the four Alien and Sedition Acts of 1798. The Naturalization Act (June 18, 1798) raised the residency period from five to fourteen years before aliens could apply for citizenship. The Alien Act of 1798 empowered the president to deport aliens even during peacetime if they were considered "dangerous to the peace and safety of the United States." The Alien Enemies Act of 1798 permitted the wartime arrest, imprisonment, and deportation of aliens who were—without more—the citizens of an enemy nation. The final and most notorious act was the Sedition Act of 1798, which made it a crime to "oppose any measure or measures of the government of the United States," or to engage in "writing, printing, uttering or publishing any false, scandalous and malicious writing or writings against the government of the United States." The first offense was punishable by a fine not exceeding five thousand dollars and up to five years' imprisonment. The second offense was punishable by a fine not exceeding two thousand dollars and up to two years' imprisonment.

Members of the Federalist Party claimed that criticism of the government was destined to topple the Constitution, while the Republicans claimed that the Federalists' effort to stifle dissent was destroying the Constitution. Although the political debates regarding these acts contained the exaggerations of partisanship, they did nonetheless provide an early occasion for legislative consideration of the First Amendment's freedom of speech and press provisions. To be sure, the Sedition Act did alter the common law by permitting truth as a defense and providing that juries would decide matters of law as well as fact. Otherwise, Representative Harrison Gray Otis (Fed., MA) argued that "there was noting in the bill contrary to the common law of the several States of the Union." By contrast, Representative Nathaniel Macon (Rep., NC) retorted that he "had no doubt on his mind that this bill was in direct opposition to the

Constitution; and that if a law like this was passed, to abridge the liberty of the press, Congress would have the same right to pass a law making an establishment of religion, or to prohibit its free exercise."[2]

Representative Samuel W. Dana (Fed., CT) stated the Federalist position on the First Amendment's relationship to sedition as follows:

> Could the framers of the [First Amendment] intend to guarantee, as a sacred principle, the liberty of lying against the government? What do gentlemen understand by "freedom of speech and of the press?" Is it license to injure others or the Government, by calumnies, with impunity? Let it be remembered that the uttering of malicious falsehoods, to the injury to the Government, is the offense which it now intended to restrain; for, if what is uttered can be proved true, it will not, according to this bill, be punished as libelous.[3]

What concerned the Republicans—justifiably, as it turned out—was not so much the abstract principle of the bill, but its practical application. For, as Representative Albert Gallatin (Rep., PA) stated, in regard to an article in the *Aurora* criticizing President Adams, which Representative Dana used as an example of seditious libel:

> It [the article] contained more information and more sense, and gave more proofs of a sound understanding and strong mind, than ever the gentleman from Connecticut [Dana] had displayed, or could display, on this floor. Furthermore, Rep. Gallatin was altogether at a loss to know what was criminal in [the *Aurora* article], though he might easily see why it was obnoxious [to the Federalists]. Was it erroneous or criminal to say that debts and taxes were the ruinous consequences of war? Or that some members in both Houses of Congress uniformly voted in favor of an extension of the powers of the Executive, and of every proposed expenditure of money? Was it not true?

Representative Gallatin argued that error, if there be any, should and could be combated with truth, asserting that the American government had subsisted and become strong because "it had been

able to repel opposition by the single weapon of argument." Moreover, he went on to say that this bill

> was subversive of the principles of the Constitution itself. If you put
> the press under any restraint in respect to the measures of members
> of Government; if you thus deprive the people of the means of ob-
> taining information of their conduct, you in fact render their right
> of electing nugatory; and this bill must be considered only as a
> weapon used by a party now in power, in order to perpetuate their
> authority and preserve their present places.

Prosecution under the Sedition Act was vigorously pursued,
mostly against politicians and journalists allied with the Jeffersonian
Republicans. The first to be charged under the act were journalists:
Benjamin Bache (1769–1798), a grandson of Benjamin Franklin,
founder and editor of the Philadelphia *General Advertiser*, later
named the *Aurora*, and John Daly Burk, editor of the New York
Time Piece. Both men were charged with libeling President Adams
yet were never brought to trial. The actual number of indictments,
trials, and convictions under the 1798 act is unclear. The stated
claims number from seventeen to twenty-five indictments, with ten
to twenty or so convictions.[4] There were many notable cases prosecuted under the 1798 sedition law: for example, the trials of Matthew Lyon (1798), Thomas Cooper (1800), Anthony Haswell
(1800), and James Thompson Callender (1800).[5] Lyon was an Irish
member of Congress from Vermont who was fined one thousand
dollars and sentenced to four months in prison for making the
following statement:

> [W]henever I shall, on the part of our Executive, see every consid-
> eration of public welfare swallowed up in a continual grasp for
> power, in an unbounded thirst for ridiculous pomp, foolish adula-
> tion, and selfish avarice—when I shall behold men of real merit daily
> turned out [of] office for no other cause than independency of sen-
> timent—when I shall see men of firmness, merit, years, abilities, and
> experience, discarded in their applications for office, for fear they
> possess that independence, and men of meanness preferred for the
> ease with which they can take up and advocate opinions, the con-
> sequence of which they know but little of—when I shall see the
> sacred name of religion employed as a State engine to make man-

kind hate and persecute each other, I shall not be their humble advocate![6]

The trial of James Thompson Callender, an irascible Scottish immigrant and Jeffersonian activist, is one of the better-known trials, with an especially interesting twist. The interplay between the "independent" federal judiciary and legal procedure illustrated the political climate under which these prosecutions were conducted. The sedition law had provided that the jury could determine the law and also the facts; Callender's attorney, William Wirt, argued, "Since, then, the jury have a right to consider the law, and since the constitution is law, the conclusion is certainly syllogistic, that the jury have a right to consider the constitution." To this, Supreme Court Justice Samuel Chase (1741–1811), a signer of the Declaration of Independence and a strong Federalist, who was sitting as circuit judge, curtly responded, "A *non sequitur*, sir!" The non sequitur was apparently that Wirt's legal conclusion did not logically follow from the Justice's political attitude.

Justice Chase participated in another notable prosecution under the Sedition Act: the case of Thomas Cooper, who was found guilty and fined four hundred dollars and sentenced to prison for six months. Cooper had criticized President Adams's handling of public finances in borrowing money at an excessive rate of interest, maintaining a standing army, and interfering with the independence of the judiciary. Justice Chase again took an aggressive posture as the presiding judge, this time requiring Cooper to prove his assertions "beyond a marrow [doubt]" before they could acquit him. As things turned out, Justice Chase got as good as he gave. Although the Senate did not convict him, the Republican-dominated House of Representatives impeached Chase in 1804 on charges that he transcended the legitimate powers of his judicial office.

The breadth of prosecutions under the Sedition Act was not limited to Republican politicians and politically active journalists. Its sweep caught many who were even Federalist supporters.[7] An egregious example involves German Americans living in eastern Pennsylvania. Although the German American population that was largely located in Berks and Bucks Counties supported the more conservative policies of the Federalist Party, their divergence from the New England orthodoxy in other ways made them politically suspect. When such concerns led them to send petitions to Congress and hold mass meetings opposing the Alien and Sedition Acts, the Federalists responded with a military expedition. They arrested and took sixty people to Philadelphia, the nation's capital at the time. The Federalists tried many, some for treason, and sentenced one person to death.[8]

After the election of Thomas Jefferson in 1800, the Alien and Sedition Acts either lapsed by their terms in 1801 or were repealed by the Republican-dominated Congress. President Jefferson stated, "I discharged every person under punishment or prosecution under the sedition law, because I considered, and now consider, that law to be a nullity, as absolute and as palpable as if Congress had ordered us to fall down and worship a golden image." He pardoned all who had been convicted, and Congress ultimately appropriated compensation to many victims to repay the fines levied, thus ending what Justice William O. Douglas labeled as one of the "sorriest chapters" in our history.[9]

The Sedition Act of 1798

An act for the punishment of certain crimes against the United States.

Section 1. Be it enacted . . . , That if any persons shall unlawfully combine or conspire together, with intent to oppose any measure or measures of the government of the United States, which are or shall be directed by proper authority, or to impede the operation of any law of the United States, or to intimidate or prevent any person holding a place or office in or under the government of the United States, from undertaking, performing or executing his trust or duty; and if any person or persons, with intent as aforesaid, shall counsel, advise or attempt to procure any insurrection, riot, unlawful assembly, or combination, whether such conspiracy, threatening, counsel, advice, or attempt shall have the proposed effect or not, he or they shall be deemed guilty of a high misdemeanor, and on conviction, before any court of the United States having jurisdiction thereof, shall be punished by a fine not exceeding five thousand dollars, and by imprisonment during a term not less than six months nor exceeding five years; and further, at the discretion of the court may be holden to find sureties for his good behaviour in such sum, and for such time, as the said court may direct.

Section 2. That if any person shall write, print, utter, or publish, or shall cause or procure to be written, printed, uttered or published, or shall

knowingly and willingly assist or aid in writing, printing, uttering or publishing any false, scandalous and malicious writing or writings against the
government of the United States, or either house of the Congress of the
United States, or the President of the United States, with intent to defame
the said government, or either house of the said Congress, or the said
President, or to bring them, or either of them, into contempt or disrepute;
or to excite against them, or either or any of them, the hatred of the good
people of the United States, or to excite any unlawful combinations
therein, for opposing or resisting any law of the United States, or any act
of the President of the United States, done in pursuance of any such law,
or of the powers in him vested by the constitution of the United States,
or to resist, oppose, or defeat any such law or act, or to aid, encourage or
abet any hostile designs of any foreign nation against the United States,
their people or government, then such person, being thereof convicted
before any court of the United States having jurisdiction thereof, shall be
punished by a fine not exceeding two thousand dollars, and by imprisonment not exceeding two years.

Section 3. That if any person shall be prosecuted under this act, for the
writing or publishing any libel aforesaid, it shall be lawful for the defendant, upon the trial of the cause, to give in evidence in his defence, the
truth of the matter contained in the publication charged as a libel. And
the jury who shall try the cause, shall have a right to determine the law
and the fact, under the direction of the court, as in other cases.

Section 4. That this act shall continue to be in force until March 3, 1801,
and no longer. . . .

Approved July 14, 1798.

NOTES

1. Justice Robert Jackson, writing for the court in *Johnson v. Eisentranger* (1950,
p. 774); Justice William O. Douglas, dissenting in *Gertz v. Robert Welch, Inc.* (1974,
p. 356); and Thomas Jefferson, 4 *Elliot's Debates on the Federal Constitution* 541
(1876).

2. John Chester Miller, *Crisis in Freedom: The Alien and Sedition Acts* (Boston:
Little, Brown, 1951), p. 63.

3. Ibid., p. 66.

4. Larry Gragg, 1998. "Order vs. Liberty." *American History Feature* (http://
www.thehistorynet.com/AmericanHistory/articles/1998/1098_text.ht) [accessed
May 27, 2000]; James Morton Smith, *Freedom's Fetters: The Alien and Sedition Laws
and American Civil Liberties* (Ithaca: Cornell University Press, 1956).

5. See Francis Wharton, *State Trials of the United States* (New York: B. Franklin,
1970), reprint, pp. 333, 659, 684, 688.

6. Justice Black dissenting in *Communist Party v. Control Board* (1961, pp. 155–156).

7. John Chester Miller, *Crisis in Freedom: The Alien and Sedition Acts* (Boston: Little, Brown, 1951), p. 223.

8. Stanley Elkins and Eric McKitrick, *The Age of Federalism* (New York: Oxford University Press, 1993).

9. Letter to Mrs. John Adams, July 22, 1804, 4 *Jefferson's Works* (Washington ed.), pp. 555, 556. *Watts v. United States* (1969, p. 709), concurring opinion. See, for example, Act of July 4, 1840 accompanied by H. R. Rep. No. 86, 26th Cong., 1st Sess. (1840).

THE ESPIONAGE ACT OF 1917

Like the Sedition Act of 1798, the Espionage Act of 1917 was conceived in the midst of war, or the anticipation of war. In 1798, war with France was believed, or at least feared, to be on the horizon. Similarly, Congress passed the 1917 act barely more than two months after President Wilson's call for war and the April 6 Joint Resolution of Congress declaring war on Germany. The similarities did not end there. Like the 1798 law, its twentieth century descendant was used more to quell internal political dissent than to protect the nation from any real external threat. The caption of the 1917 act stated that it was intended to "punish acts of interference with the foreign relations, the neutrality, and the foreign commerce of the United States, to punish espionage, and better to enforce the criminal laws of the United States, and for other purposes."

The 1917 Espionage Act, as amended by the Sedition (or Espionage) Act of 1918 initiated what some have called the "national surveillance state."[1] Viewed in historical context, this situation is not surprising. To be sure, the nation was in the midst of a war with Germany, but, more than that, the war was perceived as part of an even larger threat: the combined attempt of various radical philosophies—emanating from Europe, and in particular from Russia after the October 1917 Revolution—to gain sway in the United States. Perhaps the most feared "foreign" philosophy was anarchism, which followed the teachings of the French social philosopher Pierre Joseph Proudhon (1809–1865) and the Russian philosopher Prince Pyotr Alekseyevich Kropotkin (1842–1921). Anarchists generally follow the notion that governments interfere with legitimate social order rather than enhance it. In the words of Proudhon: "As man seeks justice in equality, so society seeks order in anarchy. Anarchy—the absence of a sovereign—such is the form of government to which we are every day approximating."[2] Europeans like Russian-born Emma Goldman (1869–1940) and Alexander Berkman (1870–1936) were characteristic of contemporary anarchists.[3] Goldman, active among German, then Russian, anarchists, copublished with Berkman the anarchist magazine *Mother Earth*, which got them both deported in 1917. Berkman had also spent fourteen years in prison for attempting to kill steel company executive Henry Clay Frick to avenge the deaths of seven steelworkers, whom Pinkerton Detectives hired by Frick had shot during the Homestead Strike at a mill owned by the magnate Andrew Carnegie.

These and other major events fueled congressional concern about anarchist activities. In addition to Goldman's speeches and Berkman's attempted murder, they included the 1901 assassination of President William McKinley (1843–1901) by a Polish-born anarchist, Leon Czolgosz (1873–1901). Czolgosz barely survived a mob beating at the assassination scene at the World's Fair in Buffalo, New York, and further beatings at Auburn Prison. He died in a public execution photographed by Thomas Edison on October 29, 1901.[4] Although Czolgosz claimed to be a disciple of Emma Goldman, the anarchists in New York had actually spurned his association. Nevertheless, the assassination no doubt partly caused the general concern that prompted Congress to enact a law in 1903 barring foreign anarchists from the country and permitting deportation of alien anarchists.[5] Ironically, the police arrested Goldman and Berkman on June 15, 1917, the day the Espionage Act became law, for violating the recently enacted draft law.[6] They were convicted, and after serving two years in the prison at Jefferson City, Missouri, they were—along with more than two hundred foreign radicals—deported under the 1903 deportation law, which for the first time made the expression of opinions a ground for exclusion (deportation) of aliens.[7]

Although anarchists were perceived as the greatest threat to national security, it was not easy to classify them. For, as Representative Henry Allen Cooper (R-WI) of Wisconsin pointed out on the House floor, the famous and highly regarded writer and philosopher of Transcendentalism, Ralph Waldo Emerson (1803–1882), was an anarchist, but one who believed in "quiet, deliberate, calm, dispassionate argument." Moreover, according to Representative Cooper, the world-renowned Russian pacifist Lev Tolstoi (1828–1910) was also an anarchist. Insisting that any statute should discriminate between different radicals, Representative Cooper pleaded with his colleagues to consider not using "that word 'anarchistic,' without some qualifying adjective." Thus arose in the debate the appellation "kindly, sweet-tempered anarchist."[8] Nonetheless, the Espionage Act targeted not only those who advocated the violent overthrow of all government but even anyone who hoped governments would wither away on their own.

Although the Espionage Act was a lengthy bill that affected core freedoms of speech and press, it engendered little debate as it worked its way through the House and Senate (H.R. 291 and S. 2). For example, when supporters brought the bill before the House of Representatives on April 30, it appeared that there was to be no debate at all. In fact, when the House dispensed with the first reading, the Speaker declared, "If no gentleman desires to debate the bill, the Chair will put it to a vote." Only when Representative Martin Barnaby Madden (R-IL) remonstrated that "there ought to be considerable discussion of this bill" did any debate ensue. According to Madden, "it is one of the most important bills that has ever come before the Congress. . . . It affects the liberties of the people of the United States to an extent that they have never been affected before in all our history."[9] In the Senate, Senator James A. Reed (D-MO), complaining that the bill's supporters urged the Judiciary Committee to great haste and the full House likewise, stated that "I am very earnest about the proposition that we are now engaged in passing legislation under stress and under excitement . . . and it ought generally to be limited to the emergency now confronting us."[10] Even so, there was relatively little debate, and the legislation was passed by Congress in short order.

Most of the debate that related to the First Amendment revolved around two issues: prior restraint (censorship) and the ability of Congress to delegate to the president the authority to designate what actions would constitute sedition. As proposed—S. 2, subdivision (c)—the bill contained a provision that empowered the president to promulgate the specific offenses. The concern for such a legislative delegation was voiced by Senator Charles Thomas (D-CO), who asked the bill's sponsor, "Does the Senator think we have the power, even in an emergency of this kind, to invest the Chief Magistrate with the right to make a regulation the nonobservance of which will lead to the imposition of these tremendous penalties?" The responses to Thomas's concern ranged from that of Senator Lee Overman (D-NC), "If we cannot give such power [to the president], then God help this country," to that of Senator Frank Brandegee (R-CT), who believed that the Supreme Court, based on precedent, would not sustain such a delegation.[11]

Certain parts of the proposed legislation—including subdivision (c), dealing with prior restraint—did not survive as part of the final enactment. Members of Congress formed a consensus around the opinion of Senator William Borah (R-ID), which carried the day. Senator Borah argued that "it is not within the power of Congress to limit the right of the freedom of the press. If the [constitutional] fathers intended anything, beyond question it was to prevent Congress from passing any law, because that is the language—[Congress] shall pass no law—limiting the freedom of the press." Referring to the delegation provision, Senator Borah went on to say, "Does not it clearly provide in advance of publication, that unless the censor—to wit, the President—consents, either directly or through his regulations, that upon certain subjects publication shall not be had. And if you can make the President a censor you can make anybody else a censor." Nevertheless, when it came to post-publication punishment, Senator Borah also had this to say: "Now, you may, if Congress has any jurisdiction at all, punish for results of publication, but you cannot set up licensors."

As enacted on June 15, 1917, the omnibus statute contained thirteen titles and seventy-nine sections covering a variety of war-related activities, from pure espionage and seditious libel to passports, foreign commerce, and vessels in port. Most of the act's provisions were not directly related to First Amendment issues. For example, Title II governed the anchorage and movement of vessels in U.S. ports and territorial waters. Titles III and IV prohibited acts that harmed the nation's foreign commerce. Title V contained various provisions relating to neutrality. Titles VI and VII regulated trade in armaments. Titles IX and X regulated passports and provided punishment for fraudulent use of any government scal, while Title XIII contained some general provisions such as a definition of the act's geographical application and a severability clause typical of most omnibus statutes.[12]

Four titles of the Espionage Act of 1917 collided with the First Amendment. Title I, entitled "Espionage," prohibited typical espionage activities in Sections 1 through 3. These prohibited obtaining information about the nation's armed forces or national defense establishments, such as locations of house troops, vessels, and munitions for the purpose of injuring the United States. Also penalized was the act of obtaining, receiving, or communicating such information. A violation of the first three sections in time of war carried the death penalty, with up to thirty years of incarceration as an alternative.[13]

Sections 3 and 4 of Title I prohibited acts of expression that are characteristically labeled seditious. Section 3 proscribed making false statements to interfere with the operation of the war effort by inciting disloyalty or obstructing military enlistment, while Section

4 created liability for conspiracy to commit such acts. The punishment for sedition was a fine of up to ten thousand dollars, imprisonment up to twenty years, or both. Section 1 of Title VIII also contained a sedition provision. It penalized making any false statement under oath, whether oral or written, in the interest of a nation with which the United States is at war if the statement is harmful to U.S. interests. The punishment for making these statements was up to five years in prison, five thousand dollars, or both.

Title XI authorized search warrants to aid investigation and conviction of violations of the act, and it set forth the grounds and procedure to be followed. One clause became particularly important in investigation and prosecution of Section 3 (sedition) cases. This provision authorized the use of search warrants "when[ever] the *property* was used as the means of committing a *felony*." Executive officers and judges alike interpreted the section as including seditious statements, and "property" as embracing books, newspaper articles, and pamphlets. The other sedition title (Title XII) declared nonmailable "every letter, writing, circular, postal card, picture, print, engraving, photograph, newspaper, pamphlet, book, or other publication, matter, or thing of any kind" that violated the espionage law. Section 2 of Title XII specifically banned these media if they contained "any matter advocating or urging treason, insurrection, or forcible resistance to any law." The penalty for violating Title XII was a fine up to five thousand dollars, imprisonment up to five years, or both.

The Espionage Act of 1917

TITLE I. ESPIONAGE

Section 1. That (a) whoever, for the purpose of obtaining information respecting the national defense with intent or reason to believe that the information to be obtained is to be used to the injury of the United States, or to the advantage of any foreign nation, goes upon, enters, flies over, or otherwise obtains information, concerning . . . the national defense of the United States; or (e) whoever [violates this section], shall be punished by a fine of not more than $10,000, or by imprisonment for not more than two years, or both.

Section 2. (a) Whoever, with intent or reason to believe that it is to be used to the injury of the United States or to the advantage of a foreign nation, communicated, delivers, or transmits, or attempts to, or aids, or induces another to, communicate, deliver or transmit, to any foreign government, or to any faction or party or military or naval force within a foreign country, whether recognized or unrecognized by the United States, or to any representative, officer, agent, employee, subject, or citizen thereof, either directly or indirectly and document, writing, code book, signal book, sketch, photograph, photographic negative, blue print, plan, map, model, note, instrument, appliance, or information relating to the national defense, shall be punished by imprisonment for not more than twenty years: Provided, That whoever shall violate the provisions of subsection (a) of this section in time of war shall be punished by death or by imprisonment for not more than thirty years; and (b) whoever, in time of war, with intent that the same shall be communicated to the enemy, shall collect, record, publish or communicate, or attempt to elicit any information with respect to the movement, numbers, description, condition, or disposition of any of the armed forces, ships, aircraft, or war materials of the United States, or with respect to the plans or conduct, or supposed plans or conduct of any naval or military operations, or with respect to any works or measures undertaken for or connected with, or intended for the fortification of any place, or any other information relating to the public defense, which might be useful to the enemy, shall be punished by death or by imprisonment for not more than thirty years.

Section 3. Whoever, when the United States is at war, shall willfully make or convey false reports or false statements with intent to interfere with the operation or success of the military or naval forces of the United States or to promote the success of its enemies and whoever when the United States is at war, shall willfully cause or attempt to cause insubordination, disloyalty, mutiny, refusal of duty, in the military or naval forces of the United States, or shall willfully obstruct the recruiting or enlistment service of the United States, to the injury of the service or of the United States, shall be punished by a fine of not more than $10,000 or imprisonment for not more than twenty years, or both . . .

TITLE XI. SEARCH WARRANTS.

Section 1. A search warrant authorized by this title may be issued by a judge of a United States district court, or by a judge of a State or Territorial court of record, or by a United States commissioner for the district wherein the property is located . . .

TITLE XII. USE OF MAILS.

Section 1. Every letter, writing, circular, postal card, picture, print, engraving, photograph, newspaper, pamphlet, book, or other publication, matter, or thing, of any kind, in violation of any of the provisions of this Act is hereby declared to be nonmailable matter and shall not be conveyed in the mails or delivered from any post office or by any letter carrier. . . .

Section 2. Every letter, writing, circular, postal card, picture, print, engraving, photograph, newspaper, pamphlet, book, or other publication, matter, or thing, of any kind, containing any matter advocating or urging treason, insurrection, or forcible resistance to any law of the United States is hereby declared to be nonmailable.

Section 3. Whoever shall use or attempt to use the mails or Postal Service of the United States for the transmission of any matter declared by this title to be nonmailable, shall be fined not more than $5,000 or imprisoned not more than five years, or both.

Approved June 15, 1917.

NOTES

1. Norman L. Rosenberg, *Protecting the Best Men: An Interpretative History of the Law of Libel* (Chapel Hill: University of North Carolina Press, 1986), Chapter 9.

2. "Anarchism," Encyclopædia Britannica Online (http://www.eb.com:195/bol/topic?artcl=117285&seq_nbr=1&page=n&isctn=2) [accessed 11 June 2000].

3. In 1901 Peter Kropotkin, on his visit to America, addressed a letter to Alexander Berkman, then in Western Penitentiary. Emma Goldman, *Mother Earth Bulletin*, Vol 1, no. 5 (February 1919).

4. "People and Events," in *America 1900*, Public Broadcasting Company (http://www.pbs.org/wgbh/amex/1900/peopleevents/pande16.html) [accessed 11 June 2000].

5. An Act to Regulate the Immigration of Aliens into the United States (March 3, 1903). This statute was subjected to a First Amendment attack that was turned down by the United States Supreme Court in *United States. ex Rel. Turner v. Williams* (1904).

6. Selective Draft Law of 1917. See the Selective Draft Law Cases, *Arver et al. v. United States* (1918), which upheld the act against, among others, a First Amendment claim that exempting ministers of religion and theological students under certain conditions, and relieving from strictly military service members of certain religious sects whose tenets deny the moral right to engage in war, violates the First Amendment by establishing or interfering with religion.

7. See "The Emma Goldman Papers," in *War Resistance, Anti-Militarism, and Deportation, 1917–1919* (http://sunsite.berkeley.edu/Goldman/Exhibition/deportation.html) [accessed 11 June 2000]. The battle against the radicals was led by a young federal agent named J. Edgar Hoover (1895–1972) who had been recently hired by Attorney General A. Mitchell Palmer as a special assistant to head up the de-

partment's General Intelligence Division. On the second anniversary of the Bolshevik Revolution (7 November 1919), Hoover's team arrested more than ten thousand suspected radicals in raids conducted in twenty-three cities. Hoover made the deportation of Goldman and Berkman a cause célèbre, personally presenting the deportation case against them before the Commissioner of Immigration. Hoover was rewarded for his efforts with an appointment as assistant director of the Federal Bureau of Investigation in 1921 and the directorship in 1924, which he held until his death in 1972.

8. *Congressional Record*, 65th Cong., 1st sess., 1917. Vol. 50, pt. # (April 30, 1917, p. 1596).

9. Ibid., p. 1590.

10. Ibid., (June 11, 1917, p. 3439).

11. Ibid., (April 18, 1917, pp. 782–783).

12. Severability clauses provide that where one section of a law is declared invalid, the remaining sections are "separable into legally distinct rights or obligations," which permits them to remain in force.

13. Ethel and Julius Rosenberg were executed in 1953 for violating the Espionage Act of 1917 by transmitting secret military information, including about the atom bomb, to the Soviet Union. *Rosenberg v. United States* (1953).

THE SEDITION ACT OF 1918

A successful prosecution for seditious statements or publications under Section 3, Title I, of the 1917 Espionage Act required three things: (1) the language must have been *willfully* uttered; (2) the language itself must have been of a character to *cause* some results denounced by the act; and (3) the language must have *been uttered on an occasion* that would lead reasonable people to conclude that it *might* produce a proscribed result (*United States v. Schutte*, 252 F. 212, 213, D. N.D. 1918). These requirements often proved to be more difficult than the government could satisfy at trial. Thus, in many situations, judicial proceedings under the act were met with displeasure among many congressional leaders who expected some show for their effort.

A typical example of the judicial decisions that caused legislative disfavor was Montana Federal District Judge George Bourquin's dismissal of an indictment in *United States v. Hall*, 248 F. 150 (D. Mont. January 27, 1918). Hall had been indicted for declaring that

> he would flee to avoid going to the war, that Germany would whip the United States, and he hoped so, that the President was a Wall Street tool, using the United States forces in the war because he was a British tool, that the President was the crookedest . . . ever President, that he was the richest man in the United States, that the President brought us into the war by British dictation, that Germany had the right to sink ships and kill Americans without warning, and that the United States was only fighting for Wall Street millionaires and to protect [J.P. Morgan & Company's] interests in England. (248 F. 150, 151)

Judge Bourquin ruled that the statute prohibited false reports and false statements of facts to be a crime, not mere opinions, beliefs, intentions, and arguments. In this case, the defendant's opinions were made in a small Montana village with a population of sixty people that was sixty miles from the nearest rail station. Moreover, the judge considered the defendant's statements as no more than banter with his landlady and argument in the local saloon—"oral kitchen gossip" and "saloon debate," as he termed them. In short, Judge Bourquin determined that Hall could not have intended any effect on military or naval affairs, much less possess the ability to have any such effect. The judge viewed Hall's actions as comparable to a person shooting a .22 caliber pistol at someone two or three miles away.

The *Hall* decision and others outraged many members of Congress. Senator Thomas J. Walsh (D-MT), referring to these cases in general and Judge Bourquin's decision in particular, characterized it as a "strained construction which has been given to the espionage act by some of the Federal courts, under which effective aid in the German propaganda that is notoriously being conducted in this country are permitted unmolested to disseminate the poison with which they have become infected." Moreover, members of Congress and the public were becoming increasingly alarmed by perceived threats to national security. For example, Senator Lee Overman (R-NC), who, on behalf of the Judiciary Committee was in charge of the espionage and sedition bills, observed at the time that although he once thought there were 100,000 spies in the country, he now believed there were 400,000.[1] Senator Overman insisted that "the country is full of traitors, scoundrels, and spies, and when [we] try to pass a law to convict them and stop it, there is great delay. We have got to do something. There is mob law now everywhere in the country, and I am afraid of mob law. If Congress does not do something, the people will take it in their hands."[2]

Congress did do something. It amended the Espionage Act of 1917 with the Sedition Act of 1918 by strengthening the antisedition provisions, particularly Section 3. Whereas the former section mainly prohibited acts that directly related to naval and military activities, the amendment made it a crime to

> utter, print, write, or publish any disloyal, profane, scurrilous, or abusive language about the form of government of the United States, or the Constitution of the United States, or the military or naval forces of the United States . . . urge, incite, or advocate any curtailment of production . . . or advocate, teach, defend, or suggest the doing of any of the acts or things in this section enumerated, and whoever shall by word or act support or favor the cause of any country with which the United States is at war or by word or act oppose the cause of the United States.

Congress made all of the provisions of the 1917 act applicable to the amendment, which meant, for example, that use of the mail in violation of the new Section 3 was illegal, and the search warrant provision would be available to prosecutors investigating violations of the new Section 3 activities as well. A new section (4) was added to Title XII that permitted the postmaster general to deny incoming as well as outgoing mail privileges to violators. The 1918 amendment also added a Section 4 to Title XII that called for the termination of any government employee who "utters any unpatriotic or disloyal language" or criticized the army, navy, or flag in any manner.

All told, there were nearly a thousand criminal convictions under the 1917–1918 espionage acts. Moreover, the U.S. Supreme Court turned aside all constitutional attacks. In one of the most famous cases, *Schenck v. United States* (1919), the court upheld the original Section 3 against a constitutional attack under the First Amendment by the general secretary of the Socialist Party and others who, during August 1917, distributed and mailed antidraft circulars to men in the process of being recruited for military service.

The Supreme Court in *Schenck*, with Justice Oliver Wendell Holmes Jr. writing the opinion, rejected the constitutional challenge to the espionage act on the basis that the nation was at war. Otherwise, had it been peacetime, the circular would most likely have come within the First Amendment's protective umbrella. Just one week after the *Schenck* decision, the Supreme Court upheld a conviction in the case of *Debs v. United States* (1919), which, unlike *Schenck*, involved no action, only speech. Also, unlike *Schenck*, this case was decided under the 1918 amendment. Another case, *Abrams v. United States* (1919), is significant, for it involves the conviction of five Russian immigrants who were protesting not the war with Germany but the assistance that the United States was providing counterrevolutionary forces in Russia by sending troops to Siberia.[3] Writing for the Court in the decision upholding Abrams's conviction, Justice John Clarke made short shrift of the First Amendment claim and also the argument that the immigrants did not intend the leaflet to affect the war with Germany. Justice Clarke, referring to the defendant's call for shutting down the munitions plants, stated that "even if their primary purpose and intent was to aid the cause of the Russian Revolution, the plan of action which they adopted necessarily involved, before it could be realized, defeat of the war program of the United States [against Germany]" (p. 621).

A significant parallel among the 1917 and 1918 acts and the 1798 act is the fact that each snared a member of Congress. Representative Matthew Lyon, an Irish immigrant and loyal Jeffersonian Republican, was prosecuted and convicted of violating the Sedition Act of 1798, and Representative Victor Berger (1860–1929, Soc., WI), the first socialist elected to Congress, was prosecuted and convicted and sentenced to twenty years of hard labor for violating section 3 of the 1918 act. Lyon was jailed for four months and fined one thousand dollars. While in jail, Lyon was reelected to Congress. Berger's conviction was overturned in 1921 upon a finding by the Supreme Court that the trial judge had a personal bias against him and his codefendants.[4] Berger regained his congressional seat in 1923 after winning another election to the House of Representatives.

After 1,956 cases commenced by federal prosecutors under the espionage and sedition acts and 877 convictions,[5] the sedition section was repealed. To close the World War I chapter on sedition, President Warren G. Harding (1865–1923) pardoned many of those convicted under the acts, including Eugene Debs, who were still serving time in federal prison.[6]

The Sedition Act of 1918

Be it enacted that section three of [the 1917 Espionage Act] be, and the same is hereby, amended so as to read as follows:

Section 3. Whoever, when the United States is at war, shall willfully make or convey false reports or false statements with intent to interfere with the operation or success of the military or naval forces of the United States, or to promote the success of its enemies, or shall willfully make or convey false reports, or false statements, or say or do anything, or incite insubordination, disloyalty, mutiny, or refusal of duty, in the military or naval forces of the United States, or shall willfully obstruct, or attempt to obstruct, the recruiting or enlistment service of the United States, and whoever, when the United States is at war, shall willfully utter, print, write, or publish any disloyal, profane, scurrilous, or abusive language about the form of government of the United States, or the Constitution of the United States, or the military or naval forces of the United States, or the flag of the United States, or the uniform of the Army or Navy of the United States, or any language intended to bring the form of government of the United States, or the Constitution of the United States, or the military or naval forces of the United States, or the flag of the United

States, or the uniform of the Army or Navy of the United States into contempt, scorn, contumely, or disrepute, or shall willfully utter, print, write, or publish any language intended to incite, provoke, or encourage resistance to the United States, or to promote the cause of its enemies, or shall willfully display the flag of any foreign enemy, or shall willfully by utterance, writing, printing, publication, or language spoken, urge, incite, or advocate any curtailment of production in this country of any thing or things, product or products, necessary or essential to the prosecution of the war in which the United States may be engaged, with intent by such by such curtailment to cripple or hinder the United States in the prosecution of the war, and whoever shall willfully advocate, teach, defend, or suggest the doing of any of the acts or things in this section enumerated and whoever shall by word or act support or favor the cause of any country with which the United States is at war or by word or act oppose the cause of the United States therein, shall be punished by a fine of not more than $10,000 or imprisonment for not more than twenty years, or both.

Provided, That any employee or official of the United States Government who commits any disloyal act or utters any unpatriotic or disloyal language, or who in an abusive and violent manner criticizes the Army or Navy or the flag of the United States shall be at once dismissed from the service. . . .

Title XII of the [1917 Espionage Act], be, and the same is hereby, amended by adding thereto the following section:

Section 4. When the United States is at war, the Postmaster General may, upon evidence satisfactory to him that any person or concern is using the mails in violation of any of the provisions of this Act, instruct the postmaster at any post office at which mail is received address to such person or concern to return to the postmaster at the office at which they were originally mailed all letters or other matter so addressed, with the words "Mail to this address undeliverable under Espionage Act" plainly written or stamped upon the outside thereof, and all such letters or other matter so returned to such postmasters shall be by them returned to the senders thereof under such regulations as the Postmaster General may prescribe. Approved May 16, 1918.

NOTES

1. *Congressional Record*, 65th Cong., 2nd sess., 1918. Vol. 56, pt. 12 (March 28, 1918, p. 4191).

2. Ibid. (April 4, 1918, p. 4570).

3. See George F. Kennan, *Soviet-American Relations, 1917–1920* (Princeton: Princeton University Press, 1989).

4. *Berger et al. v. United States* (1921).

5. Zechariah Chafee Jr., *Free Speech in the United States* (Cambridge: Harvard University Press, 1954), p. 52n.

6. See David Gray Adler, "The President's Pardon Power," in *Inventing the American Presidency*, Thomas E. Cronin, ed. (Lawrence: University Press of Kansas, 1989).

THE ALIEN REGISTRATION (SMITH)
ACT OF 1940

World War I was concluded with the signing of the Armistice on November 11, 1918, at Rethondes, France, but the rancorous attitude of many in the United States toward aliens and radicals did not abate. Turmoil in the ranks of the labor movement and race riots were perceived as directly related to the radicalism of the Communist Party. In 1915 the Russian Bolshevik Vladimir Ilich Ulyanov (1870–1924), better known as Nikolai Lenin, called for the formation of a new international organization to promote civil wars against bourgeois governments through propaganda directed toward soldiers and workers. After the Bolshevik success in the Russian Revolution of 1917, an international organization of communist parties—variously called the Third International, the Communist International, or COMINTERN—was established in 1919 for such a purpose.

Postwar revolutionary activity under the COMINTERN banner occurred throughout the United States and Europe. It was in this "buoyant and heady atmosphere" that the Communist Party U.S.A. was formed in 1919.[1] It was the same "buoyant and heady atmosphere" that led to the so-called Red Scare in 1919–1920, which has been characterized as "a nationwide anti-radical hysteria provoked by a mounting fear and anxiety that a Bolshevik revolution in America was imminent—a revolution that would destroy property, church, home, marriage, civility, and the American way of life."[2] Deportation of radicals was the principal tool available to the federal government for combating this perceived internal threat.[3] Thus, the government resorted to wholesale raids of homes of suspected radicals and intellectuals, such as Attorney General Mitchell Palmer's raid of 1919.

Between the two wars with Germany, the anticommunists searched for a law that would provide a knockout punch in their fight to rid the country of those who they perceived would overthrow the government outside the political process. The Espionage Act of 1917 as amended by the Sedition Act of 1918 could not be effectively used after World War I because, by its terms, it applied only to activities "when the United States is at war." Proposed legislation in Congress was not lacking, however. For example, during late 1919 and early 1920, more than seventy sedition bills were introduced in Congress.[4] Yet it was two decades before Congress enacted a second peacetime sedition law.

The Alien Registration Act of 1940, commonly referred to as the Smith Act, made advocating the violent overthrow of the government or belonging to any group that advocated the violent overthrow of the government a crime with punishment of up to ten thousand dollars and ten years in prison. The Smith Act also continued the 1917 Espionage Act's proscription of undermining the morale of the armed forces. The Smith Act far exceeded anything related to its title: registration of aliens. As Zechariah Chafee pointed out, it was no more concerned with registration than was the Espionage Act of 1917. With spying, Chafee claimed that the Smith Act contained the "most drastic restrictions on freedom of speech ever enacted in the United States during peace."[5] While the 1940 act was technically a peacetime regulation, it—like its 1798 counterpart—was debated and enacted as war flared in Europe. If the United States had been at war in 1940, the Smith Act might have been rendered at least partly unnecessary by the applicability of the 1917 Espionage Act. The Smith Act, however, was specifically calculated to destroy the Communist Party U.S.A., war or no war. Moreover, unlike its 1798 counterpart, the 1940 act would not expire in two years. For the most part, the Smith Act currently remains intact at 18 U.S.C. § 2385 (2000).

Barely two months before World War II began with Germany's invasion of Poland, and nearly two and a half years before the Japanese bombing of Pearl Harbor, Representative Howard W. Smith (D-VA) introduced a bill that eventually became the law bearing his name.[6] Agitation against perceived subversion was running high, as evidenced by a comment on the House floor by Rep. T.F. Ford of California that the "mood of the House is such that if you brought in the Ten Commandments today and asked for their repeal and attached to that request an [anti-]alien law, you could get it."[7] Section 1 of the Smith Act was concerned with combating the harmful effect of seditious activity on the armed services; it was very similar to Section 3 of the 1917 act. The Navy Department had been concerned since 1935 with the distribution of leaflets by communists that urged military personnel to refuse to fight in any war waged by the "bosses of capitalism."[8] As tensions increased in Europe, an anxious military establishment joined the FBI in lobbying Congress to take action to thwart such calls for less military preparedness.[9] Although debate was highly contentious, H.R. 5138 passed the House on July 29, 1939, by a vote of 272 to 48.[10] The conference bill was approved by the House on June 22, 1940, by a vote of 382 to 4. The bill was summarily passed in the Senate without a roll-call vote.

Title I of the act contained the general antisedition law, which was similar to the 1798 act and Section 3 of the 1918 act. While the words differ among the three acts, their effect is similar: suppression of political dissent. Chafee, claiming that the 1940 act provided for guilt by mere association, declared that "the precise language of a sedition law is like the inscription on a sword. What matters is the existence of the weapon. Once the sword is placed in the hands of the people in power, then, whatever it says, they will be able to reach and slash at almost any unpopular person who is speaking or writing anything that they consider objectionable criticism of their policies."[11]

In general terms, Section 1 of the Smith Act prohibited any interference with the loyalty of military personnel. Section 2 made it a crime to advocate or teach the desirability of violently overthrowing the U.S. government. Section 3 made it unlawful to attempt to commit the prohibited acts or to enter into a conspiracy to commit any of the prohibited acts. Section 4 authorized confiscation of written or printed materials used to violate the act under the search warrant provision of the Espionage Act of 1917, and Section 5 provided for punishment upon conviction of up to ten thousand dollars, ten years in prison, or both.

The alliance with the Soviet Union during World War II initially checked the application of the Smith Act to the Communist Party U.S.A. However, as soon as the end of the war appeared and Truman began his foreign policy strategy of "containing" Soviet influence, prosecutions of Communist Party members began on the domestic front. Following a massive FBI investigation that began several years before and resulted in a legal brief of 1,850 pages with 846 exhibits, a federal grand jury in New York returned indictments on July 20, 1948, against eleven leaders of the Communist Party U.S.A. for violating the Smith Act. The Supreme Court, in *Dennis v. United States* (1951), upheld the convictions obtained by the government under these indictments, stating without much ado that "certainly an attempt to overthrow the Government by force, even though doomed from the outset because of inadequate numbers or power of the revolutionists, is a sufficient evil for Congress to prevent" (p. 509). During the period from October 1949 to June 30, 1956, the government had obtained 102 convictions of communist leaders under the Smith Act.[12] As a result of these numbers, the Communist Party was effectively crippled.

With the *Dennis* decision, the Smith Act had initially achieved its design, yet it soon became almost useless, due in part to its success but also to later decisions by the Supreme Court that significantly restricted its scope. Six years after *Dennis*, the convictions of several Communist Party leaders were set aside by the Supreme Court, while others were ordered acquitted. The Court held, in *Yates v. United States* (1957), that the offense in Section 2(a)(3) relating to organizing or helping to organize any society, group, or assembly of persons that teaches, advocates, or encourages the overthrow or destruction of any government in the United States by force or violence was restricted to the initial organizational efforts, not the continuing recruitment of members. Thus, the three-year statute of limitations barred prosecution of the fourteen leaders. The Court also held that the trial judge committed an error in not distinguishing in his charge to the jury between advocacy as a call to action and as an abstract principle. According to Justice John Marshall Harlan II, speaking for the Court, "the statute was aimed at the advocacy and teaching of concrete action for the forcible overthrow of the Government, and not of principles divorced from action" (pp. 319–320).[13]

The Alien Registration (Smith) Act of 1940

An act to prohibit certain subversive activities; to amend certain provisions of law with respect to the admission and deportation of aliens; to require the fingerprinting and registration of aliens; and for other purposes.

Be it enacted by the Senate and House of Representatives of the United States of America in Congress assembled,

Title I. Section 1. (a) It shall be unlawful for any person, with intent to interfere with, impair, or influence the loyalty, morale, or discipline of the military or naval forces of the United States—

(1) to advise, counsel, urge, or in any manner cause insubordination,

disloyalty, mutiny, or refusal of duty by any member of the military or naval forces of the United States; or

(2) to distribute any written or printed matter which advises, counsels, or urges insubordination, disloyalty, mutiny, or refusal of duty by any member of the military or naval forces of the United States.

(b) For the purpose of this section, the term "military or naval forces of the United States" includes the Army of the United States, as defined in section 1 of the National Defense Act of June 3, 1916, as amended (48 Stat. 153; U.S.C. title 10 section 2), the Navy, Marine Corps, Coast Guard, Naval Reserve, and Marine Corps Reserve of the United States; and, when any merchant vessel is commissioned in the Navy or is in the service of the Army or the Navy, includes the master, officers, and crew of such vessel.

Section 2. (a) It shall be unlawful for any person—

(1) to knowingly or willfully advocate, abet, advise, or teach the duty, necessity, desirability, or propriety of overthrowing or destroying any government in the United States by force or violence, or by the assassination of any officer of any such government;

(2) with the intent to cause the overthrow or destruction of any government in the United States, to print, publish, edit, issue, circulate, sell, distribute, or publicly display any written or printed matter advocating, advising, or teaching the duty, necessity, desirability, or propriety of overthrowing or destroying any government in the United States by force or violence;

(3) to organize or help to organize any society, group, or assembly of persons who teach, advocate, or encourage the overthrow or destruction of any government in the United States by force or violence; or to be or become a member of, or affiliate with, any such society, group, or assembly of persons, knowing the purposes thereof.

(b) For the purposes of this section, the term "government in the United States" means the Government of the United States, the government of any State, Territory, or possession of the United States, the government of the District of Columbia, or the government of any political subdivision of any of them.

Section 3. It shall be unlawful for any person to attempt to commit, or to conspire to commit, any of the acts prohibited by the provisions of this title.

Section 4. Any written or printed matter of the character described in section 1 or section 2 of this Act, which is intended for the use in violation of this Act, may be taken from any house or any other place in which it may be found, or from any person whose possession it may be, under a search warrant issued pursuant to the provisions of Title XI of the [1917 Espionage] Act entitled "An act to punish acts of interference with the foreign relations, the neutrality and the foreign commerce of the United States, to punish espionage, and better enforce the criminal laws of the United States, and for other purposes," approved June 15, 1917 (40 Stat. 228, U.S.C. Title 18, ch. 18).

Section 5. (a) Any person who violates any of the provisions of this title shall, upon conviction thereof, be fined not more than $10,000 or imprisoned for not more than ten years, or both.

(b) No person convicted of violating any of the provisions of this title shall, during the five years next following his conviction, be eligible for employment by the United States, or by any department or agency thereof (including any corporation the stock of which is wholly owned by the United States).

Title IV. Section 40. If any provision of this act, or the application thereof to any person or circumstances, is held invalid, the remainder of the Act, and the application of such provision to other persons or circumstances, shall not be affected thereby.

Section 41. This Act may be cited as the "Alien Registration Act, 1940." Approved June 28, 1940.

NOTES

1. Irving Howe and Lewis Coser, *The American Communist Party: A Critical History (1919–1957)* (Boston: Beacon Press, 1957), p. 27.
2. Murray B. Levin, *Political Hysteria in America: The Democratic Capacity for Repression* (New York: Basic Books, 1971), p. 29.
3. The current deportation law in 1920 was very similar in language to the Smith Act. It excluded, among others, aliens who were anarchists, who believed or advocated the forceful or violent overthrow of the government, and those who were members of or affiliated with any organization that entertains a belief in, teaches, or advocates the forceful or violent overthrow of the government. (See 8 U.S.C. § 1227 for the general deportable alien statute and § 1227(a)(4)(A)(iii) for the section covering those advocating and teaching the forceful or violent overthrow of the government.)
4. The principal legislative effort at the time was the Graham-Sterling Bill, which sought to inflict up to ten thousand dollars in fines and as many as twenty years in prison on anyone seeking to overthrow the government. This bill died after being unfavorably reported by the Rules Committee. See Levin, Chapter 2.
5. Zechariah Chafee Jr., *Free Speech in the United States* (Cambridge: Harvard University Press, 1941), p. 441.
6. Smith's bill (H.R. 5138), along with thirty-eight others, were pending in Congress during July 1939. 84 *Cong. Rec.* 953.
7. 84 *Cong. Rec.* 10370 (July 28, 1939).

8. Chafee, *Free Speech*, pp. 448–449.

9. Debate in the Congress regarding Title I. Pro: Representative Samuel Hobbs (D-AL), 84 *Cong. Rec.* 10357 (July 28, 1939); and Representative William Blackney (R-MI), 10365. Con: Representative Edouard Izac (D-CA) (the Army and Navy "wet-nurse bill," 84 *Cong. Rec.* 9540, 10379, 10381); Representative Donald O'Toole (D-NY), 10376.

10. 84 *Cong. Rec.* 10455.

11. Chafee, *Free Speech*, pp. 467, 474.

12. Michal R. Belknap, *Cold War Political Justice: The Smith Act, the Communist Party, and American Civil Liberties* (Westport, CT: Greenwood Press, 1977), p. 176.

13. An interesting aside is the fact that dissenting in *Yates* (stating, "The conspiracy includes the same group of defendants as in the *Dennis* case. . . . They, nevertheless, served in the same army and were engaged in the same mission") was Justice Thomas C. Clark, who was appointed to the high court on August 24, 1949, but was the attorney general who initiated the prosecution and indictment in *Dennis* on July 20, 1948.

THE INTERNAL SECURITY (MCCARRAN) ACT OF 1950

No sooner had the United States completed waging a war against external threats in Europe for the second time in the twentieth century than it waged a second war against perceived internal threats at home as well. This time Congress acted in 1950 to combat what many called the second Red Scare when it overrode President Harry Truman's veto and Senator Hubert Humphrey's (D-MN) abortive filibuster of the Internal Security (McCarran) Act of 1950.[1] Unlike previous anti-sedition statutes, the McCarran Act was explicitly aimed at the Communist Party and implicitly at the USSR. The 1798 Sedition Act was directed at "any person . . . writing, printing, uttering or publishing any false, scandalous and malicious writing or writings against the government." Likewise, the 1918 Sedition Act was directed to "whoever, when the United States is at war, shall willfully utter, print, write, or publish any disloyal, profane, scurrilous, or abusive language about the form of government of the United States." The general provisions of the Smith Act of 1940 applied to "any person [who] knowingly or willfully advocate[s], abet[s], advise[s], or teach[es] the duty, necessity, desirability, or propriety of overthrowing or destroying any government in the United States by force or violence." The McCarran Act, on the other contrary, began with a congressional finding of fact[2] that "there exists a world Communist movement" whose "direction and control . . . is vested in and exercised by the Communist dictatorship of a foreign country."[3] Beyond that finding, Congress also determined that all persons who participated in the "world Communist movement" automatically "repudiat[ed] their allegiance to the United States, and in effect transfer[red] their allegiance to the foreign country in which is vested the direction and control of the world Communist movement."

Just as the previous landmark laws concerning internal security had been enacted either during a declared war or when hostilities appeared imminent, there was growing concern among many people in 1950 that internal and external threats would lead the United States into a third world war. External events appeared unmistakable. Hostilities had already broken out in Korea when North Korean communists who had been recently installed (September 1948) by the Soviet government invaded South Korea. Beijing had just fallen (January 1949) to Mao Zedong's (1893–1976) communist insurgents as they pushed the recognized government of General Chiang Kai-shek's (1887–1975) forces to the small island of Taiwan. Greece had been embroiled in a communist-provoked civil war, and Turkey was under Soviet pressure to yield bases and naval passage through the Dardanelles. Stalin had recently engineered the formation of COMINFORM (Communist Information Bureau) as an apparent replacement of the Third Communist International (COMINTERN) that had been dismantled during the war. In western Europe, a successful communist coup ousted the government of Czechoslovakia, and the Soviets had attempted to expel its former allies from Berlin by instituting a land blockade around the city. Apart from all that, the Soviet Union's successful deployment of an atomic bomb in 1949 added to international tension at mid-century.

On the domestic front, events appeared every bit as ominous. Prominent public officials were being exposed as communist sympathizers and Communist Party members. Avowed communist Whittaker Chambers accused Alger Hiss of being a Communist Party member. Hiss had served the government in different posts, including advising President Roosevelt at Yalta and serving as temporary secretary-general of the United Nations at the San Francisco Conference. In 1948 Harry Dexter White, an economist with the Department of Treasury who, as counterpart to the British economist John Maynard Keynes, drafted the organizational plan for the International Monetary Fund established at the famous 1944 Bretton Woods Conference, was accused of being a Soviet spy. An up-and-coming Justice Department attorney, Judith Coplon, was convicted in 1948 for stealing classified government documents and conspiring to transmit them to foreign powers. These and other events—such as the arrest of Julius and Ethel Rosenberg for selling atom bomb secrets to the Soviet Union; Churchill's "Iron Curtain" speech[4] at Westminster College in Fulton, Missouri; the uproar over the movie stars who were brought before the House Un-American Activities Committee amid allegations of treason; and Senator Joseph McCarthy's famous assertion to the Wheeling, West Virginia, Republican Women's Club that he had the names of 205 State Department communists—brought affairs to a critical mass.

President Truman denounced the McCarran Act in his veto message as "the greatest danger to freedom of the press, speech, and assembly since the Alien and Sedition Acts of 1798." Although the president found fault with the McCarran Act, he had actually intensified the midcentury Red Scare himself by initiating the Truman Doctrine, which he outlined in an address to members of Congress on March 12, 1947, as a pledge to "free peoples who are resisting attempted subjugation by armed minorities or by outside pressures." Congress immediately implemented this pledge with a $400,000 aid program for communist-threatened Greece. Moreover, Truman committed economic and military advisers to any unstable nation whose system was deemed susceptible to communist influence. In his speech, Truman outlined the communist threat as follows:

> The [communist] way of life is based upon the will of a minority forcibly imposed upon the majority. It relies upon terror and oppression, a controlled press and radio, fixed elections, and the suppression of personal freedom. I believe that it must be the policy of the United States to support free peoples who are resisting attempted subjugation by armed minorities or by outside pressures.

THE SUBVERSIVE ACTIVITIES CONTROL ACT OF 1950

Although this act threatened the very existence of the Communist Party in the United States, it stopped short of outright abolition. Title I of the McCarran Act, The Subversive Activities Control Act of 1950, primarily sought to counter communist influence by making it unlawful under the act to knowingly "conspire, or agree with any other person, to perform any act which would substantially contribute to the establishment within the United States of a totalitarian dictatorship."[5] It required all communist-affiliated organizations to register with the attorney general on a form that revealed their officers and individual members of the preceding twelve months, with a complete financial accounting. Additionally, members of communist-affiliated organizations were forbidden to be employed by the national government, defense contractors, and labor unions. Public officeholders were required to reveal membership in those organizations. Party members were not permitted to obtain passports for travel, and organizations affiliated with the Communist Party were denied various tax privileges contained in the Internal Revenue Code. Communist organizations were also denied mail privileges unless they noted the name of the organization, indicating thereon that it was a "Communist organization." This disclosure also applied to broadcasts by communists on radio and television.

The Subversive Activities Control Act of 1950

TITLE I—SUBVERSIVE ACTIVITIES CONTROL

Section 1. (a) This title may be cited as the "Subversive Activities Control Act of 1950." . . .

NECESSITY FOR LEGISLATION

Section 2. As a result of evidence adduced before various committees of the Senate and House of Representatives, the Congress hereby finds that:

(1) There exists a world Communist movement which, in its origins, its development, and its present practice, is a world-wide revolutionary movement whose purpose it is, by treachery, deceit, infiltration into other groups (governmental and otherwise), espionage, sabotage, terrorism, and any other means deemed necessary, to establish a Communist totalitarian dictatorship in the countries throughout the world through the medium of a world-wide Communist organization.

(2) The establishment of a totalitarian dictatorship in any country results in the suppression of all opposition to the party in power, the subordination of the rights of individuals to the state, the denial of fundamental rights and liberties which are characteristic of a representative form of government, such as freedom of speech, of the press, of assembly, and of religious worship, and results in the maintenance of control over the people through fear, terrorism, and brutality. . . .

(4) The direction and control of the world Communist movement is vested in and exercised by the Communist dictatorship of a foreign country . . .

(9) In the United States those individuals who knowingly and willfully participate in the world Communist movement, when they so participate, in effect repudiate their allegiance to the United States, and in effect transfer their allegiance to the foreign country in which is vested the direction and control of the world Communist movement.

(10) In pursuance of communism's stated objectives, the most pow-

erful existing Communist dictatorship has, by the methods referred to above, already caused the establishment in numerous foreign countries of Communist totalitarian dictatorships, and threatens to establish similar dictatorships in still other countries.

(11) The agents of communism have devised clever and ruthless espionage and sabotage tactics which are carried out in many instances in form or manner successfully evasive of existing law . . .

(13) There are, under our present immigration laws, numerous aliens who have been found to be deportable, many of whom are in the sub to roam the country at will without supervision or control.

(14) One device for infiltration by Communists is by procuring naturalization for disloyal aliens who use their citizenship as a badge for admission into the fabric of our society.

(15) The Communist movement in the United States is an organization numbering thousands of adherents, rigidly and ruthlessly disciplined. Awaiting and seeking to advance a moment when the United States may be so far extended by foreign engagements, so far divided in counsel, or so far in industrial or financial straits, that overthrow of the Government of the United States by force and violence may seem possible of achievement, it seeks converts far and wide by an extensive system of schooling and indoctrination. Such preparations by Communist organizations in other countries have aided in supplanting existing governments. The Communist organization in the United States, pursuing its stated objectives, the recent successes of Communist methods in other countries, and the nature and control of the world Communist movement itself, present a clear and present danger to the security of the United States and to the existence of free American institutions, and make it necessary that Congress, in order to provide for the common defense, to preserve the sovereignty of the United States as an independent nation, and to guarantee to each State a republican form of government, enact appropriate legislation recognizing the existence of such worldwide conspiracy and designed to prevent it from accomplishing its purpose in the United States.

DEFINITIONS

Section 3. For the purposes of this title . . .

(3) The term "Communist-action organization" means:

(a) any organization in the United States . . . which (i) is substantially directed, dominated, or controlled by the foreign government or foreign organization controlling the world Communist movement referred to in section 2 of this title, and (ii) operates primarily to advance the objectives of such world Communist movement as referred to in section 2 of this title; and

(b) any section, branch, fraction, or cell of any organization defined in subparagraph (a) of this paragraph which has not complied with the registration requirements of this title.

(4) The term "Communist-front organization" means any organization in the United States (other than a Communist-action organization as Cold War and the Battle against Subversion defined in paragraph (3) of this section) which (A) is substantially directed, dominated, or controlled by a Communist-action organization, and (B) is primarily operated for the purpose of giving aid and support to a Communist-action organization, a Communist foreign government, or the world Communist movement referred to in section 2 of this title.

(5) The term "Communist organization" means a Communist-action organization or a Communist front organization.

CERTAIN PROHIBITED ACTS

Section 4. (a) It shall be unlawful for any person knowingly to combine, conspire, or agree with any other person to perform any act which would substantially contribute to the establishment within the United States of a totalitarian dictatorship, the direction and control of which is to be vested in, or exercised by or under the domination or control of, any foreign government, foreign organization, or foreign individual: Provided, however, that this subsection shall not apply to the proposal of a constitutional amendment.

(f) Neither the holding of office nor membership in any Communist organization by any person shall constitute per se a violation of subsection (a) of this section or of any other criminal statute. The fact of the registration of any person under section 7 or section 8 of this title as an officer or member of any Communist organization shall not be received in evidence against such person in any prosecution for any alleged violation of subsection (a) or subsection (c) of this section or for any alleged violation of any other criminal statute.

EMPLOYMENT OF MEMBERS OF COMMUNIST ORGANIZATIONS

Section 5. (a) When a Communist organization, as defined in paragraph (5) of section 3 of this title, is registered or there is in effect a final order of the Board requiring such organization to register, it shall be unlawful:

(1) For any member of such organization, with knowledge or notice that such organization is so registered or that such order has become final:

(A) in seeking, accepting, or holding any nonelective office or employment under the United States, to conceal or fail to disclose the fact that he is a member of such organization; or

(B) to hold any nonelective office or employment under the United States; or

(C) in seeking, accepting, or holding employment in any defense facility, to conceal or fail to disclose that he is a member of such organization; or

(D) if such organization is a Communist-action organization, to engage in any employment in any defense facility.

(2) For any officer or employee of the United States or of any defense facility, with knowledge or notice of such final order of the Board—

(A) to contribute funds or services to such organization; or

(B) to advise, counsel, or urge any person, with knowledge or notice that such person is a member of such organization, to perform, or to omit to perform, any act if such act or omission would constitute a violation of any provision of subparagraph (1) of this subsection. . . .

DENIAL OF PASSPORTS TO MEMBERS OF COMMUNIST ORGANIZATIONS

Section 6. (a) When a Communist organization as defined in paragraph (5) of section 3 of this title, or there is in effect a final order of the Board requiring such organization to register, it shall be unlawful for any member of such organization, with knowledge or notice that such organization is so registered or that such order has become final:

(1) to make application for a passport, or the renewal of a passport, to be issued or renewed by of or under the authority of the United States; or

(2) to use or attempt to use any such passport. . . .

REGISTRATION AND ANNUAL REPORTS OF COMMUNIST ORGANIZATIONS

Section 7. (a) Each Communist-action organization (including any organization required, by a final order of the Board, to register as a Communist-action organization) shall, within [thirty days], register with the Attorney General, on a form prescribed by him by regulations, as a Communist action organization.

(b) Each Communist-front organization (including any organization required, by a final order of the Board, to register as a Communist-front organization) shall, within [thirty days], register with the Attorney General, on a form prescribed by him by regulations, as a Communist-front organization . . .

(d) The registration made under subsection (a) or line (b) shall be accompanied by a registration statement, to be prepared and filed in such manner and form as the Attorney General shall by regulations prescribe, containing the following information:

(1) The name of the organization and the address of its principal office.

(e) It shall be the duty of each organization registered under this section to file with the Attorney General on or before February 1 or the year following the year in which it registers, and on or before February 1 of each succeeding year, an annual report . . .

REGISTRATION OF MEMBERS OF COMMUNIST-ACTION ORGANIZATIONS

Section 8. (A) Any individual who is or becomes a member of any organization concerning which (1) there is in effect a final order of the Board requiring such organization to register under 7(a) of this title as a Communist-action organization . . . shall within sixty days after said order has become final, or within thirty days after becoming a member of such organization, whichever is later, register with the Attorney General as a member of such organization . . .

PENALTIES

Section 15. (a) If there is in effect with respect to any organization or individual a final order of the Board requiring registration under section 7 or section 8 of this title:

(1) such organization shall, upon conviction of failure to register, to file any registration statement or annual report, or to keep records as required by section 7, be punished for each such offense by a fine of not more than $10,000, and

(2) each individual having a duty under sub section (h) of section 7 to register or to file any registration statement or annual report on behalf of such organization, and each individual having a duty to register under section 8, shall, upon conviction of failure to so register or to file any such registration statement or annual report, be punished for each such offense by a fine of not more than $10,000, or imprisonment for not more than five years, or by both such fine and imprisonment.

Approved September 23, 1950.

NOTES

1. The McCarran Act was named after its chief sponsor, Senator Pat McCarran (D-NV), perhaps the Senate's most powerful anticommunist, who served in the Senate from 1932 until his death in 1952 and was for several years the chairman of the Senate Internal Security Subcommittee. Representative John S. Wood (D-GA), chairman of the House Un-American Activities Committee, sponsored the bill in the House of Representatives.

2. Congressional findings of fact are binding on the courts. As the Supreme Court stated in the case of *Communist Party v. Subversive Activities Control Board* (1961, pp. 94–95) with respect to the congressional findings relating to the nature of the world communist movement and the threat it poses to the security of the United States: "It is not for the courts to reexamine the validity of these legislative findings and reject them, they are the product of extensive investigation by Committees of Congress over more than a decade and a half. We certainly cannot dismiss them as unfounded or irrational imaginings." (Citations omitted.)

3. The statutory definition of a "totalitarian dictatorship" obviously described the Communist Party of the Soviet Union and its dictatorial leader, Iosif Vissarionovich Dzhugashvili (Joseph Stalin) perfectly well. It defined the "totalitarian dictatorship" as "characterized by (A) the existence of a single political party, organized on a dictatorial basis, and with so close an identity between such party and its policies and the government policies of the country in which it exists, that the party and the government constitute an indistinguishable unit, and (B) the forcible suppression of opposition to such party."

4. The "iron curtain" metaphor was coined by Winston Churchill in a speech to the students and faculty of Westminster College in Fulton, Missouri, on March 4, 1946, in which he asserted: "From Stettin in the Baltic to Trieste in the Adriatic, an Iron Curtain has descended across the Continent. Behind that line lie all the capitals of the ancient states of Central and Eastern Europe. Warsaw, Berlin, Prague, Vienna, Budapest, Belgrade, Bucharest and Sofia, all these famous cities and the populations around them lie in what I must call the Soviet sphere." Spencer Warren, "The Ever-Relevant Message," *The National Interest* (Winter 1995/96).

5. The Subversive Activities Control Act was repealed by the Friendship Act, Pub. L. 103–199, Tit. VIII, § 803(1), Dec. 19, 1993.

THE EMERGENCY DETENTION ACT OF 1950

Title II of the McCarran Act, known as the Emergency Detention Act of 1950, contained a legislative finding or declaration that the communist threat had created a

> clear and present danger to the security of the United States and to the existence of free American institutions [making it] necessary that Congress, in order to provide for the common defense, to preserve the sovereignty of the United States as an independent nation, and

to guarantee to each State a republican form of government, enact appropriate legislation recognizing the existence of such world wide conspiracy and designed to prevent it from accomplishing its purpose in the United States.

This was indeed remarkable legislative language directed toward a recent wartime ally and with one whom it had recently entered into an agreement under which the United States would "supply the Government of the Union of Soviet Socialist Republics with . . . defense articles, defense services, and defense information," and the Soviet Union would "contribute to the defense of the United States of America and the strengthening thereof, and will provide . . . articles, services, facilities or information" in connection therewith.[1]

The Emergency Detention Act empowered the president to declare an "internal security emergency," whenever one of three events occurred: when there was a congressional declaration of war, an invasion, or an insurrection within the country. In case of such emergency, the president was authorized to apprehend and detain any "person as to whom there is reasonable ground to believe that such person probably will engage in, or probably will conspire with others to engage in, acts of espionage or of sabotage." The statute required the government to take all apprehended persons before a committing magistrate who could order their discharge or detention after a hearing. If detention was ordered, an appeal by the detainee to the newly created Detention Review Board, and ultimately to the judiciary, was available.

The Emergency Detention Act of 1950

FINDINGS OF FACT AND DECLARATION OF PURPOSE

Section 101. As a result of evidence adduced before various committees of the Senate and the House of Representatives, the Congress hereby finds that: . . .

(10) The experience of many countries in World War II and thereafter with so-called "fifth columns" which employed espionage and sabotage to weaken the internal security and defense of nations resisting totalitarian dictatorships demonstrated the grave dangers and fatal effectiveness of such internal espionage and sabotage.

(11) The security and safety of the territory and Constitution of the United States, and the successful prosecution of the common defense, especially in time of invasion, war, or insurrection in aid of a foreign enemy, require every reasonable and lawful protection against espionage, and against sabotage to national-defense material, premises, forces and utilities, including related facilities for mining, manufacturing, transportation, research, training, military and civilian supply, and other activities essential to national defense.

(12) Due to the wide distribution and complex interrelation of facilities which are essential to national defense and due to the increased effectiveness and technical development in espionage and sabotage activities, the free and unrestrained movement in such emergencies of members or agents of [Communist] organizations and The Cold War and the Battle against Subversion stage operations would make adequate surveillance to prevent espionage and sabotage impossible and would therefore constitute a clear and present danger to the public peace and the safety of the United States. . . .

(14) The detention of persons who there is reasonable ground to believe probably will commit or conspire with others to commit espionage or sabotage is, in a time of internal security emergency, essential to the common defense and to the safety and security of the territory, the people and the Constitution of the United States.

(15) It is also essential that such detention in an emergency involving the internal security of the Nation shall be so authorized, executed, restricted, and reviewed as to prevent any interference with the constitutional rights and privileges of any persons, and at the same time shall be sufficiently effective to permit the performance by the Congress and the President of their constitutional duties to provide for the common defense to wage war, and to preserve, protect, and defend the Constitution, the Government, and the people of the United States.

DECLARATION OF "INTERNAL SECURITY EMERGENCY"

Section 102. (a) In the event of any one of the following:

(1) Invasion of the territory of the United States or its possessions,

(2) Declaration of war by Congress, or

(3) Insurrection within the United States or aid of a foreign enemy, and if, upon the occurrence of one or more of the above, the President shall find that the proclamation of an emergency pursuant to this section is essential to the preservation, protection and defense of the Constitution, and to the common defense and safety of the territory and

people of the United States, the President is authorized to make public proclamation of the existence of an "Internal Security Emergency."

(b) A state of "Internal Security Emergency" (hereinafter referred to as the "emergency") so declared shall continue in existence until terminated by proclamation of the President or by concurrent resolution of the Congress.

DETENTION DURING EMERGENCY

Section 103. (a) Whenever there shall be in existence such an emergency, the President, acting through the Attorney General, is hereby authorized to apprehend and by order detain, pursuant to the provisions of this title, each person as to whom there is reasonable ground to believe that such person probably will engage in, or probably will conspire with others to engage in, acts of espionage or of sabotage.

(b) Any person detained hereunder (hereinafter referred to as "the detainee") shall be released from such emergency detention upon:

(1) the termination of such emergency proclamation of the President or by concurrent resolution of the Congress; or

(2) an order of release issued by the Attorney General;

(3) a final order of release after hearing by the Board of Detention Review, hereinafter established;

(4) a final order of release by a United States court, after review of the action of the Board of Detention Review, or upon a writ of habeas corpus.

PROCEDURE FOR APPREHENSION AND DETENTION

Section 104. (a) The Attorney General, or such officer or officers of the Department of Justice as he may from time to time designate, are authorized during such emergency to execute in writing and issue:

(1) a warrant for the apprehension of each person as to whom there is reasonable ground to believe that such person probably will engage in or probably will conspire with others to engage in, acts of espionage or sabotage; and

(2) an application for an order to be issued pursuant to subsection (d) of this section for the detention of such person for the duration of such emergency.

Each such warrant shall issue only upon probable cause, supported by oath or affirmation, and shall particularly describe the person to be apprehended or detained. . . .

Section 109. (a) Any Board created under this title is empowered:

(1) to review upon petition of any detainee any order of detention issued pursuant to section 104 (d) of this title;

(2) to determine whether there is reasonable ground to believe that such detainee probably will engage in, or conspire with others to engage in espionage or sabotage;

(3) to issue orders confirming, modifying, or revoking any such order of detention; and

(4) to hear and determine any claim made pursuant to this paragraph by any person who shall have been detained pursuant to this title and shall have been released from such detention, for loss of income by such person resulting from such detention if without reasonable grounds. Upon the issuance of any final order for indemnification pursuant to this paragraph, the Attorney General is authorized and directed to make payment of such indemnity to the person entitled thereto from such funds as may be appropriated to him for such purpose. . . .

Section 111. (a) Any petitioner aggrieved by an order of the Board denying in whole or in part the relief sought by him, or by the failure or refusal of the Attorney General to obey such order, shall be entitled to the judicial review or judicial enforcement provided hereinunder in this section.

Approved September 23, 1950.

NOTE

1. "Mutual Aid Agreement between the United States and the Union of Soviet Socialist Republics: June 11, 1942," The Avalon Project at the Yale Law School (http://www.yale.edu/lawweb/avalon/wwii/amsov42.htm) [accessed July 25, 2000].

THE COMMUNIST CONTROL ACT OF 1954

The significance of the McCarran Act lies more for its role as a barometric reading of public sentiment at the height of the "Cold War" (a metaphorical term coined by Truman advisor Bernard Baruch in reference to the geopolitical competition between the United States and the USSR) than for anything that was achieved in its application.

Initially, it appeared that the Subversive Activities Control Act of 1950 would receive a favorable reception in the Supreme Court. The first decision was a long time in coming, nonetheless. It was indeed favorable. In *Communist Party v. Subversive Activities Control Board* (1961), the Court sustained the registration requirement of Section 7 on the basis that it "is a regulatory, not a prohibitory statute. It does not make unlawful pursuit of the objectives that § 2 defines" (p. 55). Typically, the Court refused to consider the constitutionality of aspects of the statute that were not necessary for a decision; namely, in this situation, the provisions of Title I that applied to individuals' registration.

The Supreme Court soon, however, began to strike down various aspects of Title I that related to individuals. First, the passport ban in Section 6 was declared invalid in *Aptheker v. Secretary of State* (1964). The Court stated in *Aptheker* that the ban "too broadly and indiscriminately restricts the right to travel and thereby abridges the liberty guaranteed by the Fifth Amendment" (p. 505). Herbert Aptheker, editor of the Communist Party's intellectual journal *Political Affairs*, and Elizabeth Flynn, a member of the party's National Executive Committee, had their passport applications rejected by the State Department solely on the basis of their Communist Party affiliation. Rejecting the government's contention that Aptheker and Flynn could escape the ban by resigning from the Communist Party, the Supreme Court indicated that requiring someone to yield the First Amendment's freedom of association would not pass constitutional muster. As Justice Arthur Goldberg, speaking for the Court, put it: "Since freedom of association is itself guaranteed in the First Amendment, restrictions imposed upon the right to travel cannot be dismissed by asserting that the right to travel could be fully exercised if the individual would first yield up his membership in a given association" (p. 507). In short, the Court rejected the government's contention "that a member of a registering organization could recapture his freedom to travel by simply . . . abandoning his membership in the organization. Since freedom of association is itself guaranteed in the First Amendment" (378 U.S. 500, 507).

The Communist Party continued its refusal to register under Section 7 after the adverse decision in *Communist Party v. Subversive Activities Control Board*. Thus, the SACB sought to compel registration of its individual members under Section 8. The refusal of the party's president, William Albertson, and other members to comply led to an order by the SACB that found its way to the Supreme Court in *Albertson v. Subversive Activities Control Board* (1965). The Court, in *Albertson*, held that the Section 8 registration requirement violated the Fifth Amendment privilege against self-incrimination. Although the Supreme Court practically abolished the membership requirements of the McCarran Act, the Smith Act's membership clause—Section 2(a)(3)—was still intact. To be sure, prosecution under the Smith Act was more difficult because the government had to prove that a person was actively engaged in the proscribed conduct "teaching, advocating, or encouraging the overthrow or destruction of the government . . . by force or violence" instead of simply relying on membership in the Communist Party.

Yet, that very point turned out to be the Smith Act's salvation. For the Supreme Court stated, in *Scales v. United States* (1961), "The membership clause of the Smith Act on its face . . . neither proscribes membership in Communist organizations, as such, but only in organizations engaging in advocacy of violent overthrow, nor punishes membership in that kind of organization" except as to one "knowing the purposes thereof. . . . We have also held that the proscribed membership must be active, and not nominal, passive or theoretical" (pp. 207–208). This dependency on the facts required by the Smith Act, as distinguished from the McCarran Act's automatic membership provision, was made abundantly clear in *Noto v. United States* (1961), in which the Court overturned a conviction under the Smith Act on the basis that facts did not warrant a finding that Noto's Communist Party was engaged in the proscribed activity.

The Subversive Activities Control Act continued to have problems. In *United States v. Robel* (1967), a holding that is consistent with *Albertson* and *Scales*, the Supreme Court invalidated Section

5(a)(1)(D), which banned employment by members of a communist organization from working in a defense facility. Robel, a Communist Party member, refused to cease employment at the shipyard where he was employed after the secretary of defense had designated it a "defense facility" as defined under the Act. Robel's indictment for illegally working in a defense facility was dismissed by the U.S. District Court and upheld by the Supreme Court on the basis that the statute created automatic guilt by the mere fact of party membership in violation of Robel's First Amendment right of association.

As the various sections of the Subversive Activities Control Act continued to wind their way through the court system slowly, the Emergency Detention Act was listlessly languishing on the books. As mentioned, the closest it came to being available for use was when President Truman declared a national emergency on December 16, 1950. However, it was never used even then. For one thing, Congress never declared a state of war in the Korean conflict. For another, it could be that Truman simply saw no usefulness in doing so. In any event, the act lay dormant until Congress repealed it on September 25, 1971. Not content with the lack of progress in carrying out the Internal Security Act of 1950, Congress enacted the Communist Control Act of 1954, which sought an absolute ban of the domestic version of the Communist Party from the political process.

The Subversive Activities Control Act had a most interesting, and most appropriately ironic, ending. It was repealed in 1993 by an act called the Friendship Act, the full title being the Act for Reform in Emerging New Democracies and Support and Help for Improved Partnership with Russia, Ukraine, and the Other New Independent States. These democratically disposed new friends were none other than the former republics of the archenemy: the USSR. After a half-century hiatus, these erstwhile enemies were friends again.

The Friendship Act did not repeal the Communist Control Act of 1954. It did, however, declare that the

> Congress finds and affirms that provisions such as those described in this section, including—the Communist Control Act of 1954 (Public Law 83–637), ... should not be construed as being directed against Russia, Ukraine, or the other independent states of the former Soviet Union, connoting an adversarial relationship between the

United States and the independent states, or signifying or implying in any manner unfriendliness toward the independent states. (See Pub. L. 103–199, § 103(c), 22 U.S.C. § 58011 [2000 ed.].)

In other words, we may still have our communists to contend with, but, alas, they are apparently our very own.

Although the Communist Control Act remains on the statute books, its continuing impact is little, if any. There is perhaps no more fitting ending to this segment of congressional landmarks and the First Amendment than a quotation from U.S. District Judge Copple in *Blawis v. Bolin*, 358 F. Supp. 349 (U.S.D.C. Arizona 1973) as he refused to permit the Communist Control Act to keep a Communist Party candidate off the ballot:

In the absence of a showing that these people, forming this party in Arizona or the United States, are guilty of the forbidden advocacy, the statutes are merely the suppression of a hated minority. "All political ideas cannot and should not be channeled into the programs of our two major parties. History has amply proved the virtue of political activity by minority, dissident groups, who innumerable times have been in the vanguard of democratic thought and whose programs were ultimately accepted. . . . The absence of such voices would be a symptom of grave illness in our society." (Quoting *Sweezy v. New Hampshire ex rel. Wyman*, 354 U.S. 234, 250–251 [1957]). It should not be forgotten that the "radical trade-unionists" of our earlier history did not "overthrow the free enterprise system," but are now charged in some quarters with being staunch members of its Establishment.

The Communist Control Act of 1954

Section 841. Findings and declarations of fact:
The Congress finds and declares that the Communist Party of the United States, although purportedly a political party, is in fact an instrumentality of a conspiracy to overthrow the Government of the United States. It constitutes an authoritarian dictatorship within a republic, demanding for itself the rights and privileges accorded to political parties, but denying to all others the liberties guaranteed by the Constitution. Unlike political parties, which evolve their policies and programs through public means,

by the reconciliation of a wide variety of individual views, and submit those policies and programs to the electorate at large for approval or disapproval, the policies and programs of the Communist Party are secretly prescribed for it by the foreign leaders of the world Communist movement. Its members have no part in determining its goals, and are not permitted to voice dissent to party objectives. Unlike members of political parties, members of the Communist Party are recruited for indoctrination with respect to its objectives and methods, and are organized, instructed, and disciplined to carry into action slavishly the assignments given them by their hierarchical chieftains. Unlike political parties, the Communist Party acknowledges no constitutional or statutory limitations upon its conduct or upon that of its members. The Communist Party is relatively small numerically, and gives scant indication of capacity ever to attain its ends by lawful political means. The peril inherent in its operation arises not from its numbers, but from its failure to acknowledge any limitation as to the nature of its activities, and its dedication to the proposition that the present constitutional Government of the United States ultimately must be brought to ruin by any available means, including resort to force and violence. Holding that doctrine, its role as the agency of a hostile foreign power renders its existence a clear present and continuing danger to the security of the United States. It is the means whereby individuals are seduced into the service of the world Communist movement, trained to do its bidding, and directed and controlled in the conspiratorial performance of their revolutionary services. Therefore, the Communist Party should be outlawed.

Section 842. Proscription of Communist Party, its successors, and subsidiary organizations:

The Communist Party of the United States, or any successors of such party regardless of the assumed name, whose object or purpose is to overthrow the Government of the United States, or the government of any State, Territory, District, or possession thereof, or the government of any political subdivision therein by force and violence, are not entitled to any of the rights, privileges, and immunities attendant upon legal bodies created under the jurisdiction of the laws of the United States or any political subdivision thereof; and whatever rights, privileges, and immunities which have heretofore been granted to said party or any subsidiary organization by reason of the laws of the United States or any political subdivision thereof, are terminated: Provided, however, that nothing in this section shall be construed as amending the Internal Security Act of 1950, as amended (50 U.S.C. 781 et seq.).

Section 843. Application of Internal Security Act of 1950 to members of Communist Party and other subversive organizations; "Communist Party" defined:

(a) Whoever knowingly and willfully becomes or remains a member of (1) the Communist Party, or (2) any other organization having for one of its purposes or objectives the establishment, control, conduct, seizure, or overthrow of the Government of the United States, or the government of any State or political subdivision thereof, by the use of force or violence, with knowledge of the purpose or objective of such organization shall be subject to all the provisions and penalties of the Internal Security Act of 1950, as amended (50 U.S.C. 781 et seq.), as a member of a "Communist-action" organization.

(b) For the purposes of this section, the term "Communist Party" means the organization now known as the Communist Party of the United States of America, the Communist Party of any State or subdivision thereof, and any unit or subdivision of any such organization, whether or not any change is hereafter made in the name thereof.

Section 844. Determination by jury of membership in Communist Party, participation, or knowledge of purpose:

In determining membership or participation in the Communist Party or any other organization defined in this Act, or knowledge of the purpose or objective of such party or organization, the jury, under instructions from the court, shall consider evidence, if presented, as to whether the accused person:

(1) Has been listed to his knowledge as a member in any book or any of the lists, records, correspondence, or any other document of the organization;

(2) Has made financial contribution to the organization in dues, assessments, loans, or in any other form;

(3) Has made himself subject to the discipline of the organization in any form whatsoever;

(4) Has executed orders, plans, or directives of any kind of the organization;

(5) Has acted as an agent, courier, messenger, correspondent, organizer, or in any other capacity in behalf of the organization;

(6) Has conferred with officers or other members of the organization in behalf of any plan or enterprise of the organization;

(7) Has been accepted to his knowledge as an officer or member of the organization or as one to be called upon for services by other officers or members of the organization;

(8) Has written, spoken or in any other way communicated by signal, semaphore, sign, or in any other form of communication orders, directives, or plans of the organization;

(9) Has prepared documents, pamphlets, leaflets, books, or any other type of publication in behalf of the objectives and purposes of the organization;

(10) Has mailed, shipped, circulated, distributed, delivered, or in any other way sent or delivered to others material or propaganda of any kind in behalf of the organization;

(11) Has advised, counseled or in any other way imparted information, suggestions, recommendations to officers or members of the organization or to anyone else in behalf of the objectives of the organization;

(12) Has indicated by word, action, conduct, writing or in any other way a willingness to carry out in any manner and to any degree the plans, designs, objectives, or purposes of the organization;

(13) Has in any other way participated in the activities, planning, actions, objectives, or purposes of the organization;

(14) The enumeration of the above subjects of evidence on membership or participation in the Communist Party or any other organization as above defined, shall not limit the inquiry into and consideration of any other subject of evidence on membership and participation as herein stated.

Approved August 24, 1950.

2

Symbolic Speech

We saw in the chapter on internal security how speech that ordinarily may not be regulated can become so closely associated with otherwise illegal actions that the two merged to an extent that Congress may regulate both speech and actions as "nonspeech."[1] The protection extended to symbolic speech, on the other hand, flows in the opposite direction. Certain actions that may ordinarily be prohibited can become so closely associated with speech that both are protected as speech. In other words, just as ordinarily protected speech will not always shield otherwise illegal acts, certain otherwise illegal acts may be permitted so as not to suppress their expressive value. Thus, protecting symbolic speech broadens the scope of expression that is protected by the First Amendment.

Protecting symbolic or expressive speech, as it is sometimes called, is a relatively recent development in First Amendment law. In 1931 the U.S. Supreme Court, recognizing that a government may "provide for the punishment of those who indulge in utterances which incite to violence and crime and threaten the overthrow of organized government by unlawful means," nevertheless invalidated a statute that prohibited the display of a red flag in a public or meeting place "as a sign, symbol or emblem of opposition to organized government" (*Stromberg v. California*, 1931, pp. 369–370). In 1969 the Supreme Court upheld the right of junior high school students to wear black armbands to protest the Vietnam War, stating that "the wearing of armbands in the circumstances of this case was [so] . . . closely akin to 'pure speech' that it . . . is entitled to comprehensive protection under the First Amendment" (*Tinker v. Des Moines Independent Community School District*, 1969, pp. 505–506).

Although most controversies involving symbolic speech have concerned state statutes or actions by state officials, Congress has enacted two landmark statutes affecting freedom of expression by symbolic acts. One is the 1965 Draft Card Mutilation Act, which prohibited burning draft cards during the Vietnam War era, and the other is the Flag Protection Act of 1968, which prohibited desecration of the United States flag. The Supreme Court upheld the draft card statute but invalidated the Flag Protection Act. The Supreme Court laid down four guidelines by which the two congressional enactments were judged. Thus, a statutory enactment that regulates symbolic speech is justified if (1) it is within the constitutional power of the government; (2) it furthers an important or substantial governmental interest; (3) the governmental interest is unrelated to the suppression of free expression; and (4) the incidental restriction on alleged First Amendment freedoms is no greater than is essential to the furtherance of that interest (*United States v. O'Brien*, 1968, p. 377).

THE DRAFT CARD MUTILATION
ACT OF 1965

If any one trait can singularly mark the 1960s, it was the willingness of minority groups and those holding minority opinions to resort to direct action in furtherance of their political goals and aspirations. From the civil rights movement, led by descendants of slaves, to the women's liberation movement, led by upper-middle-class white women, from violence by the urban poor to the antiwar violence of affluent university students, the nation was flooded with direct action and protest. A significant example of this phenomenon was the Free Speech Movement, which began as a general protest by students against bureaucratic authority at the University of California–Berkeley in the autumn of 1964. The event that prompted the protest was a new university policy that banned student information tables in the twenty-six-foot strip of university property at its main entrance and also prohibited literature and activities that advocated or opposed off-campus political issues. By December 3, 1964, the confrontation between students and administrative officials had escalated to the point that 768 Berkeley students forcibly occupied the central administration building. After the protesters were arrested for illegally occupying an administrative office, more than eight thousand students formed a picket line around university entrances, bringing university business to a practical standstill.

The Berkeley strike was, from the students' perspective, at least, highly successful. It was, in fact, the first successful strike by students at a major U.S. university. On January 3, 1965, the new acting chancellor at Berkeley announced in his inaugural address that the steps at Sproul Hall would be designated as an open discussion area for students during certain hours of the day and also that information tables would be permitted. As the sentiments of Berkeley's student strike spread to other campuses across the nation, the war in Vietnam became the focus of attention for a general protest by the nation's college youth against established authority, of which draft resistance was perhaps the most popular form. Draft resistance and related activities during the Vietnam era were enormous compared to previous wartime occasions. By 1965 the number of incidents that involved draft resistance had already grown to more than forty times World War II levels. For example, one estimate indicates that the rate of conscientious objectors grew from 14 and 15 percent of inductions in World Wars I and II, respectively, to more than 130 conscientious objector exemptions for every 100 inductions in 1972.[2] Moreover, these statistics do not reflect the number of draft resisters who resisted or evaded military service through illegal means. As military inductions grew by almost 374 percent between 1960 and 1966, the number of potential inductees—particularly university students—willing to engage in illegal conduct, from burning their draft cards to fleeing to Canada, increased dramatically.[3]

Congress responded to the growing incidents of draft resistance by enacting the Draft Card Mutilation Act of 1965 as an amendment to the Universal Military Training and Service Act of 1948, which had made it a criminal offense to knowingly destroy or mutilate a certificate issued by the Selective Service System.[4] The 1965 amendment substituted a new, more inclusive clause to section 12(b)(3) that strengthened the previous version by subjecting to criminal liability not only one who "forges, alters, or in any manner changes" a draft registration card, but also one who "knowingly destroys, [or] knowingly mutilates" one.

The draft card mutilation statute became the subject of a First Amendment test when David O'Brien and several others burned their draft cards in order to protest the war in Vietnam before a large Boston crowd on March 31, 1966. After O'Brien was indicted, he maintained that the statute violated his First Amendment right to engage in symbolic speech. He unsuccessfully argued that congressional efforts to safeguard the draft system by forbidding people to burn draft cards unduly interfered with his freedom of expression. In rejecting this claim, the Supreme Court stated that "because of the Government's substantial interest in assuring the continuing availability of issued Selective Service certificates, [and] because amended § 462 (b) is an appropriately narrow means of protecting this interest and condemns only the independent non-communicative impact of conduct within its reach, and because the non-communicative impact of O'Brien's act of burning his registration certificate frustrated the Government's interest, a sufficient governmental interest has been shown to justify O'Brien's conviction" (*United States v. O'Brien*, 1968, p. 382).

The Draft Card Mutilation Act of 1965

(b) Any person (1) who knowingly transfers or delivers to another, for the purpose of aiding or abetting the making of any false identification or representation, any registration certificate, alien's certificate of non-residence, or any other certificate issued pursuant to or prescribed by the provisions of this title, or rules or regulations promulgated hereunder; or (2) who, with intent that it be used for any purpose of false identification or representation, has in his possession any such certificate not duly issued to him; or (3) who forges, alters, knowingly destroys, knowingly mutilates, or in any manner changes any such certificate or any notation duly and validly inscribed thereon; or (4) who, with intent that it be used for any purpose of false identification or representation, photographs, prints, or in any manner makes or executes any engraving, photograph, print, or impression in the likeness of any such certificate, or any colorable imitation thereof; or (5) who has in his possession any certificate purporting to be a certificate issued pursuant to this title, or rules and regulations promulgated hereunder, which he knows to be falsely made, reproduced, forged, counterfeited, or altered; or (6) who knowingly violates or evades any of the provisions of this title or rules and regulations promulgated pursuant thereto relating to the issuance, transfer, or possession of such certificate, shall, upon conviction, be fined not to exceed $10,000 or be imprisoned for not more than five years, or both. Whenever on trial for a violation of this subsection the defendant is shown to have or to have had possession of any certificate not duly issued to him, such possession shall be deemed sufficient evidence to establish an intent to use such certificate for purposes of false identification or representation, unless the defendant explains such possession to the satisfaction of the jury.
Approved August 30, 1965.

NOTES

1. See *United States v. O'Brien* (1968).
2. Paul W. Shaffer, "Draft Resistance in the Vietnam Era" (1964) (http://www.seas.upenn.edu:8080/~pws/60s/intro.html) [accessed September 24, 2000].
3. Selective Service System, Induction Statistics (http://www.sss.gov/induct.htm) [accessed September 24, 2000].
4. The registration and classification certificates, collectively referred to as a "draft card," is a three-by-two-inch white card providing some basic information such as the name of the registrant, the registrant's classification, the date of registration, and the number and address of the local issuing board.

THE FLAG PROTECTION ACT OF 1968

Burning the national flag constitutes symbolic or expressive conduct that triggers the First Amendment. Thus, any congressional enactment that adversely impacts that expression is subjected to exacting or strict scrutiny by the courts (*United States v. Eichman*, 1990). However, flag protection statutes have not always been subjected to strict scrutiny under the First Amendment. Congress considered, but did not enact, legislation in 1878 that would have prohibited use of the flag to promote commercial enterprises. During World War I, Congress passed a law that made public mutilation of the flag a misdemeanor in the District of Columbia. In 1942, Congress enacted a provision that contained guidelines for what was considered the proper use of the flag. Finally, in the midst of the antiwar demonstrations of students against the Vietnam War, Congress enacted a statute that provided criminal penalties for mistreatment of the flag. This legislation, the Flag Protection Act of 1968, prohibited "knowingly cast[ing] contempt upon any flag of the United States by publicly mutilating, defacing, defiling, burning or trampling upon it." Congress, mindful of the critical distinction between speech and action, attempted to draft a statute that would pass First Amendment scrutiny by separating the two. The report that accompanied the bill when it was reported to the Senate by the Judiciary Committee asserted that the

> bill does not prohibit speech, the communication of ideas, or political dissent or protest. The bill does not prescribe orthodox conduct or require affirmative action. The bill does prohibit public acts of physical dishonor or destruction of the flag of the United States. The language of the bill prohibits intentional, willful, not accidental or inadvertent public physical acts of desecration of the flag. Utterances are not proscribed. Specific examples of prohibited conduct under the bill would include casting contempt upon the flag by burning or tearing it and by spitting upon or otherwise dirtying it. There is nothing vague or uncertain about the terms used in the bill.[1]

Between its enactment in 1968 and its 1989 amendments, several federal decisions upheld the statute against claims that it violated the First Amendment. Barely four months after enactment of the 1968 Flag Protection Act, Norma Louise Ferguson was arrested during an antiwar protest on the front steps of the federal courthouse in San Francisco for publicly burning the national flag. The district court, in *United States v. Ferguson* (1969), rejected her First Amendment argument, stating, "this court cannot accept the view that the actions charged can be labeled 'speech' merely because [the] defendant intends thereby to express an idea. However, even assuming that the defendant's conduct was sufficient to bring into play the protection of the First Amendment, the court held the statute valid under the test set forth in [*United States v. O'Brien* (1968)]" (p. 1113).

On October 3, 1968, Abbie Hoffman—a defendant in the notorious 1968 Chicago Seven trial—was arrested under the 1968 Flag Protection Act (and later convicted) for wearing a shirt made from a flag at the Cannon Office Building as he prepared to testify under a subpoena by the House Un-American Activities Committee. The circuit court of appeals, in *Hoffman v. United States*, 445 F.2d 226 (D.C. Cir. 1971), reversed Hoffman's conviction and avoided a direct First Amendment challenge by finding that wearing the shirt did not come within the statutory definition of "casting contempt" on the flag.

The Washington, D.C., circuit court, in *Joyce v. United States* (1971), upheld the statute in a more direct challenge involving the flag itself. Standing at the corner of 15th Street and Pennsylvania Avenue during the presidential inaugural parade, Thomas Wayne Joyce tore an American flag (three inches by five inches) off a small flagstaff he was carrying, threw the staff to the ground, and then tore the flag into two pieces. He spoke no words at the time, and his only explanation at the trial was that "he had a predetermined intention to appear down at the parade route in order to demonstrate, express some idea, [or] communicate an idea with the flag" (pp. 978–979). The circuit court approved the trial court's finding that Joyce's behavior violated the Flag Protection Act, and it further held that the statute did not violate the First Amendment inasmuch as it only prohibited acts, noting that "the constitutional freedom for speech and press [does not] extend its immunity to speech or writing [that is] used as an integral part of conduct in violation of a valid criminal statute"[2] (p. 984).

While the federal courts appeared to look with favor upon the Flag Protection Act of 1968, the U.S. Supreme Court was busy invalidating one state flag-protection statute after another. For example, in 1969, it reversed a conviction under New York law involving a protester who burned a U.S. flag to protest the shooting of a civil rights leader in Mississippi[3]; in 1974 it invalidated a Massachusetts statute used to convict a young student who wore a small U.S. flag sewn on the seat of his blue jeans[4]; and that same year it invalidated a Washington statute under which a college student was convicted for hanging a three-by-five-foot flag upside down from his dormitory room with a peace symbol attached with black tape in protest of the Cambodian incursion and the Kent State tragedy.[5] In fact, a Supreme Court ruling invalidating a Texas statute in *Texas v. Johnson* (1989) prompted Congress to enact the Flag Protection Act of 1968.[6]

In *Johnson*, the Court, basing its decision on the First Amendment, invalidated a Texas statute that prohibited the desecration of venerated objects, including the United States flag "in a way that the actor knows will seriously offend one or more persons likely to observe or discover his action."[7] Johnson was arrested, tried, and convicted in 1988 for desecrating a national flag at the Republican national convention in Dallas by dousing the flag with kerosene, then setting it on fire as protesters chanted, "America, the red, white, and blue, we spit on you." The Court, in *Johnson*, held that the conduct in these circumstances possessed sufficient communicative elements to bring the First Amendment into play and create a situation of symbolic speech. The court indicated that the determinative question was whether "an intent to convey a particularized message was present, and [whether] the likelihood was great that the message would be understood by those who viewed it" (p. 404).

Following the decision in *Texas v. Johnson*, Congress drafted the 1989 amendment to the Flag Protection Act with a view that it would pass constitutional muster because it contained no explicit limitation on the content of speech as did the Texas statute. While the Texas statute required that one only had to act in a manner as to knowingly and "seriously offend one or more persons likely to observe or discover [one's] action," the new federal flag protection statute attempted only to restrict "action" by providing that the offense consisted of mutilating, defacing, physically defiling, burning the flag, or maintaining or trampling it on the floor or ground. The statute involved symbolic expression, Congress conceded, but because its focus was on action rather than pure speech, it should not be subjected to strict scrutiny.[8]

The Supreme Court, however, was not persuaded by the congressional declaration. It declared the 1989 Flag Protection Act invalid in a case involving a political demonstration on the east steps of the U.S. Capitol in which Shawn Eichman and others, including Gregory Lee Johnson of the *Texas v. Johnson* case, burned several U.S. flags to protest a variety of foreign and domestic policies. The court, in *United States v. Eichman* (1990), quoting *Texas v. Johnson* in part, declared that "although the Flag Protection Act contains no explicit contest-based limitation on the scope of prohibited conduct, it is nevertheless clear that the Government's asserted interest is 'related to the suppression of free expression' " (p. 315). Since then, there have been repeated but unsuccessful attempts in Congress to overturn the *Johnson* and *Eichman* cases and effectively reinstate the Flag Protection Act by enacting proposals to amend the Constitution. The current proposal states as follows:

> Resolved by the Senate and House of Representatives of the United States of America in Congress assembled (two-thirds of each House concurring therein),
> SECTION 1. CONSTITUTIONAL AMENDMENT.
> The following article is proposed as an amendment to the Constitution of the United States, which shall be valid to all intents and purposes as part of the Constitution when ratified by the legislatures of three-fourths of the several States within seven years after the date of its submission for ratification:
> "Article—The Congress shall have power to prohibit the physical desecration of the flag of the United States."

The Flag Protection Act of 1968 as Amended in 1989

Section 2. Criminal Penalties with Respect to the Physical Integrity of the United States Flag.
(a)(1) Whoever knowingly mutilates, defaces, physically defiles, burns, maintains on the floor or ground, or tramples upon any flag of the United States shall be fined under this title or imprisoned for not more than one year, or both.

(2) This subsection does not prohibit any conduct consisting of the disposal of a flag when it has become worn or soiled.

(b) As used in this section, the term "flag of the United States" means any flag of the United States, or any part thereof, made of any substance, of any size, in a form that is commonly displayed.

Section 3. Expedited Review of Constitutional Issues.

(d)(1) An appeal may be taken directly to the Supreme Court of the United States from any interlocutory or final judgment, decree, or order issued by a United States district court ruling upon the constitutionality of subsection (a).

(2) The Supreme Court shall, if it has not previously ruled on the question, accept jurisdiction over the appeal and advance on the docket and expedite to the greatest extent possible.

Approved July 5, 1968, and October 28, 1989, respectively.

NOTES

1. Senate Report No. 1287, 90th Cong., 1st Sess. 3. See also H. R. Rep. No. 350, 90th Cong., 1st Sess. 3, which has similar language.

2. The original bill in Congress contained a provision prohibiting flag desecration by words, but such provision was deleted upon advice of the attorney general of the United States. See H. R. Rep. No. 35, 90th Cong., 1st Sess. 7 (1967).

3. *Street v. New York* (1969).

4. *Smith v. Goguen* (1974).

5. *Spence v. Washington* (1974). Cambodia is a reference to President Nixon's 1970 military invasion of Cambodia, and Kent State is a reference to the student protest of this invasion at Kent State University in Ohio in May 1970, at which National Guardsmen killed four students.

6. As Congressman James Quillen (R-TN)—then chairman of the powerful Rules Committee, which had introduced the 1968 flag bill—put it, the *Johnson* decision stirred up such a "tempest" that the public became "outraged" and demanded that Congress act to rectify matters. Representative Brooks, chairman of the Committee on the Judiciary, stated that "it has been our position throughout consideration of this legislation that the Congress should act quickly to amend the law in order to respond to the Supreme Court's decision in Texas versus Johnson and protect the physical integrity of the flag." Congressional Record—House, Thursday, October 12, 1989, 101st Cong., 1st Sess., 135 Cong. Rec. H 6989.

7. Tex. Penal Code Ann. § 42.09 (1980).

8. See H. R. Rep. No. 101–123, 101st Cong., 1st Sess. 2 (1989); S. Rep. No. 101–152, 101st Cong., 1st Sess. 4 (1989). See generally, Hearings on Measures to Protect the Physical Integrity of the American Flag, Hearings Before the Comm. on the Judiciary, United States Senate, 101st Cong., 1st Sess. 1–754; Statutory and Constitutional Responses to the Supreme Court Decision in *Texas v. Johnson,* Hearings Before the Subcomm. on Civil and Constitutional Rights of the Comm. on the Judiciary, House of Representatives, 101st Cong., 1st Sess. 1–572 (1989).

3

Election Campaign Activities

As important as all the activities impacted by the landmark statutes discussed in this book are, none could be more crucial for a functioning democracy than those that affect political campaigns for election to public office. For, as James Madison stated, "The value and efficacy of [elections] depend on the knowledge of the comparative merits and demerits of the candidates for public trust, and on the equal freedom, consequently, of explaining and discussing these merits and demerits of the candidates respectively."[1] The Supreme Court has put it thus: "Whatever differences may exist about interpretations of the First Amendment, there is practically universal agreement that a major purpose of that Amendment was to protect the free discussion of governmental affairs. This of course includes discussions of candidates, structures and forms of government, the manner in which government is operated or should be operated, and all such matters relating to political processes" (*Mills v. Alabama*, 1996, pp. 218–219).

Article I, Section 4, of the Constitution grants Congress the power to regulate elections of members of the Senate and House of Representatives.[2] Although the Supreme Court at one time indicated that party primary or nominating elections were not "elections" within the meaning of Article I, Section 4 (*Newberry v. United States*, 1921), it later held that primary elections were within the Constitution's grant of authority to Congress to regulate elections (*United States v. Classic*, 1941). The Court has also recognized broad congressional power to legislate in connection with the elections of the president and vice president (*Burroughs v. United States*, 1934).

As the Court observed in *Monitor Patriot Co. v. Roy* (1971), "it can hardly be doubted that the [First Amendment's] constitutional guarantee has its fullest and most urgent application precisely to the conduct of campaigns for political office" (p. 272).

Yet, just as with most—if not all—First Amendment cases, the amendment's goal of free and unfettered expression immediately runs headlong into other cherished values. In this case, it runs afoul of the notion of political equality, which in this context means that everyone should have an equal voice in the political process. "The principle of equality in political suffrage rights has the constitutional footing of the 'one man, one vote' principle" (*Buckley v. Valeo*, 1975, p. 841). Or, as the Supreme Court stated when it declared the poll tax unconstitutional, "Ours is a nation that respects the drive of private profit and the pursuit of gain, but does not exalt wealth thereby achieved to undue preference in fundamental rights" (*Harper v. Virginia Board of Elections*, 1966).[3] Congress has stated two other public concerns that it uses to support restrictions on campaign financing. One is the need to prevent corruption, so that money does not buy an illegitimate public interest, and the other is the need to keep the overall campaign cost at a level that permits more candidates to participate. In short, Congress seeks to limit improper influence on candidates, prevent corruption, and broaden the opportunity for political candidacy to as many people as possible.

Enacting statutes that balance the dual values of individual liberty and individual equality in the electoral process is no easier task than is legislating in other First Amendment areas. Moreover, there is just as much uncertainty and debate about the practical effects of campaign money on the political system as there is about the pernicious effects of pornography and seditious libel. Besides the arguments over practical effects, the issue of money in politics is further clouded by a mysterious and contradictory attitude toward the *role* of money in politics. The dominance of money in election campaigns is something that most politicians dislike yet seek to maximize at every turn, as witnessed by the long and rich history of significant legislative enactments followed by studied noncompliance on the part of the very campaigners who passed the laws.

Money and politics have always been logical, perhaps necessary, bedfellows. National icons, as well as most candidates for public office, have apparently felt a need to spend money in a variety of ways to get their message and candidacy across. George Washington reputedly engaged in the typical colonial practice of "swilling the planters with bumbo," a beverage mixture of rum, water, sugar, and nutmeg, while spending twenty-five pounds on two elections to the Virginia House of Burgesses, thirty-nine pounds on another, and fifty pounds on a fourth one.[4] Abraham Lincoln's 1864 reelection, with the backing of northern business leaders who had been awarded enormously lucrative government contracts, achieved the distinction of being the first "million-dollar" presidential campaign in the United States. Lincoln's party demanded not only sizable contributions from corporate beneficiaries but also 5 percent of the pay by those who had been appointed to federal jobs.[5]

Over the years, political campaigns have increasingly become more dependent on money. This is due to three major factors. First, as the political process has become more democratic, the need for money has become more dominant. Because of the extension of voting rights to most white males during the Jacksonian era, to African Americans and women, to eighteen- to twenty-year-olds, and even to those who could not afford a poll tax, the potential electorate has grown enormously in U.S. history. Another factor in the electorate's growth was the 1913 amendment providing for the popular election of members to the U.S. Senate. Second, just as enlargement of the electoral franchise required larger campaign treasuries to reach the voters, increased opportunity for business with the government during the late 1800s, a period referred to as the "Gilded Age" because it depicts the extravagant and corrupt nature of America's industrial age, followed by the burgeoning regulatory state, brought more entrepreneurs and their corporations into the political process, mainly by way of financial contributions in election campaigns. Finally, the advent of radio and then television-based campaigns brought on the need for massive amounts of money, with less and less need for political organizations and party workers.

It is an abiding concern of many that the notion of political equality in an effort to influence the government rings hollow given the economic reality of uneven national wealth distribution. No doubt there is economic disparity in the country. The *New York Times* estimated that the nation's richest 1 percent in 1774 owned 14 percent of the wealth. By the end of the 1980s, the amount of wealth held by the richest 1 percent had risen to 36 percent. Although this rise in ownership as a percentage had not been a continuous climb,[6] the disparity between the very wealthy and the remainder of society continues to be unabated, at the very least. An analysis of the Federal Reserve Board's 1998 Survey of Consumer Finances by a professor of economics at New York University indicates that the amount of wealth held by the upper 1 percent in 1998 exceeded 38 percent. In fact, the wealthiest 20 percent of the population possesses more than 83 percent of the wealth, leaving less than 17 percent of the wealth for the remaining 80 percent of the people.[7]

The fact that economic disparity has an effect in the political process should hardly surprise anyone. Thus, as we will see later, one of the primary goals of recent congressional restrictions on the amount of money that can be contributed and spent in political campaigns has been to equalize the ability of a greater number of citizens to participate in the electoral process. Nonetheless, the effect of uneven distribution of wealth continues as reflected in a recent report by the Federal Election Commission. Immediately prior to the Republican party's 2000 nominating convention, the report showed that 739 individuals had contributed two-thirds of the party's $137-million-dollar, soft-money campaign chest.[8] Thus, in spite of the legislation that was intended to curtail the influence of concentrated wealth, it continues to play a major role in political campaigns.

Many factors can affect not just the role of money but also its source. For example, it is easy to understand that the wealthy contribute more, for they have more to contribute. Furthermore, one may argue (as many do) the wealthy also have more at stake in the governing process. For example, in 1999, the richest 1 percent (1.2 million families) paid 21 percent of all federal taxes, while the poorest 60 percent (69 million families) paid 17 percent. Yet the 69 million families might respond that, considering how much expendable income remains after taxes are paid, taxes hit them the hardest.[9] This debate is not going to be further elaborated here, but these statistics do help to frame the First Amendment's applicability to the cross-section of economic and political reality. Another major factor, and the one that is of concern to us here, is the claimed constitutional right of individuals to use their money in electoral politics regardless of their level of wealth. The First Amendment stands as a pillar for the right of all individuals—rich or poor—to participate in political campaigns through financial donations.

The First Amendment applies to campaign financing in two different ways. On the one hand, campaign restrictions relating to financial contributions impact the First Amendment's right of association. Although the right of *association* is not specifically mentioned in the First Amendment, the right of *assembly* is, and that has been construed to include a broad range of situations that go by the name of "associational" rights that affect political campaigns. This right is based on the principle "that [e]ffective advocacy of both public and private points of view, particularly controversial ones, is undeniably enhanced by group association" (*National Association for the Advancement of Colored People v. Alabama*, 1958, p. 460). The Supreme Court explained the right of association as involving "more than the 'right of assembly'—a right that extends to all irrespective of their race or ideology. [It], like the right of belief, is more than the right to attend a meeting; it includes the right to express one's attitudes or philosophies by membership in a group or by affiliation with it or by other lawful means. Association in that context is a form of expression of opinion; and while it is not expressly included in the First Amendment its existence is necessary in making the express guarantees fully meaningful" (*Griswold v. Connecticut*, 1965, p. 484). In the chapter on internal security we saw this right of association applied to the Smith Act's membership clause in *Scales v. United States* (1961), and the Communist Control Act's ban on Communist Party members working with defense contractors in *United States v. Robel* (1967).

On the other hand, restrictions on campaign expenditures place a burden on the First Amendment's freedom of speech provision as well as its protection of the right of association. An expenditure, unlike a contribution, is viewed as direct speech. As the Supreme Court explained it, "the transformation of contributions into political debate involves speech by someone other than the contributor," whereas spending limits tend to "infringe on the [spender's] freedom to discuss candidates and issues" (*Buckley v. Valeo*, 1976, p. 19). As a result of this distinction, personal expenditures are considered more important to the exercise of First Amendment privileges, and, as such, enactments restricting expenditures have received stricter scrutiny than other restrictions.

Aside from the manner in which the contribution-expenditure distinction relates to the First Amendment, there are other aspects of the election process that Congress has attempted to regulate. In fact, a view of the different parts of an election that can and have been regulated appears much like a labyrinth. Contributions may be restricted on the basis of the following:

1. How much an individual may contribute to a candidate, a political committee (a party or an election campaign committee), or an independent group (a public interest group or a political action committee, or PAC, of a corporation or a union).

2. How much a political party or an independent group may contribute to the candidate.

3. How much an individual, a candidate, a political committee, or an independent group may spend on a candidate's campaign, on a general election, or on some issue that may be closely connected to a particular candidate or political party.

4. How much money a political committee or an independent group may spend on these matters.

5. How much candidates may spend on their own campaigns.

Other aspects that have been regulated are the following: the extent to which corporations and labor unions may or may not make financial contributions; the extent to which financial records must be maintained and disclosed before, during, and after elections; and the methods and degree of administrative and penal enforcement. Congress has also provided for public financing of certain elections out of the general tax revenue, along with regulations that restrict participation by and toward federal employees in electoral politics.

Most landmark enactments followed a significant historic event. Beginning with the Naval Appropriations Act of 1867, followed by a dozen or so congressional enactments, Congress has sought to diminish in one way or another the role of money in election campaigns. Congress has enacted five laws that are given landmark status because either they were the first attempts of their kind to regulate some aspect of campaign finance or they constituted an extremely broad-based or extensive regulatory regime. By banning corporate contributions, the Tillman Act of 1907 was the first outright ban on campaign contributions. The Publicity Act of 1910 was the first statute that sought to impose spending limits on campaigns, limiting United States senatorial campaigns to ten thousand dollars and house campaigns to five thousand dollars. The Corrupt

Practices Act of 1925 was the first enactment to contain extensive record-keeping and disclosure requirements. Although statutes as early as the midnineteenth century limited the ability of candidates to coerce participation by federal employees, the Hatch Act of 1939 and its 1940 amendments were the first to actually prohibit federal employees from participating in election campaigns. The 1974 collective amendments to the Federal Election Campaign Act of 1971 constitute a most remarkable landmark act in that it was by far the most comprehensive congressional enactment regarding electoral politics. It contained firm limits on contributions and expenditures, set up elaborate record-keeping and disclosure requirements, placed public financing of presidential elections and preelection activity on a firm footing, and established the Federal Election Commission to supervise the entire regulatory scheme.

NOTES

1. *6 Writings of James Madison* 397 (G. Hunt, ed., 1906).
2. See *Smiley v. Holmes* (1932); *Ex parte Yarbrough* (1884).
3. Other decisions in which financial requirements were held inimical to the political process include: *Phoenix v. Kolodziejski* (1970), disallowing restricting voting on general obligation municipal bonds to real property taxes; *Bullock v. Carter*, 405 U.S. 134 (1972), and *Lubin v. Panish* (1974), restricting the use of filing fees as a prerequisite to getting on the ballot.
4. Gil Troy, "Money and Politics: The Oldest Connection," *Wilson Quarterly* (Summer 1997) (http://wwics.si.edu/OUTREACH/WQ/WQSELECT/TROY.HTM) [accessed August 7, 2000]. It might be noted that fifty pounds spent by Washington in the late eighteenth century would be approximately equivalent to more than seven thousand dollars today. (As noted later, Congress limited congressional campaign expenditures to five thousand dollars and ten thousand dollars for House and Senate seats more than a century and a half after Washington first served in the Virginia House of Burgesses.) For Washington's campaign, in an age before expensive communications media and modes of travel, fifty pounds is a lot of "bumbo," especially for a man who supposedly did not seek public office.
5. Ibid.
6. During the 1920s, just prior to the stock market crash that brought on the Great Depression, the percentage stood at more than 42 percent, and by the late 1970s it had fallen to less than 18 percent (Sylvia Nasal, "The Rich Get Richer, But Never the Same Way Twice," *New York Times*, National Edition, August 16, 1992, p. E3).
7. Edward N. Wolff, "Recent Trends in Wealth Ownership, 1983–1998," a Working Paper for the Jerome Levy Economics Institute (http://www.levy.org/docs/wrkpap/papers/300.html) [accessed August 5, 2000].
8. *Soft money* is the name given to contributions and expenditures on indirect

political activities, such as voter registration and issue advocacy, that are presumably not directed toward or intended to benefit any particular candidate.

9. Robert J. Samuelson, "Rule by the Rich? No," *Washington Post*, April 18, 2000, p. A21 (http://www.washingtonpost.com/wp-dyn/articles/) [accessed August 6, 2000].

THE TILLMAN ACT OF 1907

The concentration of wealth in the hands of a small part of the population was a major concern at the end of the nineteenth century. Two notable American historians described it as follows: "The nation was fabulously rich but its wealth was gravitating rapidly into the hands of a small portion of the population, and the power of wealth threatened to undermine the political integrity of the Republic."[1] Congress had already responded to this phenomenon with such laws as the Sherman Antitrust Act of 1890 and the Income Tax Act of 1894. Moreover, by the time Congress enacted the Tillman Act, there were two campaign statutes on the books that regulated election campaigns. One, the Naval Appropriations Act of 1867, which contained a prohibition on soliciting naval employees in Washington, D.C., had been enacted partly in response to electioneering practices, especially the "shakedown" of naval employees during the 1864 election. The other was enacted on the heels of President James Garfield's death in September 1881 from a gunshot wound, which he had received by the hand of a disgruntled office-seeker in July at a Washington, D.C., railway station. Just as President McKinley's 1901 assassination by the hand of an avowed alien anarchist led to the enactment of the 1903 law deporting anarchists and forbidding others to enter, President Garfield's assassination led to the Pendleton Act in 1883, which created a nonpoliticized civil service program and banned certain campaign activities on government property.

The enormous growth of campaign expenditures during the elections of 1896, 1900, and 1904 was a precursor to the Tillman Act's prohibition on corporate contributions. The elections of 1896 and 1900 were notable for the ability of McKinley's campaign manager, Marcus Hanna—a Cleveland, Ohio, industrialist and chairman of his party's national committee—to obtain extremely large sums of money from corporate donors. In the 1896 election, which was the first five-million-dollar election, Hanna supposedly used a mathematical formula to calculate the amount that a corporation should contribute based on the relationship between the donating corporation's wealth and the overall national prosperity. In fact, he is said to have returned one-fifth of a $250,000 donation by Standard

Oil because the company's share of the national prosperity had turned out to be lower than expected.

Although President Theodore Roosevelt had been a beneficiary of huge corporate contributions in 1904, he responded to large-scale criticism by calling for election reform in his first annual message to Congress. The House Committee on Elections immediately began conducting a hearing to consider various proposals to limit the influence of corporate money in elections. The supporting testimony was exemplified by the strong words of Samuel Gompers, president of the American Federation of Labor: "The necessity for some law upon the subject is patent [obvious] to every man who hopes for the maintenance of the institutions under which we live. It is doubtful to my mind if the contributions and expenditures of vast sums of money in the nominations and elections for our public offices can continue to increase without endangering the endurance of our Republic in its purity and in its essence."[2]

Congress responded with the Tillman Act of 1907. The Tillman Act was named after its most ardent supporter, Benjamin "Pitchfork" Tillman, the combative senator from South Carolina who was censured by the Senate in 1902 for a mutual assault in the Senate chamber with John McLaurin, his colleague from South Carolina. The Tillman Act prohibited corporations and banks that were chartered by the federal government from contributing to any political campaign at any level of government, and although Congress did not have the authority to regulate state-incorporated companies from participating in state and local elections, it did forbid them to participate in all federal elections. Violations of the Tillman Act carried a fine of up to $5,000, for the corporation, as well as a fine of $250 to $1,000, imprisonment for not more than one year, or both, for corporate officials.

The Tillman Act of 1907[3]

An act to prohibit corporations from making money contributions in connection with political elections.

Be it enacted, that it shall be unlawful for any national bank, or any corporation organized by authority of any laws of Congress, to make a money contribution in connection with any election to any political office. It shall also be unlawful for any corporation whatever to make a money contribution in connection with any election at which Presidential and Vice Presidential electors or a representative in Congress is to be voted for or any election by any State legislature of a United States Senator. Every corporation which shall make any contribution in violation of the foregoing provisions shall be subject to a fine not exceeding five thousand dollars, and every officer or director of any corporation who shall consent to any contribution by the corporation in violation of the foregoing provisions shall upon conviction be punished by a fine of not exceeding one thousand and not less than two hundred and fifty dollars, or by imprisonment for a term of not more than one year, or both such find an imprisonment in the discretion of the court.

Approved January 26, 1907.

NOTES

1. Samuel Eliot Morison and Henry Steele Commager, *The Growth of the American Republic*, vol. 2, 4th ed., (New York: Oxford University Press, 1950), p. 355.

2. Hearings before the House Committee on Elections, 59th Cong., 1st Sess. 12, at 28–31. Gompers' words would boomerang on the labor movement with the enactment of the Smith-Connally Act in 1943 and the Labor Management Relations (Taft-Hartley) Act of 1947, which banned campaign contributions by labor unions.

3. Although the prohibitive provisions of the Tillman Act are still a part of current law, they have been practically nullified by the First Amendment's protection of so-called soft money, as we will see later.

THE PUBLICITY ACT OF 1910

The Publicity Act of 1910 as amended in 1911 was the first federal legislation to require a disclosure of campaign receipts. Moreover, its 1911 amendments imposed, for the first time, limits on the amount of money that congressional candidates could spend on their campaigns.[1] Though mild by modern standards, the 1910 act was very bold for its day. It required all national and interstate political committees that sought to influence elections for seats in the House of Representatives to maintain detailed records of all campaign receipts and all expenditures of ten dollars or more. Campaign records were required to be filed within thirty days after the election with the clerk of the House, who was to maintain them for public inspection during the next fifteen months. Persons violating the act were subject to up to one year in prison, a fine of one thousand dollars, or both.

The 1910 act might have been rather timid by most standards, but the 1911 amendments were not. They extended the act's provisions to Senate campaigns as well as to primary elections and nominating conventions for both House and Senate candidates. The amendments also strengthened disclosure and publicity by requiring campaign records to be filed with the House clerk and Senate secretary ten to fifteen days before an election, and updated every six days thereafter until a final postelection report was filed within thirty days of the election. Furthermore, the 1911 amendments placed a monetary limit on campaign expenditures. Candidates could spend no more for their election than was permitted by the state law in their jurisdiction, but in no event—state law notwithstanding—could House candidates spend more than five thousand dollars, and Senate candidates more than ten thousand dollars. Section 8 of the 1911 amendments contained another new regulatory provision prohibiting pledges or promises of "any office or position to any person, or to use his influence or to give his support to any person for any office or position for the purpose of procuring the support of such person, or of any person, in his candidacy."

Although it was a very progressive enactment, the Publicity Act did not prove to be very effective in regulating campaign expenditures. For one thing, it had no enforcement mechanism, and for another, it could be easily sidestepped by a candidate's putative ignorance of who was spending what and how much on the campaign. Moreover, in states where one-party rule prevailed, such as the solidly Democratic South, the act was almost completely eviscerated by the Supreme Court's decision in *Newberry v. United States* (1921), which held that the authority of Congress to regulate the manner of holding elections under Article I, Section 4 of the Constitution did not extend to primary elections. The Supreme Court eventually overturned *Newberry* with its decision in *United States v. Classic* (1941), yet, as we will see, it was not until 1971 that Congress acted to regulate contributions in primary election campaigns.

The Publicity Act of 1910

An act providing for publicity of contributions made for the purpose of influencing elections at which Representatives in Congress are elected.

Be enacted, that the terms "political committees" under the provisions of this Act shall include the national committees of all political parties and the national congressional campaign committees of all political parties and all committees, associations, or organizations which shall in two or more states influence the result or attempt to influence the result of an election at which Representatives in Congress are to be elected.

Section 2. That every political committee as defined in this act shall have a chairman and a treasurer. It should be the duty of the treasurer to keep a detailed and exact amount of all money or its equivalent received by or promised to such committee or any member thereof, or by or to any person acting under its authority or in its behalf, and the name of every person, firm, association, or committee from whom received, and of all expenditures, disbursements, and promises of payments or disbursements made by the committee or any member thereof, or by any person acting under its authority or in its behalf, and to whom paid, distributed or dispersed. No officer or member of such committee, or other person acting under its authority or on its behalf, shall receive any money or its equivalent, or expend or promise to expend any money on behalf of such committee, until after a chairman and treasurer of such committee shall have been chosen.

Section 3. That every payment or disbursements made by a political committee exceeding ten dollars in amount to be evidenced by a receipted bill stating the particulars of expense, and every such record, voucher, receipt, or account shall be preserved for fifteen months after the election to which it relates.

Section 4. That whoever, acting under the authority or on behalf of such political committee, whether as a member thereof or otherwise, receives any contribution, payment, loan, gift, advance, deposit, or promise of money or its equivalent shall, on demand, and in any event within five days after the receipt of such contribution, payment, loan, gift, advance, deposit, or promise, render to the treasurer of such political committee a detailed account of the same, together with the name and addresses from whom received, and said treasurer shall forthwith enter the same in a ledger or record to be kept by him for that purpose.

Section 5. That the treasurer of every such political committee shall, not more than fifteen days and not less than ten days next before an election at which representatives in Congress are to be elected in two or more states, file in the office of the Clerk of the House of Representatives at Washington, District of Columbia, with said Clerk, an itemized detailed statement; and on each sixth day thereafter until such election said treasurer shall file with said Clerk a supplemental itemized detailed statement. Each of said statements shall conform to the requirements of the following section of this Act, except that the supplemental statement herein required need not contain any item of which publicity is given in a previous statement. Each of said statements shall be full and complete, and shall be signed and sworn to by said treasurer.

It shall also be the duty of said treasurer to file a similar statement with said Clerk within thirty days after such election, such file statement also to be signed and sworn to by said treasurer and to conform to the requirements of the following section of this Act. The statement so filed with the Clerk of the House shall be preserved by him for fifteen months and shall be a part of the public records of his office and shall be open to public inspection. . . .

Section 8. The word "candidate" as used in this section shall include all persons whose names are presented for nomination for Representative or Senate or in Congress of United States at any primary election or nominating convention, or for endorsement or election at any general or special election held in connection with the nomination or election of a person to fill such office, whether or not such persons are actually nominated, endorsed, or elected.

Every person who shall be a candidate for nomination at any primary election or nominating convention, or for election at any general or special election, as a Representative in the Congress of United States, shall, not less than ten nor more than fifteen days before the day for holding such primary election or nominating convention, and not less than ten nor more than fifteen days before the date of the general or special election at which candidates for Representative are to be elected, file with the clerk of the House of Representatives at Washington, District of Columbia, a full, correct and itemized statement of all moneys and things of value received by him or by anyone for him with his knowledge and consent, from any source, in aid or support of his candidacy together with the names of all those who have furnished the same in whole or in part; and such statement shall contain a true and itemized account of all monies and things of value given, contributed, expended, used, or promised by such candidate, or by his agent, representative, or other person for and in his behalf with his knowledge and consent, together with the names of all those to whom any and all such gifts, contribution, payments, or promises were made, for the purpose to procuring his nomination or election.

Every person who shall be a candidate for nomination at any primary election or nomination convention, or for endorsement at any general or special election or election by the legislature of any State, as Senator in the Congress of United States, shall, not less than ten nor more than fifteen days before the day for holding such primary election or nominating convention, and not less than ten nor more than fifteen days before the day of the general or special election at which he is seeking endorsement, and not less than five nor more than 10 days before the date upon which the first vote is to be taken in two houses of the legislature before which he is a candidate for election as Senator, file with Secretary of the Senate at Washington, District of Columbia, a full, correct and itemized statement of all moneys and things of value received by him or by anyone for him with his knowledge and consent, from any source, in aid or support of his candidacy together with the names of all those who have furnish the same in whole or in part; and such statement shall contain a true and itemized account of all monies and things of value given, contributed, expended, used, or promised by such candidate, or by his agent, representative, or other person for and in his behalf with his knowledge and consent, together with the names of all those to whom any and all such gifts, contribution, payments, or promises were made, for the purpose to procuring his nomination or election.

Every such candidate for nomination at any primary election or nominating convention, or for endorsement or election at any general or special election, or for election by the legislature to any state, shall, within fifteen days after such primary election or nominating convention, and within thirty days after such general or special election, and within thirty days after the date on which the legislature should have elected a Senator, file with the clerk of the House of Representatives or with the Secretary of the Senate, as the case may be, a full, correct and itemized statement of all moneys and things of value received by him or by anyone for him with his knowledge and consent, from any source, in aid or support of his candidacy together with the names of all those who have furnished the same in whole or in part; and such statement shall contain a true and itemized account of all monies and things of value given, contributed, expended, used, or promised by such candidate, or by his agent, representative, or other person for and in his behalf with his knowledge and consent, together with the names of all those to whom any and all such gifts, contribution, payments, or promises were made, for the purpose to procuring his nomination or election.

Every such candidate shall include therein a statement of every promise or pledge made by him, or by anyone for him with his knowledge and consent or to whom he has given authority to make any such promise or pledge, before the completion of any such primary election or nominating convention or general or special election or election by legislature, relative to the appointment or recommendation for appointment of any person to any position of trust, honor, or profit, either in the county, State or Nation, or in any political subdivision thereof, or in any private or corporate employment, for the purpose of procuring the support of such person or of any person in his candidacy, and if any such promise or pledge shall have been made the name or names, the address or addresses, and the occupation or occupations, of the person or persons to whom such promise or pledge shall have been made, shall be stated, together with a description of the position relating to which such promise or pledge has been made. In the event that no such promise or pledge has been made by such candidate, the fact shall be distinctly stated.

No candidate for Representative in Congress or for Senator of United States shall promise any office or position to any person, or to use his influence or to give his support to any person for any office or position for the purpose of procuring the support of such person, or of any person, in his candidacy; nor shall any candidate for Senator of United States give, contribute, expend, use, or promise any money or thing of value to assist in procuring the nomination of election of any particular candidate for the legislature of the State in which he resides, but such candidate, may, within the limitation and restrictions and subject to the requirements of this act, contribute to political committees having charge of the distribution of campaign funds.

No candidate for Representative in Congress or Senator of the United States shall give, contribute, expend, use, or promise, or cause to be given, contributed, expended, used, or promised, in procuring his nomination and election, any sum, in the aggregate, in excess of the amount which he may lawfully give, contribute, expend, or promise under laws of the State in which he resides: Provided, That no candidate for Representative in Congress shall give, contribute, expend, use, or promise any sum, in the aggregate, exceeding five thousand dollars in any campaign for his nomination and election; and no candidate for Senator of the United States shall give, contribute, expend, use, or promise any sum, in the aggregate, exceeding ten thousand dollars in any campaign for his nomination and election: Provided further, That money expended by any such candidate to meet and discharge any assessment, fee, or charge made or levied upon candidates by the laws of the State in which he resides, or for his necessary personal expenses, incurred for himself alone, for travel and subsistence, stationery and postage, writing or printing (other than in newspapers), and distributing letters, circulars, and posters, and telegraph and telephone service, shall not be regarded as an expenditure within meaning of this section, and shall not be considered any part of the sum fixed as the limit of expense and need not be shown in the statements herein required to be filed. . . .

Section 10. That every person willfully violating any of the foregoing provisions of this Act shall, upon conviction, be fined not more than one thousand dollars or imprisoned not more than one year, or both.
Approved August 23, 1912.

NOTE

1. The Publicity Act of 1910, as amended, is sometimes referred to as the Corrupt Practices Act, but it should not be confused with the better-known Corrupt Practices Act of 1925, which will be discussed later.

THE CORRUPT PRACTICES ACT OF 1925

The Corrupt Practices Act of 1925, which replaced the Publicity Acts of 1910 and 1911, was a response to the *Newberry* decision and the Teapot Dome scandal that surrounded the Harding-Coolidge administrations. Although the Teapot Dome scandal did not directly involve the influence of money in election campaigns, it did involve the illegitimate influence of moneyed interests in the political process. During the administrations of Theodore Roosevelt, William Taft, and Woodrow Wilson (1901–1921), tracts of public lands in Wyoming (Teapot Dome) and California (Elk Hills and Buena Vista) had been set aside by the national government as oil reserves to be used in the event that the navy lost its regular supplies during an emergency situation. Harding's Treasury secretary, former Senator Albert Fall, persuaded Navy Secretary Edwin Denby to transfer control of the reserves over to the Treasury from the Navy, and then Fall proceeded to lease them to Harry Sinclair's Mammoth Oil Company and Edward Doheny's Pan American Petroleum Company in exchange for gifts that amounted to $400,000.

The Supreme Court declared that the oil leases were invalid on the grounds that Secretary Fall's misbehavior had tainted the transactions.[1] Fall was later convicted of accepting bribes for himself and making illegal contributions to the Republican Party, which used the money to pay some debts incurred in the 1920 campaign. Fall went to prison, and the scandal became a potent weapon in the arsenal of reformers who sought to make changes in campaign-finance laws. The scandal, along with the increasing role of money in elections, led to a legislative disposition characterized at the time by Senator Joseph T. Robinson (D-AR), one of the Senate leaders, as follows:

> We all know . . . that one of the great political evils of the time is the apparent hold on political parties which business interests and certain organizations seek and sometimes obtain by reason of liberal campaign contributions. Many believe that when an individual or association of individuals makes large contributions for the purpose of aiding candidates of political parties in winning the elections, they expect, and sometimes demand, and occasionally at least, receive,

consideration by the beneficiaries of their contributions which not infrequently is harmful to the general public interest. It is unquestionably an evil which ought to be dealt with, and dealt with intelligently and effectively.[2]

The Corrupt Practices Act of 1925 was the first attempt to place campaign-financing laws into a comprehensive statutory scheme by not only adding new provisions but also incorporating features from prior enactments. It maintained the basic preelection and postelection record-keeping and filing requirements of the Publicity Acts, but it added a requirement that political committees must file financial reports each quarter during an election year. A significant addition was the requirement that anyone who spends fifty dollars or more in two or more states for the purpose of influencing an election must also file expenditure reports with the House clerk and Senate secretary. The limits on campaign spending by candidates were maintained, but the maximum for House candidates was lowered to $2,500. The ban on pledging jobs in exchange for votes was continued, along with a new provision that banned vote-buying outright. The ban on all solicitations and receipts from federal employees was imported from the 1867 Naval Appropriations and 1883 Pendleton Acts. The Tillman Act's ban on corporate contributions was incorporated into the Corrupt Practices Act alongside the penalties for noncompliance that were part of the Publicity Acts. A new provision was added that provided for a fine of up to ten thousand dollars and two years of imprisonment for intentional violations.

The constitutionality of the Corrupt Practices Act was called into question when a member of Congress, Representative Harry F. Wurzbach of Texas, was indicted for receiving campaign contributions from a federal employee. The district court in *United States v. Wurzbach*, 31 F.2d 774 (W.D. Texas, April 3, 1929) declared the statute invalid. Although the district judge cited authority for the proposition that " 'political rights' consist in the power to participate, directly or indirectly, in the establishment or management of the Government, [and] these are the political rights which the humblest citizen possesses," he actually based his decision on the rationale of *Newberry v. United States*, holding that the Corrupt Practices Act was overly broad due to the fact that it could cover primary elections, which had been declared to be outside of governmental authority in *Newberry*. The Supreme Court, in an opinion written by Justice Oliver Wendell Holmes Jr., reversed the district court's decision in the *Wurzbach* case, thereby upholding the Corrupt Practices Act on the grounds that while *Newberry* correctly stated the principle that Congress could not regulate a purely state affair (i.e., a primary election), it could regulate the activities of candidates seeking national office.

The Corrupt Practices Act of 1925

Section 302. When used in this title—

(a) The term "election" includes a general or special election . . . , but does not include a primary election or convention of a political party;

(b) The term "candidate" means an individual whose name is presented at an election for election as Senator or Representative in . . . the Congress of the United States, whether or not such individual is elected;

(c) The term "political committee" includes any committee, association, or organization which accepts contributions or makes expenditures for the purpose of influencing or attempting to influence the election of candidates or presidential and vice presidential electors (1) in two or more States, or (2) whether or not in more than one State if such committee, association, or organization (other than a duly organized State or local committee of a political party) is a branch or subsidiary of a national committee, association, or organization;

(d) The term "contribution" includes a gift, subscription, loan, advance, or deposit, of money, or anything of value, and includes a contract, promise, or agreement, whether or not legally enforceable, to make a contribution;

(e) The term "expenditure" includes a payment, distribution, loan, advance, deposit, or gift, of money, or any thing of value, and includes a contract, promise, or agreement, whether or not legally enforceable, to make an expenditure;

(f) The term "person" includes an individual, partnership, committee, association, corporation, and any other organization or group of persons; . . .

Section 303.

(b) It shall be the duty of the treasurer of a political committee to keep a detailed and exact account of—(1) All contributions made to or for such committee; (2) The name and address of every person making any such contribution, and the date thereof; (3) All expenditures made by or on behalf of such committee; and (4) The name and address of every person to whom any such expenditure is made, and the date thereof.

(c) It shall be the duty of the treasurer to obtain and keep a receipted bill, stating the particulars, for every expenditure by or on behalf of a political committee exceeding $10 in amount. The treasurer shall preserve all receipted bills and accounts required to be kept by this section for a period of at least two years from the date of the filing of the statement containing such items. . . .

Section 305. (a) The treasurer of a political committee shall file [the detailed information described in Section 303(b)(1)-(4)] with the Clerk between the 1st and 10th days of March, June, and September, in each year, and also between the 10th and 15th days, and on the 5th day, next preceding the date on which a general election is to be held, at which candidates are to be elected in two or more States, and also on the 1st day of January, a statement containing, complete as of the day next preceding the date of filing. . . .

(c) The statement filed on the 1st day of January shall cover the preceding calendar year.

Section 306. Every person (other than a political committee) who makes an expenditure in one or more items, other than by contribution to a political committee, aggregating $50 or more within a calendar year for the purpose of influencing in two or more States the election of candidates, shall file with the Clerk an itemized detailed statement of such expenditure in the same manner as required of the treasurer of a political committee by section 305.

Section 307. (a) Every candidate for Senator shall file with the Secretary and every candidate for Representative . . . shall file with the Clerk not less than ten nor more than fifteen days before, and also within thirty days after, the date on which an election is to be held, a statement containing, complete as of the day next preceding the date of filing—(1) A correct and itemized account of each contribution received by him or by any person for him with his knowledge or consent, from any source, in aid or support of his candidacy for election, or for the purpose of influencing the result of the election, together with the name of the person who has made such contribution; (2) A correct and itemized account of each expenditure made by him or by any person for him with his knowledge or consent, in aid or support of his candidacy for election, or for the purpose of influencing the result of the election, together with the name of the person to whom such expenditure was made: except that only the total sum of expenditures for items specified in subdivision (c) of section 309 need be stated; (3) A statement of every promise or pledge made by him or by any person for him with his consent, prior to the closing of the polls on the day of the election, relative to the appointment or recommendation for appointment of any person to any public or private position or employment for the purpose of procuring support in his candidacy, and the name, address, and occupation of every person to whom any such promise or pledge has been made, together with the description of any such position. If no such promise or pledge has been made, that fact shall be specifically stated. . . .

Section 309. (a) A candidate, in his campaign for election, shall not make expenditures in excess of the amount which he may lawfully make under the laws of the state in which he is a candidate, nor in excess of the amount which he may lawfully make under the provisions of this title.

(b) Unless the laws of his State prescribe a less amount as the maximum limit of campaign expenditures, a candidate may make expenditures up to—(1) The sum of $10,000 if a candidate for Senator, or the sum of $2,500 if a candidate for Representative . . . ; or (2) An amount equal to the amount obtained by multiplying three cents by the total number of votes cast at the last general elections for all candidates for the office which the candidate seeks, but in no event exceeding $25,000 if a candidate for Senator or $5,000 if a candidate for Representative. . . .

(c) Money expended by a candidate to meet and discharge any assessment, fee, or charge made or levied upon candidates by the laws of the State in which he resides, or expended for his necessary personal, traveling, or subsistence expenses, or for stationery, postage, writing, or printing (other than for use on billboards or in newspapers), for distributing letters, circulars, or posters, or for telegraph or telephone service, shall not be included in determining whether his expenditures have exceeded the sum fixed by paragraph (1) or (2) of subdivision (b) as the limit of campaign expenses of a candidate.

Section 310. It is unlawful for any candidate to directly or indirectly promise or pledge the appointment, or the use of his influence or support for the appointment of any person to any public or private position or employment, for the purpose of procuring support in his candidacy.

Section 311. It is unlawful for any person to make or offer to make an expenditure, or to cause an expenditure to be made or offered, to any person, either to vote or withhold his vote, or to vote for or against any candidate, and it is unlawful for any person to solicit, accept, or receive any such expenditure in consideration of his vote or the withholding of his vote.

Section 312. It is unlawful for any Senator or Representative . . . or any person receiving any salary or compensation for services from money de-

rived from the Treasury of the United States, to directly or indirectly solicit, receive, or be in any manner concerned in soliciting or receiving,
any assessment, subscription, or contribution for any political purpose
whatever, from any other such officer, employee, or person.

Section 313. It is unlawful for any national bank, or any corporation
organized by authority of any law of Congress, to make a contribution in
connection with any election to any political office, or for any corporation
whatever to make a contribution in connection with any election at which
presidential and vice presidential electors or a Senator or Representative
in, or a Delegate or Resident Commissioner to, Congress are to be voted
for, or for any candidate, political committee, or other person to accept
or receive any contribution prohibited by this section. Every corporation
which makes any contribution in violation of this section shall be fined
not more than $5,000; and every officer or director of any corporation
who consents to any contribution by the corporation in violation of this
section shall be fined not more than $1,000, or imprisoned not more than
one year, or both.

Section 314. (a) Any person who [nonwillfully] violates any of the foregoing provisions . . . shall be fined not more than $1,000 or imprisoned
not more than one year, or both.

(b) Any person who willfully violates any of the foregoing provisions of
this title . . . shall be fined not more than $10,000 and imprisoned not
more than two years.

Approved February 28, 1925.

NOTES

1. See *Mammoth Oil Co. v. United States* (1927) and *Pan American Petroleum &
Transp. Co. v. United States* (1927).
2. 65 Cong. Rec. 9507–9508.

THE HATCH ACT OF 1939 AS AMENDED IN 1940

Beginning with the Naval Appropriations Act of 1867, Congress has restricted the ability of candidates for national office to solicit campaign funds from federal employees. The Hatch Act of 1939, as amended in 1940, placed certain restrictions on the ability of federal employees, employees of the District of Columbia (D.C.) government, and certain state and local government employees to participate in political activities. Any employee that violated the ban was to be immediately discharged and made subject to a permanent ban against reemployment in the same position. The 1940 amendments limited for the first time the amount of money that individuals could contribute to federal candidates or national party committees. Not diminishing the First Amendment consequences for federal employees, limits on financial contributions to candidates and expenditures by candidates and noncandidates alike would come to play an even more important role in the relationship between congressional regulation in the field of campaign politics and the First Amendment. However, as we will see, the significance of contributions and expenditures for First Amendment law did not appear until the passage of the 1971 Federal Election Campaign Act and its amendments.

The Hatch Act, named for its author, Senator Carl Atwood Hatch (1889–1963) of New Mexico, was not the first restriction on campaign activities by federal employees. As far back as 1801, President Thomas Jefferson had issued an executive order that he "expected that [all officers within the executive branch] will not attempt to influence the votes of others nor take any part in the business of electioneering."[1] Congress then enacted the Civil Service Act of 1883, which authorized the president to promulgate rules that sought to prevent federal employees in the competitive classified service from using their "official authority or influence to coerce the political action of any person or body." With the Hatch Act, all federal officers and employees, whether in the classified civil service or not, were brought within the purview of the ban on political activity.[2]

The conflict between the First Amendment and campaign regulations began to surface with the Hatch Act. The United Federal Workers of America, an unincorporated labor union representing federal employees and twelve individual plaintiffs, each of whom occupied a position in the federal government under the classified civil service, brought suit against the civil service commissioners who were charged with enforcing the Hatch Act. The union and employees claimed that the act's ban on political activity violated federal employees' freedom of speech, press, and peaceful assembly. The trial court dismissed the suit by summarily declaring the following in somewhat convoluted language:

> To say that the Congress has not the power to pass this legislation in the public interest, and in the interest of the employees of the Government whose tenure it is seeking to protect, is to say that it is not rational for the Congress to conclude that it cannot take political activity out of the employment, promotion and dismissal of Government employees without at the same time taking Government employees out of political activity. This is a question for the Congress, and not the courts, to decide. (*United Federal Workers of America et al. v. Mitchell et al.*, 1944, p. 626)

The First Amendment argument in *United Federal Workers* was met with similar rejection in an appeal to the Supreme Court in *United Public Workers of America (C.I.O.) et al. v. Mitchell et al.* (1947). Notwithstanding a vigorous dissent by Justices William O. Douglas and Hugo Black, the Supreme Court held in favor of the Hatch Act, declaring that "these fundamental human rights [i.e., right to engage in political campaign activities] are not absolutes," and that there must be a balance between the guarantees of freedom against the right of Congress to protect a democratic society against the supposed evil of political partisanship by government employees (p. 96). Justice Black's dissent was especially strong, claiming that the Hatch Act

> reduces the constitutionally protected liberty of several million citizens to less than a shadow of its substance. It relegates millions of federal, state, and municipal employees to the role of mere spectators of events upon which hinge the safety and welfare of all the people, including public employees. It removes a sizable proportion of our electorate from full participation in affairs destined to mould the fortunes of the nation. It makes honest participation in essential

political activities an offense punishable by proscription from public employment. It endows a governmental board with the awesome power to censor the thoughts, expressions, and activities of law-abiding citizens in the field of free expression, from which no person should be barred by a government which boasts that it is a government of, for, and by the people—all the people. Laudable as its purpose may be, it seems to me to hack at the roots of a Government by the people themselves. (p. 115)

Nonetheless, the views of Justices Black and Douglas did not prevail in this case, nor have they since become the prevailing view regarding federal employees.[3] Their opinions have, however, increasingly become the dominant views of the judiciary regarding campaign regulation of other campaign-financing situations, as we will see.

In 1993 Congress enacted significant changes to the Hatch Act that permitted many federal employees to take an active part in political activities in some situations. For example, they may become candidates for public office in nonpartisan elections, assist in voter registration drives, contribute money to political organizations, sign nominating petitions, and make campaign speeches for candidates in partisan elections. The amended Hatch Act continues to prohibit covered employees from using their official authority or influence to interfere with an election, soliciting or discouraging political activity of anyone doing business with the employee's agency, soliciting or receiving political contributions, and becoming a candidate for public office in partisan elections. The 1993 amendments did not change the provisions applying to state and local employees.

The Hatch Act of 1939 as Amended in 1940

Section 13. (a) It is hereby declared to be a pernicious political activity, and it shall hereafter be unlawful, for any person, directly or indirectly, to make contributions in an aggregate amount in excess of $5,000, during any calendar year, or in connection with any campaign for nomination or election, to or on behalf of any candidate for an elective Federal office (including the offices of President of the United States and Presidential and Vice Presidential electors), or to or on behalf of any committee or other organization engaged in furthering, advancing or advocating the nomination or election of any candidate for any such office or the success of any national political party. This subsection shall not apply to contributions made to or by a State or local committee or other State or local organization.

(b) For the purposes of this section—

(1) The term "person" includes an individual, partnership, committee, association, corporation, and any other organization or group of persons.

(2) The term "contribution" includes a gift, subscription, loan, advance, or deposit of money, or anything of value, and includes a contract, promise, or agreement, whether or not legally enforceable, to make a contribution.

(c) It is further declared to be a pernicious political activity, and it shall hereafter be unlawful for any person, individual, partnership, committee, association, corporation, and any other organization or group of persons to purchase or buy any goods, commodities, advertising, or articles of any kind or description where the proceeds of such a purchase, or any portion thereof, shall directly or indirectly inure to the benefit of or for any candidate for an elective Federal office (including the offices of President of the United States, and Presidential and Vice Presidential electors) or any political committee or other political organization engaged in furthering, advancing, or advocating the nomination or election of any candidate for any such office or the success of any national political party: Provided, That nothing in this sentence shall be construed to interfere with the usual and known business, trade, or profession of any candidate.

(d) Any person who engages in a pernicious political activity in violation of any provision of this section, shall upon conviction thereof be fined not more than $5,000 or imprisoned for not more than five years. In all cases of violations of this section by a partnership, committee, association, corporation, or other organization or group of persons, the officers, directors, or managing heads thereof who knowingly and willfully participate in such violation, shall be subject to punishment as herein provided.

(e) Nothing in this section shall be construed to permit the making of any contribution which is prohibited by any provision of law in force on the date this section takes effect. Nothing in this Act shall be construed to alter or amend any provisions of the Federal Corrupt Practices Act of 1925, or any amendments thereto. . . .

Section 6. Such Act of August 2, 1939, is further amended by adding at the end thereof the following new section: . . .

Section 20. No political committee shall receive contributions aggregating more than $3,000,000, or make expenditures aggregating more than $3,000,000, during any calendar year. For the purposes of this section, any contributions received and any expenditures made on behalf of any political committee with the knowledge and consent of the chairman or treasurer of such committee shall be deemed to be received or made by such committee. Any violation of this section by any political committee shall be deemed also to be a violation of this section by the chairman and the treasurer of such committee and by any other person responsible for such violation. Terms used in this section shall have the meaning assigned to them in section 302 of the Federal Corrupt Practices Act, 1925, and the penalties provided in such Act shall apply to violations of this section. Approved July 19, 1940.

NOTES

1. Quoted in *United Federal Workers of America et al. v. Mitchell et al.*, 56 F. Supp. 621, 626 (D. District of Columbia, August 3, 1944).

2. This Hatch Act should not be confused with an earlier Hatch Act (1887), concerning the study of scientific agriculture, which was named for Representative William Henry Hatch (1833–1896) of Missouri.

3. See *CSC v. Letter Carriers* (1973), which upheld a later version of the Hatch Act.

THE FEDERAL ELECTION CAMPAIGN ACT
OF 1971

Several significant changes to the Corrupt Practices Act of 1925, including the Hatch Act amendments and the Taft-Hartley Act of 1947, were the forerunners of a comprehensive revision that began in 1971. The Taft-Hartley Act of 1947 made the ban on political contributions by labor unions a permanent part of the electoral laws. The ban had been instituted by the War Labor Disputes Act of 1943—or the Smith-Connally Act, as it is popularly known—and was made permanent after a 1945 report of the House Special Committee to Investigate Campaign Expenditures that expressed much concern over the vast amount of money that some labor unions were devoting to politics. The report was reminiscent of Samuel Gompers' 1906 remonstrations about corporate money in politics, and in part stated:

> The scale of operations of some of these [labor] organizations is impressive. Without exception, they operate on a nation-wide basis; and many of them have affiliated local organizations. One was found to have an annual budget for "educational" work approximating $1,500,000, and among other things regularly supplies over 500 radio stations with "briefs for broadcasters." Another, with an annual budget of over $300,000 for political "education," has distributed some 80,000,000 pieces of literature, including a quarter million copies of one article. Another, representing an organized labor membership of 5,000,000, has raised $700,000 for its national organizations in union contributions for political "education" in a few months, and a great deal more has been raised for the same purpose and expended by its local organizations.[1]

Nonetheless, labor unions and corporations may well have the last say—at least for the time being—by way of the political action committee (PAC), a creation that was introduced by the Congress of Industrial Organization in 1943. The term *political action committee* is the popular name for "independent" campaign committees that are affiliated with neither a political party nor a candidate's committee. Although PACs are commonly affiliated with corporations and labor unions, many are associated with public interest groups that do not have a corporate affiliation. PACs were exempt from the Taft-Hartley Act because they were supposedly independent of the corporations and labor unions that created them, and their receipts came from voluntary contributions as opposed to the use of regular corporate income and union dues.

PACs became prominent, and even dominant, in campaign financing with the Federal Election Campaign Act of 1971, which set strict limits on individual contributions but left the door open for "party-related and educational activities" and other "soft money" expenditures not regulated by federal law. Indeed, the growth of PACs has been quite phenomenal. According to statistics provided by the Federal Election Commission, between 1977 and 1999 the number of union-related PACs nearly doubled, from slightly more than 200 to approximately 350. During the same period, corporate-related PACs increased from just under 600 to 1,600, and independent PACs from 100 to almost 1,000.[2] The rise in the amount of money spent by PACs on candidates to the U.S. Senate and House of Representatives is equally dramatic. During the 1977–1978 election cycle PACs spent $35.2 million, and during the 1995–1996 cycle they spent $217.8 million, an increase of 518.75 percent.[3]

Even before PACs were experiencing such extraordinary growth in number and political expenditures, the overall amount of money spent in election campaigns was growing in similar fashion. For example, during the years between 1956 and 1968, the total amount of money spent in congressional elections grew from $155 million to $300 million. This rapid growth of campaign expenditures and other events, such as a class action suit brought by Common Cause against the Democratic and Republican national committees,[4] spawned sufficient concern among members of Congress that they responded with the Federal Election Campaign Act of 1971, which was amended by the Federal Election Campaign Act Amendments of 1974.[5]

While the FECA repealed the Corrupt Practices Act of 1925 and its amendments, it retained many of its provisions, such as the prohibited promise of patronage (jobs) and contracts between a candidate and any federal department or agency. The act gave a regulatory exemption to contributions for nonpartisan- or noncandidate-based "get out the vote" and voter registration drives by unions and corporations. FECA placed a ceiling on contributions by candidates to their own campaigns for president and vice president ($50,000), along with Senate ($35,000) and House ($25,000) candidates. Congress also enacted an important companion to FECA during its ninety-second session, the Revenue Act of 1971, which would later place the presidential campaign finance system on sound footing by establishing a separate presidential campaign fund and a checkoff system that permitted taxpayers to voluntarily subsidize the fund by earmarking a portion of their income tax. No sooner had the FECA taken effect in early 1972, when news of many campaign abuses during the 1972 election began to surface. The Watergate Scandal, as the collective abuses became known, included many campaign-financing incidents involving both major political parties. In one such incident, in exchange for the president's decision to raise milk price supports, thereby overturning the secretary of agriculture's decision against the raise, members of the dairy industry pledged two million dollars to the president's campaign. The contributors split the two million dollars into numerous smaller contributions among hundreds of industry committees in order to avoid the reporting requirements under existing law. In another episode, a major corporation received a favorable antitrust ruling from the Justice Department after a $400,000 campaign pledge. In others, several corporations made contributions that were blatantly illegal, and allegations were rampant regarding illegal contributions that had been laundered in foreign bank accounts. One incident involved a prohibition that had been part of the law since as far back as the Corrupt Practices Act of 1925. A principal fund raiser had promised a prestigious ambassadorial post to a prospective contributor in return for a $100,000 contribution to be split between two senatorial candidates and the presidential campaign.[6] Such revelations, along with events like the Common Cause lawsuit, called attention to the inadequacies of the existing law. Thus, in 1974 Congress enacted the most far-reaching campaign regulations ever. These landmark amendments directly confronted the First Amendment.

The 1974 amendments established a bipartisan commission, the Federal Election Commission, composed of six full-time members to administer the election laws. It implemented the public financing program using the funds made possible by the check-off provision of the 1971 Revenue Act. FECA as amended now provided an extensive framework for financing presidential elections that included full funding in some situations and matching funds in others. Major-party candidates could qualify for funding before their campaigns began, and minor-party and independent candidates could qualify for funding based on past or current votes received. Financing under the plan included costs of nominating conventions and presidential primaries.

The most notable aspects of the 1974 amendments that were impacted by the First Amendment were contribution and spending limits. The major campaign contribution limits in federal elections were: (1) individuals could contribute no more than one thousand dollars for each primary, runoff, or general election, with an aggregate limit of $25,000 to all federal candidates each year; (2) organizations and political committees (PACs, for example) were limited to five thousand dollars for each candidate in each election, with no limit on the aggregate amount; independent expenditures made for the direct benefit of a candidate were limited to one thousand dollars[7]; cash contributions exceeding one hundred dollars were prohibited, as were foreign contributions; and the 1971 limits placed on the use of a candidate's own finances were continued.

The spending limits of candidates were equally extensive. (1) Presidential candidates were limited to: (a) ten million dollars for all primaries; (b) two million dollars for nominating conventions of the major parties, lesser amounts for others; and (3) twenty million dollars for the general election. (2) Senatorial candidates were limited to: (a) $100,000 or eight cents per eligible voter, whichever was greater in primary elections; and (b) $150,000 or twelve cents per eligible voter, whichever was greater in the general election. (3) House candidates were limited to seventy thousand dollars for primary elections, and a like amount for the general election. (4) National parties were limited to ten thousand dollars per candidate in the general election for each House candidate, the larger of twenty thousand dollars or two cents per eligible voter per Senate candidate, and two cents per voter per presidential candidate.

One day after the 1974 amendments went into effect, a blue-chip group of complainants filed a lawsuit seeking to invalidate their provisions, claiming, among other things, that significant sections, including the limitations on contribution and expenditures, violated the parties' First Amendment rights. The plaintiffs—including U.S. Senators James L. Buckley (R-NY), Senator Eugene J. McCarthy (D-MN), Representative William A. Steiger (R-WI), Committee for a Constitutional Presidency-McCarthy '76, Conservative Party of the

State of New York, Mississippi Republican Party, Libertarian Party, New York Civil Liberties Union, and the American Conservative Union—sued an equally notable group that included Francis R. Valeo, secretary of the U.S. Senate; W. Pat Jennings, clerk of the U.S. House of Representatives; Elmer B. Staats, comptroller general of the United States; Edward H. Levi, attorney general of the United States; and the Federal Election Commission (*Buckley v. Valeo*, 1976).

In *Buckley* the Supreme Court subjected campaign financing to First Amendment scrutiny as never before. The result was mixed. The Court held that (1) the provisions of FECA that imposed ceilings on political contributions to the campaigns of others did not violate First Amendment speech and association rights, because they were validly grounded by the substantial governmental interests in limiting corruption and the appearance of corruption; (2) the provisions limiting independent political expenditures by individuals and groups, and fixing ceilings on overall campaign expenditures by candidates, were unconstitutional because they were impermissible burdens on the right of free expression under the First Amendment, and could be sustained neither on the basis of the public's interests in preventing corruption nor the appearance of corruption, nor as an effort to equalize the resources of candidates; (3) the provisions limiting the amount of personal expenditures by a candidate were similarly unconstitutional under the First Amendment; (4) the reporting and disclosure provisions were not violations of First Amendment speech and association rights; and (5) the provisions of the Internal Revenue Code relating to public financing of presidential nominating conventions and primary election campaigns did not violate the First Amendment. The Court also upheld the provisions of the Internal Revenue Code that established the program for public financing of presidential elections, but it ruled against the manner in which FECA members were selected.

Following the *Buckley* decision, Congress amended FECA with the Federal Election Campaign Act Amendments of 1976 to conform with the Supreme Court's decision, and added some minor adjustments to the contribution ceilings as well as some reporting regulations relating to independent expenditures. The act was also amended by the Federal Election Campaign Act Amendments of 1980.

The Federal Election Campaign Act of 1971 as Amended

Section 591. Definitions:

(a) "election" means (1) a general, special, primary, or runoff election, (2) a convention or caucus of a political party held to nominate a candidate, (3) a primary election held for the selection of delegates to a national nominating convention of a political party, 14) a primary election held for the expression of a preference for the nomination of persons for election to the office of President, and (5) the election of delegates to a constitutional convention for proposing amendments to the Constitution of the United States;

(b) "candidate" means an individual who seeks nomination for election, or election, to Federal office, whether or not such individual is elected, and, for purposes of this paragraph, an individual shall be deemed to seek nomination for election, or election, to Federal office, if he has (1) taken the action necessary under the law of a State to qualify himself for nomination for election, or election, or (2) received contributions or made expenditures, or has given his consent for any other person to receive contributions or make expenditures, with a view to bringing about his nomination for election, or election, to such office.

(c) "Federal office" means the office of President or Vice President of the United States, or Senator or Representative in, or Delegate or Resident Commissioner to, the Congress of the United States.

(d) "political committee" means any individual, committee, association, or organization which accepts contributions or makes expenditures during a calendar year in an aggregate amount exceeding $1,000;

(e) "contribution" means—

(1) a gift, subscription, loan, advance, or deposit of money or anything of value . . . made for the purpose of influencing the nomination for election, or election, of any person to Federal office or . . . the selection of delegates to a national nominating convention of a political party or for the expression of a preference for the nomination of persons for election to the office of President of the United States;

(2) a contract, promise, or agreement, express or implied, whether or not legally enforceable, to make a contribution for such purposes;

(3) funds received by a political committee which are transferred to such committee from another political committee or other source;

(4) the payment, by any person other than a candidate or a political committee, of compensation for the personal services of another person which are rendered to such candidate or political committee without charge for any such purpose; . . .

(f) "expenditure"—

(1) means a purchase, payment, distribution, loan, advance, deposit, or gift of money or anything of value . . . made for the purpose of influencing the nomination for election, or election, of any person to Federal office or . . . the selection of delegates to a national nominating convention of a political party or for the expression of a preference for the nomination of persons for election to the office of President of the United States;

(2) means a contract, promise, or agreement, express or implied, whether or not legally enforceable, to make any expenditure; and

(3) means the transfer of funds by a political committee to another political committee; . . .

(g) "person" and "whoever" mean an individual, partnership, committee, association, corporation, or any other organization or group of persons.

Section 608. Limitations on contributions and expenditures:

(a) (1) No candidate may make expenditures from his personal funds, or the personal funds of his immediate family, in connection with his campaigns during any calendar year for nomination for election, or for election, to Federal office in excess of, in the aggregate—

(A) $50,000, in the case of a candidate for the office of President or Vice President of the United States;

(B) $35,000, in the case of a candidate for the office of Senator or for the office of Representative from a State which is entitled to only one Representative; or

(C) $25,000, in the case of a candidate for the office of Representative. . . .

(2) No candidate or his immediate family may make loans or advances from their personal funds in connection with his campaign for nomination for election, or for election, to Federal office unless such loan or advance is evidenced by a written instrument fully disclosing the terms and conditions of such loan or advance.

(3) For purposes of this subsection, any such loan or advance shall be included in computing the total amount of such expenditures only to the extent of the balance of such loan or advance outstanding and unpaid.

(4) For purposes of this subsection, "immediate family" means a can-

didate's spouse, and any child, parent or grandparent, brother, or sister of the candidate, and the spouse of such persons.

(b) (1) Except as otherwise provided by paragraphs (2) and (3), no person shall make contributions to any candidate with respect to any election for Federal office which, in the aggregate, exceed $1,000.

(2) No political committee (other than a principal campaign committee) shall make contributions to any candidate with respect to any election for Federal office which, in the aggregate, exceed $5,000.

(3) No individual shall make contributions aggregating more than $25,000 in any calendar year. For purposes of this paragraph, any contribution made in a year other than the calendar year in which the election is held with respect to which such contribution was made is considered to be made during the calendar year in which such election is held.

(c) (1) No candidate [that receives federal matching funds] shall make expenditures in excess of—

(A) $10,000,000, in the case of a candidate for nomination for election to the office of President of the United States, except that the aggregate of expenditures under this subparagraph in any one State shall not exceed twice the expenditure limitation applicable in such State to a candidate for nomination for election to the office of Senator, Delegate, or Resident Commissioner, as the case may be;

(B) $20,000,000, in the case of a candidate for election to the office of President of the United States;

(C) in the case of any campaign for nomination for election by a candidate for the office of Senator or by a candidate for the office of Representative from a State which is entitled to only one Representative, the greater of—

(i) 8 cents multiplied by the voting age population of the State (as certified under subsection (g)); or

(ii) $100,000;

(D) in the case of any campaign for election by a candidate for the office of Senator or by a candidate for the office of Representative from a State which is entitled to only one Representative, the greater of—

(i) 12 cents multiplied by the voting age population of the State (as certified under subsection (g)); or

(ii) $150,000;

(E) $70,000, in the case of any campaign for nomination for election, or for election, by a candidate for the office of Representative in any other State, Delegate from the District of Columbia, or Resident Commissioner;

(f) (1) Notwithstanding any other provision of law with respect to limitations on expenditures or limitations on contributions, the national committee of a political party and a State committee of a political party, including any subordinate committee of a State committee, may make expenditures in connection with the general election campaign of candidates for Federal office, subject to the limitations contained in paragraphs (2) and (3) of this subsection.

(2) The national committee of a political party may not make any expenditure in connection with the general election campaign of any candidate for President of the United States who is affiliated with such party which exceeds an amount equal to 2 cents multiplied by the voting age population of the United States (as certified under subsection (e)). Any expenditure under this paragraph shall be in addition to any expenditure by a national committee of a political party serving as the principal campaign committee of a candidate for the office of President of the United States.

(3) The national committee of a political party, or a State committee of a political party, including any subordinate committee of a State committee, may not make any expenditure in connection with the general election campaign of a candidate for Federal office in a State who is affiliated with such party which exceeds—

(A) in the case of a candidate for election to the office of Senator, or of Representative from a State which is entitled to only one Representative, the greater of—

(i) 2 cents multiplied by the voting age population of the State (as certified under subsection (g)); or

(ii) $20,000; and

(B) in the case of a candidate for election to the office of Representative, Delegate, or Resident Commissioner in any other State, $10,000.

(g) During the first week of January 1975, and every subsequent year, the Secretary of Commerce shall certify to the Commission and publish in the Federal Register an estimate of the voting age population of the United States, of each State, and of each congressional district as of the first day of July next preceding the date of certification. The term "voting age population" means resident population, 18 years of age or older.

(h) No candidate or political committee shall knowingly accept any contribution or make any expenditure in violation of the provisions of this section. No officer or employee of a political committee shall knowingly accept a contribution made for the benefit or use of a candidate, or knowingly make any expenditure on behalf of a candidate, in violation of any limitation imposed on contributions and expenditures under this section.

(i) Any person who violates any provision of this section shall be fined not more than $25,000 or imprisoned not more than one year, or both. Approved February 7, 1972, October 15, 1974, May 11, 1976, and January 8, 1980, respectively.

NOTES

1. H. R. Rep. No. 2093, 78th Cong., 2d Sess. 3.

2. Federal Election Commission, "Campaign Finance Reports and Data" (http://www.fec.gov/press/paccnt_grph.html) [accessed September 16, 2000].

3. Federal Election Commission, News Release of April 27, 1997 (http://www.fec.gov/press/pacye96.htm) [accessed September 16, 2000].

4. Common Cause lost the suit, in which it alleged that candidates from both major parties were systematically violating election campaign laws, but it did focus attention on many deficiencies of current law. See: *Common Cause et al., Plaintiffs, v. Democratic National Committee et al.*, 333 F. Supp. 803 (D. D.C. 1971)

5. Title I, governing Campaign Communications, has been repealed. FECA Amendments of 1974, § 205(b). Title II consists of Criminal Code Amendments respecting the election law crimes enacted in prior federal election laws, including the Corrupt Practices Act of 1925. Title III required Disclosure of Federal Campaign Funds. Title IV contained General Provisions.

6. See Final Report of the Select Comm. on Presidential Campaign Activities, S. Rep. 93–981, 93rd Cong., 2d Sess. (1974).

7. The determination of whether an expenditure is made on "behalf" of a candidate and when it simply—and coincidentally—helps a candidate incidentally has become a highly contentious and difficult problem under present law.

4

Obscenity

Three congressional landmarks exist in the field of protecting the public from obscenity. The first is the Comstock Act enacted in 1873, the second is the Anti-Dial-a-Porn Act of 1989 (the Helms Amendment to the Communications Act of 1935), and the third is the Child Online Protection Act of 1998. The Comstock Act was not the first anti-obscenity enactment by Congress. Nonetheless, it became the standard model because of the broadness of its scope and the durability of its approach. The Helms Amendment promulgated a procedure to restrict minors' access to pornographic telephone messages and conversation. The Child Online Protection Act, which is a direct descendant of the Comstock Act, is the latest broad-based effort to combat obscenity and indecency in the newest technological medium, the Internet. The events that would come to influence the congressional attacks on obscenity and indecency were largely unknown to the lawmakers in 1789, the year that they introduced the First Amendment to the U.S. Constitution in Congress. These events, involving changes that have occurred over the past two centuries, were the alterations in the legal definition of obscenity along with the public's attitude toward what is considered obscene, on the one hand, and the development of progressive technologies, on the other.

Although the First Amendment had very little, if any, bearing on the congressional battle against obscenity during the nineteenth century, it came to play a crucial role by the middle of the twentieth century. In fact, when future president James Madison introduced the speech and press clause in the House of Representatives on

June 8, 1789, little might he have imagined the role it would eventually play in regulating obscenity. In Madison's time, there was no general common-law offense against obscenity. In fact, except for a 1712 enactment in Massachusetts, Acts and Laws of the Province of Mass. Bay, c. CV, 8 (1712), Mass. Bay Colony Charters & Laws 399 (1814), obscenity law was not even a legislative subject until 1821, when Vermont enacted an anti-obscenity law. (Vermont Session Laws, 1821 Chapter I, Section 23). In fact, 1821 was also the year in which the first prosecutions occurred under the earlier Massachusetts law that made it a criminal offense to publish "any filthy, obscene, or profane song, pamphlet, libel or mock sermon in imitation or mimicking of religious services."[1] The Massachusetts law is typical of early anti-obscenity laws in that it associates obscenity with irreligious acts. Although the word *obscenity* simply suggests anything that offends accepted standards of decency or modesty to such an extent that it is repugnant, at the end of the eighteenth century it had a strictly religious connotation. However, as we will see, "obscenity" as it relates to the First Amendment has become exclusively associated with pruriency or sex. If an expression is determined to be obscene, it is not entitled to First Amendment protection.

Indecency is another statutory term that plays an important part in anti-obscenity law. We can think of indecency as simply a weak version of obscenity, not bad enough to be banned outright as obscene, but bad enough to justify some restriction, at least insofar as children are concerned. Statutes often contain many other associated terms, such as *lewd* and *lascivious*. Nevertheless, these terms are either given no legal meaning or considered as the equivalent of obscenity or indecency.

During the process of creating the Commission on Obscenity and Pornography in 1967, Congress determined that "the traffic in obscenity and pornography is a matter of national concern."[2] Over the years, Congress has shown an increasing interest in the depth and breadth of the potential impact of obscenity in society, particularly on the youth. The current situation is very unlike the early years, when the relationship between the First Amendment and obscenity was not a concern, for two reasons. First, the frequency of supposedly obscene acts was not very high, and second, almost everyone took the constitutionality of governmental actions combating obscenity for granted. Nonetheless, in 1842 Congress enacted the first national anti-obscenity law in response to a public protest over the arrival of postcards from France that were considered obscene. The Customs Law of 1842 prohibited the importation of "indecent and obscene prints, paintings, lithographs, engravings, and transparencies."[3]

It was almost a quarter century before the second congressional anti-obscenity statute was enacted. During the Civil War the postmaster general reported to Congress that soldiers were receiving many obscene materials through the mail. The congressional response was an 1865 statute that provided, "No obscene book, pamphlet [etc.] . . . shall be admitted into the mails."[4] This 1865 act, which was the first to contain a criminal provision and the first to involve the mail, provided for a five-hundred-dollar fine, imprisonment for not more than a year, or both. While there was some debate about the possibility of undesirable censorship by postal officials, the act nonetheless provided a basis for it. Postal officials used the act's authority to censor mail and, in fact, had been in the habit of doing so even before the act was passed.[5] Increasingly, however, during the past two centuries, censorship has become a highly disfavored practice in the United States even when it involves obscene materials. Judges, relying on the First Amendment, have insisted on a constitutional preference for a system of punishment after the fact rather than a system of prior restraint.[6]

NOTES

1. For a historical account of obscenity laws in the United States, see *The Report of the Commission on Obscenity and Pornography* (New York: Bantam Books, 1970), Chapter 4. Tribe, supra note 2, § 12–16, at 906 (citing *Commonwealth v. Sharpless*, 2 Serg. & Rawle 91 [Penn. 1815], as the first reported American obscenity case).

2. P.L. 90–100, §§ 1–6, 81 Stat. 253.

3. This statute—drafted by a select committee headed by Millard Fillmore (1800–1874), who later served as the thirteenth president from 1850–1853—examined needed changes in the Tariff Act and provided for a judicial procedure in the district court where objectionable material that was seized by customs officials would be adjudicated or tried by a judge and jury. The first reported case was *United States v. Three Cases of Toys* (1843).

4. 13 Stat. 507 § 16.

5. James C.N. Paul and Murray L. Schwartz, *Federal Censorship: Obscenity in the Mail* (Westport, CT: Greenwood Press, 1962), p. 251.

6. For more on censorship, see *Near v. Minnesota* (1931) and later cases that follow its holding.

THE COMSTOCK ACT OF 1873

The 1865 mail act was the precursor to what has become the landmark congressional enactment in the field of legislative measures against obscenity. Known as the Comstock Act or Comstock Law, it was enacted in 1873 following the strenuous and effective lobbying efforts of twenty-eight-year-old Anthony Comstock (1844–1915). Comstock was the organizer and secretary of the New York City YMCA's Committee for the Suppression of Vice. Following passage of the law bearing his name, Comstock became an unpaid, voluntary special postal agent dedicated to enforcing his namesake. He gained much notoriety for his moral crusades against literature and artwork that he considered obscene. In fact, Comstock boasted near the end of his life that he had "convicted enough people to fill a passenger train of sixty-one coaches, with sixty of the coaches containing sixty people each and the last almost full." He also was said to have claimed credit for destroying 160 tons of literature and 3,984,063 pictures.[1]

Comstock's name not only adorned this landmark statute; "Comstockery" came to represent anti-obscenity efforts overall. George Bernard Shaw (1856–1950)—the Irish-born British playwright who was awarded the 1925 Nobel Prize in literature for his plays of unorthodox social criticism, including *Arms and the Man* (1894), *Pygmalion* (1913), and *Saint Joan* (1923)—penned the name. Shaw had become an enemy of Comstock when the latter sought to prevent the former's *Mrs. Warren's Profession*—whose subject is organized prostitution—from performing in New York. When Comstock accused Shaw of being an "Irish smut dealer," Shaw glibly characterized the insult as "Comstockery."[2]

Comstock's lobbying method did not change much over the years. He was privileged to be allowed to set up an exhibit in the vice president's office where he displayed articles that he deemed to be examples of obscene materials that were being sent through the mail. These included publications and their advertisements of various gadgets designed to stimulate sexual potency, of contraceptives, and of other "abominations." A century later, Senator James Exon (D-NE) would do likewise on the floor of the Senate chamber. Senator Exon placed several articles in the *Congressional Record* during the debate on the Communications Decency Act, including a *Los Angeles Times* article entitled "Info Superhighway Veers into Pornographic Ditch" and several articles about telephone dial-a-porn messages that were shrewdly calculated to inflame passions. Debate on the Comstock Act was small at best and nonexistent at worst. When the Senate called it up for action in February, Senator Eugene Casserly of California stated, "We've barely had time to read this bill." Later in the session, Senator Roscoe Conkling (R-NY), lamenting the lack of a copy of the bill, stated, "If I were to be questioned now as to what [it] contains, I could aver nothing certain in regards to it."

The actual name of the Comstock Act was "An Act for the Suppression of Trade in, and Circulation of, obscene Literature and Articles of Immoral Use." The Comstock Act altered the 1865 act in several significant ways. Congress expanded the categories of obscenity, vulgarity, and indecency to include lewdness, lasciviousness, and immorality. Congress also included a ban for the first time on distributing information on and materials for birth control and abortion.[3] The act extended the previous ban on mailing and importing obscene materials to include authorization for searches, seizures, and destruction of prohibited materials. Penalties were increased in some situations by as much as one hundred dollars to five thousand dollars, one year to ten years of hard labor in prison, or both, and in others as much as six months to five years, one hundred dollars to two thousand dollars, or both.

The Comstock Act of 1873

Section 1. That whoever . . . shall sell, or lend, or give away, or in any manner exhibit, or shall offer to sell, or to lend, or give away, or in any manner exhibit, or shall otherwise publish or offer to publish in any manner, or shall have in his possession, for any such purpose or purposes, any obscene book, pamphlet, paper, writing, advertisement, circular, print, picture, drawing or other representation, figure, or image on or of paper or other material, or any cast, instrument, or other article of an immoral nature . . . shall be deemed guilty of a misdemeanor, and on conviction thereof . . . shall be imprisoned at hard labor in the penitentiary for not less than six months nor more than five years for each offense, or fined not less than one hundred dollars nor more than two thousand dollars, with costs of court.

Section 2. That no obscene, lewd, or lascivious book, pamphlet, picture, paper, print, or other publication of an indecent character, or any article or thing designed or intended for the prevention of conception or procuring of abortion, nor any article or thing intended or adapted for any indecent or immoral use or nature, nor any written or printed card, circular, book, pamphlet, advertisement or notice of any kind giving information, directly or indirectly, where, or how, or of whom, or by what means either of the things before mentioned may be obtained or made, nor any letter upon the envelope of which, or postal-card upon which indecent or scurrilous epithets may be written or printed, shall be carried in the mail, and any person who shall knowingly deposit, or cause to be deposited, for mailing or delivery, any of the hereinbefore-mentioned articles or things, or any notice, or paper containing any advertisement relating to the aforesaid articles of things, and any person who, in pursuance of any plan or scheme for disposing of any of the hereinbefore-mentioned articles or things shall take, or cause to be taken from the mail any such letter or package shall be deemed guilty of a misdemeanor, and, on conviction thereof, shall, for every offense, be fined not less than one hundred dollars nor more than five thousand dollars, or imprisoned at hard labor not less than one year nor more than ten years or both, in the discretion of the judge.

Section 3. That all persons are prohibited from importing into the United States from any foreign country, any of the hereinbefore-mentioned articles or things . . . and all such prohibited articles in the course of importation shall be detained by the officer of customs, and proceedings taken against the same under section five of this act.

Section 4. That whoever, being an officer, agent, or employee of the government of the United States, shall knowingly aid or abet any person engaged in any violation of this act, shall be deemed guilty of a misdemeanor, and on conviction thereof, for every offense, be punished as provided in section two of this act.

Section 5. That any judge of any district or circuit court of the United States, within the proper district, before whom complaint in writing of any violation of this act shall be made, to the satisfaction of such judge, and founded on knowledge or belief, and, if upon belief, setting forth the grounds of such belief, and supported by oath or affirmation of the complainant, may issue conformably to the Constitution, a warrant directed to the marshal, or any deputy marshal, in the proper district, directing him to search for, seize, and take possession of any such article or thing hereinbefore-mentioned, and to make due and immediate return thereof, to the end that the same may be condemned and destroyed by proceedings, which shall be conducted in the same manner as other proceedings in case of municipal seizure, and with the same right of appeal or writ of error. . . .

Approved March 3, 1873.

NOTES

1. Robert Corn-Revere, "New Age Comstockery: Exxon v. the Internet," Cato Institute Policy Analysis No. 232, June 28, 1995, p. 3 (http://www.wco.com/~dragon22/comstock.html) [accessed February 28, 2000].

2. Heywood Broun and Margaret Leech, *Anthony Comstock: Roundsman of the Lord* (New York: Albert & Charles Boni, 1927), pp. 18, 229–233.

3. The birth control portion of the act was repealed in 1971 by Public Law 91–662 in response to the Supreme Court's decision in *Griswold v. Connecticut* (1965). Consequently, this portion of the act is omitted.

THE ANTI-DIAL-A-PORN ACT OF 1989

Over time the interchange between technology and congressional efforts to combat obscenity and indecency has become a burning public issue. A statement in a recent House of Representatives House Report described the issue as follows:

> Congress must stand ready to "keep pace with the progress of the country, and adapt (itself) to the new [technological] developments." From regulating matters regarding ports of entry into the United States (18th Century) to the creation of a national railroad system (19th Century) to establishing communications policy (20th Century), Congress' duty remains constant: to uphold the responsibilities delegated to Congress by the people with respect to the regulation of commerce among the several States. (105th Congress, 2nd Session, 105 H. Rpt. 775, Child Online Protection Act, October 5, 1998).

A review of congressional responses to new technological developments will reveal that the responses are becoming more difficult with each technological development.

After Scottish-born Alexander Graham Bell (1847–1922) displayed the electrical transmission of speech by his telephone apparatus in 1876, communications took a radical turn. The telephone not only permitted long-distance communication (hence its name *tele*phone), but high-speed communication as well. Consequently, it was destined to become a major cultural factor in a very short time. The story of how Congress struggled with telephonic technology and questions of obscenity illustrates the difficulties involved in finding the right solution to the specific medium.

The telephone provided the medium for a new version of pornographic distribution called "dial-a-porn." Dial-a-porn, the business of offering live and prerecorded pornographic messages over the telephone, is a feature provided by telephone companies whereby vendors can offer consumers services and information over the telephone line for an additional charge. The technological nature of dial-a-porn presented Congress with a major problem in that minors could dial up the pornography providers as easily as adults could—and from the same telephone. The congressional reaction to this new technology was a 1983 amendment to the Communications Act of 1935 that prohibited making obscene telephone calls to anyone under eighteen. The act directed the Federal Communications Commission (FCC) to promulgate a procedure for restricting minors' access to dial-a-porn. The FCC adopted its initial dial-a-porn rule in 1984, permitting access (presumably by adults) to dial-a-porn messages only during the hours of 9:00 P.M. and 8:00 A.M. or to those who use a credit card to charge the calls before transmission of the message (49 Fed. Reg. 24,996, 47 C.F.R. § 64.201, 1988). The FCC's regulatory response to dial-a-porn was struck down because it was not considered the least restrictive means of protecting the minor population (*Carlin Communications, Inc. v. FCC,* 1984).

In 1985 the FCC issued a second regulation, which permitted dial-a-porn providers to send messages anytime during the day but only to persons who prepaid with a credit card (presumably adults) or to adults who obtained an access identification number (50 Fed. Reg. 42699, 42705, 1985). This regulation was also struck down by an appellate court in Philadelphia in the case of *Carlin Communications, Inc. v. FCC* (1986), once again on the grounds that the regulation was not the least restrictive means. In 1987 the FCC issued a third regulation, this time adding a special defense for dial-a-porn companies: allowing callers to receive a so-called "scrambled" message that they could convert with a descrambling device (52 Fed. Reg. 17,760, 1987). The circuit court granted a provisional approval to this regulation, subject to reopening if new technology became available (*Carlin Communications, Inc. v. FCC,* 1988). Nevertheless, one legislative enactment, three administrative regulations, and three judicial decisions later the story is not over.

In 1988 Congress boldly amended Section 223(b) of the Communications Act of 1934, outrightly prohibiting obscene or indecent telephone communications to anyone at anytime for commercial purposes. In *Sable Communications of California, Inc. v. FCC* (1989), the Supreme Court upheld the act as it applied to "obscene" material but declared the act unconstitutional as it applied to less graphic "indecent" material. While the Court reaffirmed the compelling interest of protecting children from indecent material, it nonetheless declared that the statute was not sufficiently narrow to avoid affecting the rights of adults to use such [indecent] material.

Congress responded in 1989 with yet another amendment, this time the Anti-Dial-a-Porn Act, which prohibited any telephone communication to any person under eighteen years of age, while affording a "safe harbor" defense to dial-a-porn companies if they restricted access to adults by complying with section (c), which prohibits the telephone company from providing access to dial-a-porn messages unless it has obtained permission from the telephone consumer. The circuit court upheld this latest enactment in *Dial Information Services Corp. v. Thornburgh* (1991). The Supreme Court implicitly upheld this decision by refusing to hear an appeal in *Thornburgh* (1992). The Supreme Court had actually alluded to its preferred solution in *Sable Communications* (which had invalidated an absolute ban of indecent material), where it opined that "the FCC's technological approach [use of credit cards and identification codes] restricting dial-a-porn messages to adults who seek them would be extremely effective, and only a few of the most enterprising and disobedient young people would manage to secure access to such messages" (p. 429).

One important thing to note in these various exchanges among Congress, the FCC, and the courts is the critical role of technology. Not only does the primary technology of the telephone play a major role, what we might call secondary technology also plays a crucial role in the resolution. Indeed, the basis for holding that Congress—or its agent, the FCC—did not use the least restrictive means often turns on whether some secondary technology was available and had been used. For example, as part of the circuit court's opinion in *Carlin* (1986), it held that the least restrictive means (technology) had not been used and suggested that Congress use a procedure known as "customer blocking." When the Court ruled favorably in *Thornburgh*, it did so on the basis that Congress had designated adequate and appropriate technologies. What has become a pattern with the telephone has become more apparent with other technologies, especially the Internet.

The Anti-Dial-a-Porn Act of 1989

Section 223 of the Communications Act of 1934 (47 U.S.C. 223) is amended by striking subsection (b) and inserting the following:

(b)(1) Whoever knowingly—

(A) within the United States, by means of telephone, makes (directly or by recording device) any obscene communication for commercial purposes to any person, regardless of whether the maker of such communication placed the call; or

(B) permits any telephone facility under such person's control to be used for an activity prohibited by subparagraph (A), shall be fined in accordance with title 18, United States Code, or imprisoned not more than two years, or both.

(2) Whoever knowingly—

(A) within the United States, by means of telephone, makes (directly or by recording device) any indecent communication for commercial purposes which is available to any person under 18 years of age or to any other person without that person's consent, regardless of whether the maker of such communication placed the call; or

(B) permits any telephone facility under such person's control to be used for an activity prohibited by subparagraph (A), shall be fined not more than $50,000 or imprisoned not more than six months, or both.

(3) It is a defense to prosecution under paragraph (2) of this subsection that the defendant restrict access to the prohibited communication to persons 18 years of age or older in accordance with subsection (c) of this section and with such procedures as the Commission may prescribe by regulation.

(4) In addition to the penalties under paragraph (1), whoever, within the United States, intentionally violates paragraph (1) or (2) shall be subject to a fine of not more than $50,000 for each violation. For purposes of this paragraph, each day of violation shall constitute a separate violation.

(5)(A) In addition to the penalties under paragraphs (1), (2), and (5), whoever, within the United States, violates paragraph (1) or (2) shall be subject to a civil fine of not more than $50,000 for each violation. For purposes of this paragraph, each day of violation shall constitute a separate violation.

(B) A fine under this paragraph may be assessed either—

(i) by a court, pursuant to civil action by the Commission or any attorney employed by the Commission who is designated by the Commission for such purposes, or

(ii) by the Commission after appropriate administrative proceedings.

(6) The Attorney General may bring a suit in the appropriate district court of the United States to enjoin any act or practice which violates paragraph (1) or (2). An injunction may be granted in accordance with the Federal Rules of Civil Procedure.

(c)(1) A common carrier within the District of Columbia or within any

State, or in interstate or foreign commerce, shall not, to the extent technically feasible, provide access to a communication specified in subsection (b) from the telephone of any subscriber who has not previously requested in writing the carrier to provide access to such communication if the carrier collects from subscribers an identifiable charge for such communication that the carrier remits, in whole or in part, to the provider of such communication.

(2) Except as provided in paragraph (3), no cause of action may be brought in any court or administrative agency against any common carrier, or any of its affiliates, including their officers, directors, employees, agents, or authorized representatives on account of—

(A) any action which the carrier demonstrates was taken in good faith to restrict access pursuant to paragraph (1) of this subsection; or

(B) any access permitted—

(i) in good faith reliance upon the lack of any representation by a provider of communications that communications provided by that provider are communications specified in subsection (b), or

(ii) because a specific representation by the provider did not allow the carrier, acting in good faith, a sufficient period to restrict access to communications described in subsection (b).

(3) Notwithstanding paragraph (2) of this subsection, a provider of communications services to which subscribers are denied access pursuant to paragraph (1) of this subsection may bring an action for a declaratory judgment or similar action in a court. Any such action shall be limited to the question of whether the communications which the provider seeks to provide fall within the category of communications to which the carrier will provide access only to subscribers who have previously requested such access.

(d) Sending or displaying offensive material to persons under 18
Whoever—

(1) in interstate or foreign communications knowingly—

(A) uses an interactive computer service to send to a specific person or persons under 18 years of age, or

(B) uses any interactive computer service to display in a manner available to a person under 18 years of age, any comment, request, suggestion, proposal, image, or other communication that, in context, depicts or describes, in terms patently offensive as measured by contemporary community standards, sexual or excretory activities or organs, regardless of whether the user of such service placed the call or initiated the communication; or

(2) knowingly permits any telecommunications facility under such per-

son's control to be used for an activity prohibited by paragraph (1) with the intent that it be used for such activity, shall be fined under title 18 or imprisoned not more than two years, or both.

(e) Defenses

In addition to any other defenses available by law:

(1) No person shall be held to have violated subsection (a) or (d) of this section solely for providing access or connection to or from a facility, system, or network not under that person's control, including transmission, downloading, intermediate storage, access software, or other related capabilities that are incidental to providing such access or connection that does not include the creation of the content of the communication.

(2) The defenses provided by paragraph (1) of this subsection shall not be applicable to a person who is a conspirator with an entity actively involved in the creation or knowing distribution of communications that violate this section, or who knowingly advertises the availability of such communications.

(3) The defenses provided in paragraph (1) of this subsection shall not be applicable to a person who provides access or connection to a facility, system, or network engaged in the violation of this section that is owned or controlled by such person.

(4) No employer shall be held liable under this section for the actions of an employee or agent unless the employee's or agent's conduct is within the scope of his or her employment or agency and the employer

(A) having knowledge of such conduct, authorizes or ratifies such conduct, or

(B) recklessly disregards such conduct.

(5) It is a defense to a prosecution under subsection (a)(1)(B) or (d) of this section, or under subsection (a)(2) of this section with respect to the use of a facility for an activity under subsection (a)(1)(B) of this section that a person—

(A) has taken, in good faith, reasonable, effective, and appropriate actions under the circumstances to restrict or prevent access by minors to a communication specified in such subsections, which may involve any appropriate measures to restrict minors from such communications, including any method which is feasible under available technology; or

(B) has restricted access to such communication by requiring use of a verified credit card, debit account, adult access code, or adult personal identification number.

(6) The Commission may describe measures which are reasonable, effective, and appropriate to restrict access to prohibited communications under subsection (d) of this section. Nothing in this section authorizes the

Commission to enforce, or is intended to provide the Commission with the authority to approve, sanction, or permit, the use of such measures. The Commission shall have no enforcement authority over the failure to utilize such measures. The Commission shall not endorse specific products relating to such measures. The use of such measures shall be admitted as evidence of good faith efforts for purposes of paragraph (5) in any action arising under subsection (d) of this section. Nothing in this section shall be construed to treat interactive computer services as common carriers or telecommunications carriers.

Approved November 21, 1989.

THE CHILD ONLINE PROTECTION
ACT OF 1998

Never has the congressional task been more daunting than current attempts to regulate electronic commerce on the Internet generally and the distribution of indecent materials specifically. The Internet is a giant network of computers that interconnect with each other throughout the world.[1] As of October 5, 1998, according to statistics contained in a recent report of the Committee of Commerce in the House of Representatives, the number of computers connected to the Internet stood at 29.6 million (up 215 percent from barely three years before), and the committee estimated that the number was more than seventy million in 1998.[2] Equally impressive is the variety of information and material on the Internet. It is so diverse that it encompasses everything from the most mundane to the most sublime, from the most artistic to the most prurient. The so-called adult entertainment industry on the Internet has experienced growth every bit as phenomenal as that of electronic commerce and noncommercial enterprises. As of late 1998 there were approximately 28,000 pornographic sites on the Internet, which generated approximately $925 million in annual revenues. In fact, congressional reports have provided estimates that as recently as 1996, nearly half the content available on the Internet is inappropriate for children, and the estimate had risen to almost 70 percent by April 1998.[3]

In addition to receiving Internet-based information, individuals with a computer and some basic knowledge can send or publish their own material on the Internet. The above-mentioned House report points out:

> Sexually explicit material on the Internet includes text, pictures, and communications via chat rooms. Purveyors of such material generally display many unrestricted and sexually explicit images to advertise and entice the consumer into engaging in a commercial transaction. Currently, minors can move from Web page to Web page, viewing and downloading this material without restriction. Once posted [or published] on the Internet, sexually explicit materials has [*sic*] entered all communities.[4]

Consequently, the Internet represents a major change in information distribution technology, because an individual can be both sender and receiver, and there is no centralized control at all. The major obstacle for regulating indecent material—as opposed to obscene material, which Congress can completely ban—is that Congress must attempt to permit full access to adults while trying to limit its availability to minors. In technological terms, if a transmission to minors is blocked, it is extremely difficult to unblock for adults, and vice versa. The relative ease with which obscene and indecent materials can be identified and restricted in conventional ways is not possible with Internet technology. For example, while a newsstand operator can place pornographic magazines in plain brown wrappers or keep them behind the checkout counter, and broadcasters can use the FCC's "safe harbor" policy of restricting indecent material to certain times of the day, and postal and customs officials can visually identify and physically restrain objectionable material, Internet transmissions are like pollen relentlessly flowing through the air. While removing a "pig from the parlor"[5] might be a rather easy task, removing pollen from the air without destroying the flowers it comes from is impossible.

Although the Internet has existed since the late 1960s, its use did not mushroom until the World Wide Web, which arrived in the 1980s. The Internet became very accessible for "browsing." Thus, although the World Wide Web is not even two decades old, Congress has struggled with regulating indecency on the Internet for that long. So far, Congress has enacted two major statutory efforts, with other bills pending, all of which appear to have a precarious future. In fact, the first major legislative effort to police the Internet, the Communications Decency Act (CDA) of 1996, was declared unconstitutional in *A.C.L.U. v. Reno* (*Reno I*, 1997).

The CDA was not only a response to the challenge of Internet technology, it also constituted a declaration of war against technological distribution of indecent material. The bill's Senate sponsor, Senator James Exon, (D-NE), declared:

> Before too long, a host of new telecommunications devices will be used by citizens to communicate with each other. Telephones may one day be relegated to museums next to telegraphs. Conversation is being replaced with communications, and electrical transmissions are being replaced with digital transmissions. . . . Anticipating this

exciting future of communications, the Communications Decency amendment . . . will keep pace with the coming change.[6]

Thus, Senator Exon urged his Congressional colleagues to act because "the information superhighway is . . . a revolution that in years to come will transcend newspapers, radio, and television as an information source. Therefore, I think this is the time to put some restrictions or guidelines on it."[7]

The CDA amended Section 223 of the Communications Act of 1935 to require Internet vendors that purvey any material deemed to be harmful to minors to restrict minors' access to such material. The CDA criminally prohibited (1) the knowing transmission, by means of a telecommunications device, of "obscene or indecent" communications to any recipient under 18 years of age; and (2) the knowing use of an interactive computer service to send to a specific person or persons under 18 years of age, or to display in a manner available to a person under 18 years of age, communications that, in context, depict or describe, in terms "patently offensive" as measured by contemporary community standards, sexual or excretory activities or organs. Violators of the original act faced penalties including up to two years in prison for each violation. However, the CDA provided affirmative defenses for those (1) who take good faith, reasonable, effective, and appropriate actions to restrict access by minors to the prohibited communications, and (2) who restrict such access by requiring certain designated forms of age proof, such as a verified credit card or an adult identification number or code.

Soon after the Court declared the CDA unconstitutional in *A.C.L.U. v. Reno* (*Reno I*, 1997), Congress enacted the Child Online Protection Act (COPA), which was to go into effect on November 29, 1998. COPA embodies both aspects of historical change to obscenity law that have occurred since the Comstock Law. This one statute contains the combined congressional responses to the definition of obscenity and the application of technology as they have evolved over the past two centuries. In the words of the House Report, "the Committee [on Commerce] believes that the bill strikes the appropriate balance between preserving the First Amendment rights of adults and protecting children from harmful material on the World Wide Web." The major concerns of Congress in balancing these concerns are: (1) restricting access of children while not imposing limits on the adult population; (2) defining what is harmful to minors in a way that is not vague as applied to the Internet; and (3) responding to the unique features of the Internet as a medium of communication.

The legislative findings and declarations associated with COPA provide a step-by-step formula for a constitutional analysis of congressional enactments that parallels judicial treatment. The House Committee on Commerce began its report and analysis with a Constitutional Authority Statement to the effect that the legislation was enacted pursuant to the authority granted by Article I, Section 8, Clause 3 that provides that Congress has the power to regulate interstate commerce. Section 2 of COPA contained an array of congressional findings that supported a necessary claim that "the widespread availability of the Internet presents opportunities for minors to use materials through the World Wide Web in a way that can frustrate parental supervision or control" and that "the protection of the physical and psychological well-being of minors by shielding them from materials that are harmful to them is a compelling governmental interest."

As already noted, with the presence of a compelling interest to protect children, Congress may be permitted to affect the First Amendment rights of adults only if the statute is drafted in a sufficiently narrow manner by employing the least restrictive means to reach its goal. The statutory scope of COPA is limited in two principal ways. First, Section 231(a) limits application to indecent communications that are "harmful to minors" by companies if made for "commercial purposes" only. Automatically excluded are the following communications: electronic mail, news groups, and chat rooms. Also excluded are telecommunications carriers, providers of Internet access services, persons or businesses that refer or link Internet users to various points on the Internet such as directories, indexes, references, and hypertext link services. The definition of "a commercial purpose" as defined by Section 231(e)(2) is largely based on whether or not it "make[s] the communication as a regular course of such person's trade or business." The legislative history showed that Congress had one eye on the judiciary, for it indicates that the term "engaged in the business" has been approved as a sufficiently limited classification for anti-obscenity in *United States v. Skinner* (1994). The legislative history also responded to judicial remonstrances regarding the statutory use of "material that is harmful to minors," noting not only that Congress believes that it meets the appropriate judicial definitions of obscenity and harmful to minors, but it uses a standard that the courts have tested and refined for thirty years in a way that limits the definition of indecency to materials that are clearly pornographic and inappropriate for minors.

Second, Section 231(c) grants communicators what is called an "affirmative defense," which means that if they can prove the defenses, the government cannot prosecute them under the act even if the prohibited activity (children being exposed to material harmful to minors) otherwise occurs. In short, if persons posting objectionable material on the Internet can prove that they made good faith efforts to restrict access to the materials by minors, there can be no conviction. Section 231(c)(1) sets forth three procedures that will be accepted as an affirmative defense: (1) restriction by requiring the use of a credit card, debit account, adult access code, or personal identification number; (2) by accepting a digital certificate that verifies age; and (3) "any other reasonable measures that are feasible under available technology."

The day after the president signed it into law on October 21, 1998, and barely more than a month before the effective date of COPA, the American Civil Liberties Union (ACLU), along with others including Internet site operators and content providers, sued the Department of Justice (naming Attorney General Janet Reno as the defendant), alleging that the act was unconstitutional under the First and Fifth Amendments and seeking a court injunction to prevent its application. As U.S. District Judge Lowell A. Reed Jr. framed it, "Two diametric interests—the constitutional right of freedom of speech and the interest of Congress, and indeed society, in protecting children from harmful materials—are in tension in this lawsuit" (*A.C.L.U. v. Reno, Reno II*, 1999).[8] Whatever the policy implications for Judge Reed's remarks may be, his reading of COPA resulted in a decision to grant the injunction, thus forestalling application of the act. Beginning on January 20, 1999, the district court heard five days of testimony and one day of argument by attorneys just on the motion for a preliminary injunction.[9]

On February 1, 1999, Judge Reed issued the injunction, stating that the act's opponents "have established a substantial likelihood that they will be able to show that COPA imposes a burden on speech that is protected for adults." In short, since the evidence showed that the act might be unconstitutional and cause irreparable harm to the Internet providers who represent persons and entities that use the Internet in various ways, Judge Reed granted an injunction until the case could be tried on its merits.

Soon after the district judge prohibited the enforcement of COPA in *Reno II*, the Justice Department appealed the case to the U.S. Court of Appeals for the Third Circuit in Philadelphia, where the parties argued their positions before a three-judge circuit court panel on November 4, 1999. The appellate tribunal rendered its judgment on June 22, 2000. It affirmed the trial court's preliminary injunction (*A.L.C.U. v. Reno, Reno III*, 2000). The circuit court's opinion stated:

> We are confident that the ACLU's attack on COPA's constitutionality is likely to succeed on the merits. Because material posted on the Web is accessible by all Internet users worldwide, and because current technology does not permit a Web publisher to restrict access to its site based on the geographic locale of each particular Internet user, COPA essentially requires that every Web publisher subject to the statute abide by the most restrictive and conservative state's community standards in order to avoid criminal liability. Thus, because the standard by which COPA gauges whether material is "harmful to minors" is based on identifying "contemporary community standards," the inability of Web publishers to restrict access to their Web sites based on the geographic locale of the site visitor, in and of itself, imposes an impermissible burden on constitutionally protected First Amendment speech. (217 F.3d 217 162, 166)

This opinion—given the relationship of legislation and the First Amendment—is not all that surprising. What is surprising, however, is another comment by the circuit court that seems to fly in the face of the strict scrutiny rule, and that is: "We are forced to recognize that, at present, due to technological limitations, there may be no other means by which harmful material on the Web may be constitutionally restricted." What makes this a surprise is that, as we pointed out, the strict scrutiny test requires only that the government show a compelling interest (and protecting children from the ill effects of indecent material has been repeatedly held to be a compelling interest) coupled with a legislative effort that is as narrowly drawn as possible to serve that compelling interest. Therefore, presumably, if the government has in fact shown a compelling interest and the court is of the opinion that the legislation could not be more narrowly drawn, the act should pass constitutional scrutiny even under the demanding First Amendment test.

In any event, the fate of COPA is shaky at best. Not only have the district court and the circuit court of appeals shown a likelihood of finding it unconstitutional when it is heard on its merits (if this ever comes to pass), former U.S. Attorney General Janet Reno has written a letter to Representative Thomas Bliley (R-VA), chairman of the House Committee on Commerce, indicating that the U.S. Justice Department has serious reservations about COPA's constitutionality. Indeed, with Internet and World Wide Web technology proving so difficult and coupled with the apparent libertarian views of federal judges, any success at restricting pornography on the Internet is beginning to appear quite elusive. Nonetheless, congressional efforts continue even now along other fronts. Although the more comprehensive anti-obscenity statutes are receiving a tough go with the courts, some are faring better.

The Child Online Protection Act of 1998

TITLE XIV—CHILD ONLINE PROTECTION

Section 1402. Congressional Findings.

The Congress finds that—

(1) while custody, care, and nurture of the child resides first with the parent, the widespread availability of the Internet presents opportunities for minors to access materials through the World Wide Web in a manner that can frustrate parental supervision or control;

(2) the protection of the physical and psychological well-being of minors by shielding them from materials that are harmful to them is a compelling governmental interest;

(3) to date, while the industry has developed innovative ways to help parents and educators restrict material that is harmful to minors through parental control protections and self-regulation, such efforts have not provided a national solution to the problem of minors accessing harmful material on the World Wide Web;

(4) a prohibition on the distribution of material harmful to minors, combined with legitimate defenses, is currently the most effective and least restrictive means by which to satisfy the compelling government interest; . . .

Section 1403. Requirement to Restrict Access by Minors to Materials Commercially Distributed by Means of the World Wide Web That Are Harmful to Minors.

Part I of Title II of the Communications Act of 1934 (47 U.S.C. 201 et seq.) is amended by adding at the end the following new section:

Section 231. Restriction of Access by Minors to Materials Commercially Distributed by Means of the World Wide Web That Are Harmful to Minors.

(a) Requirement To Restrict Access—

(1) Prohibited conduct.—Whoever knowingly and with knowledge of the character of the material, in interstate or foreign commerce by means of the World Wide Web, makes any communication for commercial purposes that is available to any minor and that includes any material that is harmful to minors shall be fined not more than $50,000, imprisoned not more than 6 months, or both. . . .

(3) Civil penalty.—In addition to the penalties under paragraphs (1) and (2), whoever violates paragraph (1) shall be subject to a civil penalty of not more than $50,000 for each violation. For purposes of this paragraph, each day of violation shall constitute a separate violation. . . .

(1) a telecommunications carrier engaged in the provision of a telecommunications service;

(2) a person engaged in the business of providing an Internet access service;

(3) a person engaged in the business of providing an Internet information location tool; or

(4) similarly engaged in the transmission, storage, retrieval, hosting, formatting, or translation (or any combination thereof) of a communication made by another person, without selection or alteration of the content of the communication, except that such person's deletion of a particular communication or material made by another person in a manner consistent with subsection (c) or section 230 shall not constitute such selection or alteration of the content of the communication.

(c) Affirmative Defense.—

(1) Defense.—It is an affirmative defense to prosecution under this section that the defendant, in good faith, has restricted access by minors to material that is harmful to minors—

(A) by requiring use of a credit card, debit account, adult access code, or adult personal identification number;

(B) by accepting a digital certificate that verifies age; or

(C) by any other reasonable measures that are feasible under available technology.

(2) Protection for use of defenses.—No cause of action may be brought in any court or administrative agency against any person on account of any activity that is not in violation of any law punishable by criminal or civil penalty, and that the person has taken in good faith to implement a defense authorized under this subsection or otherwise to restrict or prevent the transmission of, or access to, a communication specified in this section. . . .

(6) Material that is harmful to minors.—The term "material that is harmful to minors" means any communication, picture, image, graphic image file, article, recording, writing, or other matter of any kind that is obscene or that—

(A) the average person, applying contemporary community standards, would find, taking the material as a whole and with respect to minors, is designed to appeal to, or is designed to pander to, the prurient interest;

(B) depicts, describes, or represents, in a manner patently offensive with respect to minors, an actual or simulated sexual act or sexual contact, an actual or simulated normal or perverted sexual act, or a lewd exhibition of the genitals or post-pubescent female breast; and

(C) taken as a whole, lacks serious literary, artistic, political, or scientific value for minors.

(7) Minor.—The term "minor" means any person under 17 years of age.

Section 1404. Notice Requirement.

(a) Notice.—Section 230 of the Communications Act of 1934 (47 U.S.C. 230) is amended—

(1) in subsection (d)(1), by inserting or 231 after section 223;

(2) by redesignating subsections (d) and (e) as subsections (e) and (f), respectively; and

(3) by inserting after subsection (c) the following new subsection: "(d) Obligations of Interactive Computer Service—A provider of interactive computer service shall, at the time of entering an agreement with a customer for the provision of interactive computer service and in a manner deemed appropriate by the provider, notify such customer that parental control protections (such as computer hardware, software, or filtering services) are commercially available that may assist the customer in limiting access to material that is harmful to minors. Such notice shall identify,

or provide the customer with access to information identifying, current providers of such protections. . . ."

Section 1405. Study by Commission on Online Child Protection.

(a) Establishment—There is hereby established a temporary Commission to be known as the Commission on Online Child Protection (in this section referred to as the "Commission") for the purpose of conducting a study under this section regarding methods to help reduce access by minors to material that is harmful to minors on the Internet. . . .
Approved October 21, 1998.

NOTES

1. Sometimes the Internet is referred to as the World Wide Web, which is actually the information retrieval system that uses a "hypertext" computer-formatting language called hypertext markup language (HTML) and other computer-based programs that process the data. Nonetheless, it has become commonplace to refer to the Internet as the "Web," as in "surfing the Web." Technically speaking, however, we use the Web to navigate, or surf, the Internet.

2. 105th Congress, 2nd Session, 105 H. Rpt. 775, Child Online Protection Act, October 5, 1998.

3. Ibid.

4. Ibid.

5. The "pig from the parlor" simile was coined by Justice George Sutherland in *Euclid v. Ambler Realty* (1926, p. 388) to illustrate some things that may be appropriate in some situations but not in others. In other words, while some printed material may be appropriate for an exclusively adult audience, it may be inappropriate if children are present.

6. 140 *Congressional Record* S9746 (July 26, 1994).

7. Quoted in Peter H. Lewis, "Cybersex Stays Hot, Despite a Plan for Cooling It Off," *New York Times*, March 26, 1995.

8. It is an interesting point of U.S. culture that a federal judge would suggest that the First Amendment (freedom of expression) rights of adults—or anyone else, for that matter—and the community's interest in protecting children from harmful materials are diametrically opposed.

9. A preliminary injunction is a temporary prohibition against the act's enforcement because a judge believes that its enforcement *may* be unconstitutional. A final decision that the act is constitutional or not can come only after a full trial.

5

Intellectual Property: The Copyright Act of 1976

Intellectual property includes products of a person's intellectual efforts, such as books and articles, discoveries and inventions. Federal statutes protect the proprietary or ownership interest of authors, inventors, and discoverers in and to these intellectual properties under three basic statutes: copyright, patent, and trademark. *Copyright* is the name for the monopoly right granted by the government to authors, composers, and playwrights for a specified period of time to exclusively publish, produce, sell, or distribute original literary works, musicals, dramas, or artwork. *Patent* is the name for the right granted to inventors for the exclusive right to make, use, and sell their inventions for a certain period of time. *Trademark* is the name, symbol, or other device that identifies a seller's product. When trademarks are registered with the appropriate governmental office, they can be used only by the seller.

Laws that secure intellectual property rights might not be typically thought to involve First Amendment issues. After all, intellectual property rights are explicitly designed to enhance creative expression, not stifle it. Notwithstanding the goals of intellectual property laws, they do in fact have serious First Amendment repercussions. As we will see, laws that grant a monopoly on expression not only limit who can repeat the expression, but they can also restrict discussion of the underlying ideas that generate the expression.

Copyright and patent statutes are enacted under the authority contained in Article I, Section 8, Clause 3 of the U.S. Constitution, which provides in part that "The Congress shall have power to . . .

promote the progress of science and useful arts, by securing for limited times to authors and inventors the exclusive right to their respective writings and discoveries." The trademark statute is enacted under the Commerce Clause in Section 8, which gives Congress the power to regulate interstate commerce.[1] Statutes that grant intellectual property rights seek to "promote the progress of science and useful arts" by fostering the economic interests of the creators. As U.S. Supreme Court Justice Stanley Reed put it, "The economic philosophy behind the [copyright and patent clause] is the conviction that encouragement of individual effort by personal gain is the best way to advance public welfare through the talents of authors and inventors" (*Mazer v. Stein*, 1954, p. 219). Moreover, the Copyright Clause and its statutory progenies are considered by some not only to be compatible with the First Amendment, but to implement it as well. An example of this attitude is U.S. Supreme Court Justice Sandra Day O'Connor, who declared that "the Framers intended copyright itself to be the engine of free expression. By establishing a marketable right to the use of one's expression, copyright supplies the economic incentive to create and disseminate ideas" (*Harper & Row, Publishers, Inc. v. Nation Enterprises*, 1985, p. 556).

It is obvious that insofar as promoting the incentive to be creative is concerned, these laws most likely advance desirable and useful expression. Yet granting creators exclusive rights to their creations after they have become "public" by various methods of publication, intellectual property laws do restrict the First Amendment freedom of everyone else. In fact, the Copyright Clause and the First Amendment are literally antagonistic to each other, with the latter preventing the abridgement of any expression, and the former actually curtailing certain expression. Moreover, if one treats the two provisions literally, the First Amendment should prevail over the Copyright Clause because it is, after all, an amendment that is generally assumed to change any preexisting nonconforming provision.[2] Be that as it may, the Copyright Clause and the First Amendment have been allowed by Congress and the courts to coexist within the same document since the Bill of Rights was adopted. In this regard, much weight has been given to the fact that Congress enacted the first copyright law within eight months after proposing the First Amendment to the Constitution, and it enacted the second copyright law within two years of the adoption of the First Amendment.[3]

Insofar as copyright laws seek to enhance the right to free expression by some, they are similar to laws regulating labor-management relations, which seek to enhance one group's rights while inevitably invading the rights of others. Copyright laws encourage free expression by extending proprietary or ownership rights to authors by means of a copyright, but they can discourage free expression by everyone else on the same subject. For example, it is a common expectation for people to copy existing works for a variety of legitimate reasons, including leisure examination, study, and dissemination for educational purposes.[4] Yet the penalties of copyright violation can potentially prevent these activities. A more serious concern is the possibility that a copyright can impede discussion and use of an author's underlying idea as well as the particular expression of that idea. This potential problem was aptly captured by U.S. Supreme Court Justice William O. Douglas: "The arena of public debate would be quiet, indeed, if a politician could copyright his speeches or a philosopher his treatises and thus obtain a monopoly on the ideas they contained" (*Lee v. Runge*, 1971, p. 893). Thus, the two constitutional provisions collide.

When two constitutional provisions come into conflict, one or both must yield through a process that seeks to balance the competing interests. At one time, the economic interests of individuals under certain sections of the Constitution such as the Due Process Clause were deemed more important than the interest of the public under other sections, including the First Amendment. A good illustration of economic prominence is the case of *Charles Wolff Packing Co. v. Court of Industrial Relations* (1923), in which the Court stated that economic interests are "part of the liberty of the individual protected by the guaranty of the due process clause of the Fourteenth Amendment. . . . [Economic] freedom is the general rule, and restraint the exception. The legislative authority to abridge [economic freedom] can be justified only by exceptional circumstances."[5] That situation is now much different. Currently, "the preferred place [is] given in our [national] scheme to the great, the indispensable democratic freedoms secured by the First Amendment" (*Thomas v. Collins*, 1945, p. 530). As we will see, Congress has sought to balance these two competing interests in a way that is somewhat unique to copyright law. First, we will examine the historical context for the landmark copyright law.

The foundation of copyright law in the United States is interwoven with efforts of English monarchs to censor expression during the sixteenth and seventeenth centuries. Two parallel events combined to create, on the one hand, a greater need to censor expression alongside, and on the other, a greater ability to accomplish it. The invention of the printing press by Johannes Gutenberg in 1455 made publication and distribution of books and pamphlets so easy that it became increasingly difficult for monarchs to control the dissemination of information and ideas, many of which were deemed to be seditious and treasonable. Contemporaneous with the growth in printing was the rise of a printing guild that facilitated the crown's need.[6]

The principal guild of printers in England during the sixteenth and seventeenth centuries was the Company of Stationers of London, or the Stationers' Company. This guild became the handmaiden of royal censorship by providing the crown the opportunity to control what was published by licensing the guild's operations. Members of the printers' guild, rather than authors, were given all the rights of ownership in published works, and the crown possessed regulatory control over members of the guild by requiring them to obtain a license for each publication. A copy of the license from the crown's official roll constituted evidence that the printer had ownership of the printed matter; hence the term *copyright* and the beginning of copyright.[7] One of the earliest copyright acts, if not the first act, was a royal proclamation in 1538 that prohibited "naughty printed books." The proclamation also required printers to obtain a license from the Privy Council or Court of Star Chamber to print or distribute any printed matter.

Copyright law took a major turn in 1710 when the English Parliament enacted *An Act for the Encouragement of Learning, by Vesting the Copies* [ownership] *of Printed Books in the Authors or Purchasers of such Copies,* often simply referred to as the *Statute of Queen Anne.* (Statute, 8 Anne, c. 19.) This statute not only ended the printer's monopoly; it shifted the copyright to authors for a limited period. Prior to 1710 the common law considered the printer's copyright to be perpetual. The *Statute of Queen Anne* granted authors a copyright term of fourteen years that could be extended for another fourteen-year term if the author was still living. Thereafter the subject of the copyright belonged to what later became known as the "public domain," where everyone has the freedom to copy and use intellectual works as they please.[8]

The constitutional provision authorizing copyright protection to authors and inventors was included in the U.S. Constitution with little notice during the constitutional convention. James Madison introduced it without comment, and it was inserted in the final version with little, if any, discussion. Moreover, the clause received scant attention in the *Federalist Papers*, with Madison simply asserting in *Number 43* that the "utility of this power will scarcely be questioned." Congress implemented Article I, Section 8, by enacting the Copyright Law of 1790. Although the act, *An Act for the Encouragement of Learning, by securing the Copies of Maps, Charts and Books, to the Authors and Proprietors of Such Copies, during the Times therein mentioned,* was patterned after the *Statute of Anne,* there were significant differences. One noteworthy difference was the addition of maps and charts as covered material. The act required authors to register their title with the district court in their place of residence, and it granted copyright protection for a period of fourteen years that could be extended with a new registration.

Many changes occurred in copyright law during the period between the 1790 enactment and the landmark Copyright Act of 1976. Prints, engravings, and cuts (engraved blocks or plates used by printers, including prints that are produced by them) were added in 1802. An 1831 enactment added musical compositions, but performance rights in them were not included until 1856. The 1856 enactment also extended the initial copyright period to twenty-eight years. Between 1856 and 1870, dramatic compositions, photographs, paintings, and sculpture were included as copyrightable works. With the list of copyrightable items increasing to such a degree, Congress enacted the 1909 Copyright Act, which enacted a major revision concerning the definition of what was copyrightable. Instead of the itemized list, the category included "all the writings of an author," with the term *author* defined very broadly. This act, which formed the basic copyright law until 1976, also extended the renewal period from fourteen to twenty-eight years, making the monopoly period a total of fifty-six years.

Throughout the years of amending and modifying the copyright laws, Congress and the courts had to manage a balancing act between the monopoly created by the copyright statutes and the freedom of expression demanded by the First Amendment. Congress and the courts have primarily settled on a distinction between the ideas of an author and the expression of that idea in terms of copyright protection, and ideas that are ineligible. The noted federal judge Learned Hand, of the Second Federal Circuit, situated in New York City, put the distinction this way, in *Nichols v. Universal Pictures Corporation,* 45 F.2d 119, 121 (2nd Cir. 1930). Judge Hand's opinion created an analytical spectrum from a pure expression to an abstract idea.

> In such cases we are . . . concerned with the line between expression and what is expressed. Upon any work . . . a great number of patterns of increasing generality will fit equally well, as more and more of the incident is left out. The last may perhaps be no more than the most general statement of what the [work] is about, and at times might consist only of its title; but there is a point in this series of abstractions where they are no longer protected, since otherwise the [author] could prevent the use of his "ideas," to which, apart from their expression, his property is never extended.

To be sure, while the idea–expression distinction is quite abstract and vague as stated, it does nevertheless attempt to draw a meaningful distinction that enables people to make a determination on a basis other than simple preference for one constitutional provision or the other.[9] The Supreme Court has implicitly accepted the idea–expression distinction, declaring, "We note that Federal District Courts have rejected First Amendment challenges to the federal copyright law on the ground that 'no restraint [has been] placed on the use of an idea or concept' " (*Zacchini v. Scripps-Howard Broadcasting Co.*, 1977, p. 577).

After more than twenty years of examining the status of copyright law, Congress enacted a complete revision and restatement with the Copyright Act of 1976. Beginning in 1955, Congress received thirty-four studies with various legislative proposals to revise the 1909 Act.[10] The main impetus for revision was the enormous change brought about by advancing technologies, principally the photocopying machine, along with video and audio cassette recorders. The 1976 act is a voluminous and intricate enactment, consisting of eight chapters covering sixty pages and a host of detailed provisions. For the first time it added statutory protection to works that were unpublished—for example, private memoirs. Section 102 (b) embodied the idea–expression distinction that had been developed by the courts as a means of protecting the public's First Amendment rights.

Congress, recognizing the problem of granting monopolies even in the case of expression, and acknowledging judicial attempts to prevent this problem through the doctrine of fair use, incorporated the fair-use doctrine for the first time in section 107 of the 1976 act.[11] Congress recognized that each case must be decided within the parameters of its own factual situation. Nonetheless, section 107 sets out criteria that must be considered in making that determination. The accompanying congressional report summarized the types of uses of copyrighted works that come within the purview of fair use:

1. quotation of excerpts in a review or criticism for purposes of illustration or comment;

2. quotation of short passages in a scholarly or technical work, for illustration or clarification of the author's observations;

3. use in a parody of some of the content of the work parodied;

4. summary of an address or article, with brief quotations, in a news report;

5. reproduction by a library of a portion of a work to replace part of a damaged copy;

6. reproduction by a teacher or student of a small part of a work to illustrate a lesson;

7. reproduction of a work in legislative or judicial proceedings or reports;

8. incidental and fortuitous reproduction, in a newsreel or broadcast, of a work located in the scene of an event being reported.

Another significant right of the public to use copyrighted materials is given to libraries. Section 108 provides that under certain circumstances, libraries may reproduce or distribute a single copy of a work or a phonograph record. The library copy may not be connected with commercial profit, the library's collection must be open to the public, and the copy must contain a copyright notice.

The consequences of violating a copyright are potent. The copyright holders can recover damages that include not only their economic losses but any profits that the infringer may have gained. Copyright holders can also collect the costs of litigation, including attorneys' fees. Violators are subject to criminal penalties as well: fines of ten thousand dollars to fifty thousand dollars, prison terms of one to two years, or a combination of fine and imprisonment. Moreover, all of the material that is connected to the violation, including copies and devices that are involved in making or distributing the copies, are subject to seizure and forfeiture.

The Copyright Revision Act of 1976

CHAPTER 1. SUBJECT MATTER AND SCOPE OF COPYRIGHT

Section 102. Subject matter of copyright: In general.

(a) Copyright protection subsists, in accordance with this title, in original works of authorship fixed in any tangible medium of expression, now known or later developed, from which they can be perceived, reproduced, or otherwise communicated, either directly or with the aid of a machine or device. Works of authorship include the following categories:

(1) literary works;

(2) musical works, including any accompanying words;

(3) dramatic works, including any accompanying music;

(4) pantomimes and choreographic works;

(5) pictorial, graphic, and sculptural works;

(6) motion pictures and other audiovisual works;

(7) sound recordings; and

(8) architectural works.

(b) In no case does copyright protection for an original work of authorship extend to any idea, procedure, process, system, method of operation, concept, principle, or discovery, regardless of the form in which it is described, explained, illustrated, or embodied in such work. . . .

Section 106. Exclusive rights in copyrighted works.

Subject to sections 107 through 121, the owner of copyright under this title has the exclusive rights to do and to authorize any of the following:

(1) to reproduce the copyrighted work in copies or phonorecords;

(2) to prepare derivative works based upon the copyrighted work; . . .

Section 107. Limitations on exclusive rights: Fair-use.

. . . the fair use of a copyrighted work, including such use by reproduction in copies or phonorecords or by any other means specified by that section, for purposes such as criticism, comment, news reporting, teaching (including multiple copies for classroom use), scholarship, or research, is not an infringement of copyright. In determining whether the use made of a work in any particular case is a fair use the factors to be considered shall include—

(1) the purpose and character of the use, including whether such use is of a commercial nature or is for nonprofit educational purposes;

(2) the nature of the copyrighted work;

(3) the amount and substantiality of the portion used in relation to the copyrighted work as a whole; and

(4) the effect of the use upon the potential market for or value of the copyrighted work.

Section 108. Limitations on exclusive rights: Reproduction by libraries and archives.

(a) ... it is not an infringement of copyright for a library or archives, or any of its employees acting within the scope of their employment, to reproduce no more than one copy or phonorecord of a work, except as provided in subsections (b) and (c), or to distribute such copy or phonorecord, under the conditions specified by this section, if—

(1) the reproduction or distribution is made without any purpose of direct or indirect commercial advantage;

(2) the collections of the library or archives are (i) open to the public ... and

(3) the reproduction or distribution of the work includes a notice of copyright that appears on the copy or phonorecord that is reproduced ...

(e) [Inter-library Loans] The rights of reproduction and distribution under this section apply to the entire work, or to a substantial part of it, made from the collection of a library or archives where the user makes his or her request or from that of another library or archives, if the library or archives has first determined, on the basis of a reasonable investigation, that a copy or phonorecord of the copyrighted work cannot be obtained at a fair price, if—

(1) the copy or phonorecord becomes the property of the user, and the library or archives has had no notice that the copy or phonorecord would be used for any purpose other than private study, scholarship, or research; and

(2) the library or archives displays prominently ... a warning of copyright ...

(f) Nothing in this section—

(1) shall be construed to impose liability for copyright infringement upon a library or archives or its employees for the unsupervised use of reproducing equipment located on its premises: Provided, That such equipment displays a notice that the making of a copy may be subject to the copyright law. ...

CHAPTER 2. COPYRIGHT OWNERSHIP AND TRANSFER.

Section 201. Ownership of copyright.

(a) Initial Ownership. Copyright in a work protected under this title vests initially in the author or authors of the work ...

(b) Works Made for Hire. In the case of a work made for hire, the employer or other person for whom the work was prepared is considered the author for purposes of this title, and, unless the parties have expressly agreed otherwise in a written instrument signed by them, owns all of the rights comprised in the copyright.

(c) Contributions to Collective Works. Copyright in each separate contribution to a collective work is distinct from copyright in the collective work as a whole, and vests initially in the author of the contribution . . .

(d) Transfer of Ownership.

(1) The ownership of a copyright may be transferred in whole or in part by any means of conveyance or by operation of law, and may be bequeathed by will or pass as personal property by the applicable laws of intestate succession. . . .

Section 205. Recordation of transfers and other documents.

(a) Conditions for Recordation. Any transfer of copyright ownership or other document pertaining to a copyright may be recorded in the Copyright Office if the document filed for recordation bears the actual signature of the person who executed it, or if it is accompanied by a sworn or official certification that it is a true copy of the original, signed document. . . .

(c) Recordation as Constructive Notice. Recordation of a document in the Copyright Office gives all persons constructive notice of the facts stated in the recorded document, but only if—

(1) the document, or material attached to it, specifically identifies the work to which it pertains so that, after the document is indexed by the Register of Copyrights, it would be revealed by a reasonable search under the title or registration number of the work . . .

CHAPTER 3. DURATION OF COPYRIGHT.

Section 302. Duration of copyright: Works created on or after January 1, 1978.

(a) In General. Copyright in a work created on or after January 1, 1978, subsists from its creation and, except as provided by the following subsections, endures for a term consisting of the life of the author and 70 years after the author's death.

(b) Joint Works. In the case of a joint work prepared by two or more authors who did not work for hire, the copyright endures for a term consisting of the life of the last surviving author and 70 years after such last surviving author's death.

(c) Anonymous Works, Pseudonymous Works, and Works Made for Hire. In the case of an anonymous work, a pseudonymous work, or a work made for hire, the copyright endures for a term of 95 years from the year of its first publication, or a term of 120 years from the year of its creation, whichever expires first . . .

Section 303. Duration of copyright: Works created but not published or copyrighted before January 1, 1978.

(a) Copyright in a work created before January 1, 1978, but not theretofore in the public domain or copyrighted, subsists from January 1, 1978, and endures for the term provided by section 302. In no case, however, shall the term of copyright in such a work expire before December 31, 2002; and, if the work is published on or before December 31, 2002, the term of copyright shall not expire before December 31, 2047. . . .

CHAPTER 5. COPYRIGHT INFRINGEMENT AND REMEDIES.

Section 502. Remedies for infringement: Injunctions.

(a) Any court having jurisdiction . . . may . . . grant temporary and final injunctions on such terms as it may deem reasonable to prevent or restrain infringement of a copyright. . . .

Section 503. Remedies for infringement: Impounding and disposition of infringing articles.

(a) . . . the court may order the impounding, on such terms as it may deem reasonable . . .

(b) . . . the court may order the destruction or other reasonable disposition of all copies or phonorecords found to have been made or used in violation of the copyright owner's exclusive rights . . .

Section 504. Remedies for infringement: Damages and profits.

(a) In General. Except as otherwise provided by this title, an infringer of copyright is liable for either—

   (1) the copyright owner's actual damages and any additional profits of the infringer, as provided by subsection (b); or

   (2) statutory damages, as provided by subsection (c).

(b) Actual Damages and Profits. The copyright owner is entitled to recover the actual damages suffered by him or her as a result of the infringement, and any profits of the infringer that are attributable to the infringement and are not taken into account in computing the actual damages . . .

(c) Statutory Damages.

   (1) . . . the copyright owner may elect, at any time before final judgment is rendered, to recover, instead of actual damages and profits, an award of statutory damages . . . in a sum of not less than $750 or more than $30,000 as the court considers just. . . .

   (2) In a case where . . . the court finds, that infringement was committed willfully, the court in its discretion may increase the award of statutory damages to a sum of not more than $150,000. . . .

Section 505. Remedies for infringement: Costs and attorney's fees.
In any civil action under this title, the court in its discretion may allow the recovery of full costs by or against any party other than the United States or an officer thereof. Except as otherwise provided by this title, the court may also award a reasonable attorney's fee to the prevailing party as part of the costs.

Section 506. Criminal offenses.
(a) Criminal Infringement. Any person who infringes a copyright willfully either—

(1) for purposes of commercial advantage or private financial gain, or

(2) by the reproduction or distribution, including by electronic means, during any 180-day period, or 1 or more copies or phonorecords of 1 or more copyrighted works, which have a total retail value of more than $1,000,

shall be punished as provided under section 2319 of title 18, United States Code. For purposes of this subsection, evidence of reproduction or distribution of a copyrighted work, by itself, shall not be sufficient to establish willful infringement.

(b) Forfeiture and Destruction. When any person is convicted of any violation of subsection (a), the court in its judgment of conviction shall, in addition to the penalty therein prescribed, order the forfeiture and destruction or other disposition of all infringing copies or phonorecords and all implements, devices, or equipment used in the manufacture of such infringing copies or phonorecords.

Approved October 19, 1976.

NOTES

1. This examination will be limited to copyright acts inasmuch as they involve freedom of expression in a more direct way than either trademark or patent laws.

2. Melville B. Nimmer and David Nimmer, *Nimmer on Copyright*, vol. 1, § 1.10[A], pp. 66.44–45.

3. Copyright Act of 1802. See *Burrow-Giles Lithographic Co. v. Sarony*, 1884, p. 57. Congress proposed the amendment on September 25, 1789, and enacted the copyright act on May 31, 1790. The First Amendment became effective when approved by the eleventh state (Virginia) on December 15, 1791. The Copyright Act of 1802 was enacted on April 29, 1802.

4. Copyright infringement and plagiarization should not be confused. Copyright infringement is the unlawful copying of the expressive works of another, whether credit to the author by way of attribution is given or not. Plagiarization is the act of claiming another's expression or idea as one's own, whether the idea or expression is copyrighted or not.

5. The comments of Chief Justice William Howard Taft in *Charles Wolff Packing Co. v. Court of Industrial Relations*, 1923, p. 534.

6. A guild is an association of persons of the same trade or pursuits, formed to protect mutual interests and maintain standards. It established a monopoly of trade in its locality or within a particular branch of industry or commerce; it set and maintained standards for the quality of goods and the integrity of trading practices in that industry; it worked to maintain stable prices for its goods and commodities; and it sought to control town or city governments in order to further the interests of the guild members and achieve their economic objectives.

7. Theodore F. T. Plucknett, *A Concise History of the Common Law* (Boston: Little, Brown and Company, 1956) p. 499.

8. The "public domain" has become important as designating materials that for reasons of obvious public policy are too important to the public interest to permit proprietary interest to overcome the public's freedom to use as they may. For example, an early U.S. Supreme Court decision held without discussion that printed reports of its decisions could not be the subject of copyright (*Wheaton v. Peters*, 1834).

9. Other tests exist, but the idea–expression distinction has continued to be the primary test utilized by the courts. Moreover, the Supreme Court has yet to rule on either the specific aspects of the relevant test or the specific application of First Amendment to copyright laws.

10. For legislative history, see S. Rep. No. 94–473, H. R. Rep. No. 94–1476.

11. See 94th Cong. H. Rep. 94–1476.

6

Labor-Management Relations

Just as symbolic speech clouds the speech–nonspeech distinction, labor laws do something very similar, by seeking to enhance freedoms of speech and association. Instead of restricting freedom of speech and the right to associate, many labor laws seek to enhance these rights by granting workers the liberty to join unions and bargain collectively with their employers about the terms and conditions of employment. Nonetheless, as we will see, though extending rights to workers in a general way, many of these same laws have the reverse effect by limiting the rights of some workers and employers in the process.

During the nation's first century or so, labor law was a common law matter—in other words, a creature of judicial decision making.[1] At common law, workers had very few rights, especially when it came to joining together in efforts to bargain collectively with employers.[2] Thus, workers' attempts to form unions were usually met with judicial hostility. Unions and union activity were viewed by federal judges as combinations engaged in illegal conspiracies (under the common law and later under the Sherman Antitrust Act) that restrained interstate commerce.[3] At times judges would declare union activity to be a violation of employers' liberty of contract under the Fifth Amendment's due process clause. Judicial injunctions that ordered union members to cease their activities were a favorite and effective tool for employers and law enforcement officials. Thus, when union members engaged in strikes or boycotts, employers were able to obtain injunctions from judges quickly, almost on a moment's notice, and usually without any prior notice to union members. Once an injunction was issued, armed forces were often used to carry them out.

Judicial hostility prevailed even in the face of First Amendment claims, such as one that was made by Samuel Gompers, president of the American Federation of Labor, in 1907. Gompers was charged with violating an injunction that prohibited him from publishing a flyer that listed the names of merchants whom union leaders did not want workers to patronize. When he was indicted and tried for criminal contempt, he defended on the ground that the injunction violated his freedom of speech under the First Amendment. In upholding Gompers' conviction, the Supreme Court summarily dismissed his First Amendment claim, stating that the "attack on this part of the injunction raises no question as to an abridgment of free speech, but involves the power of a court of equity to enjoin the defendants from continuing a boycott which, by words and signals, printed or spoken, caused or threatened irreparable damage" to employers (*Gompers v. Buck's Stove & Range Co.*, 1911, p. 437).

Toward the end of the nineteenth century, popular opinion and legislative attitudes began to favor speech and association rights for workers. Legislation on the national and state levels appeared that sought to give workers the right to organize, bargain collectively, and engage in concerted activities such as strikes and boycotts. For example, the Clayton Antitrust Act of 1914 specifically declared that unions were not "combinations in restraint of trade," and Section 4 of the Norris-LaGuardia Act of 1932 severely restricted the authority of federal courts to issue any injunctions in labor matters, and restated in unambiguous language the right of labor to be free of injunctions.[4]

Although these legislative initiatives were also met with judicial hostility, unions and union membership grew by leaps and bounds, especially in the rail industry, which, in many ways, became the prototypical model for workers in other industries. During World War I, when the federal government assumed managerial control of the nation's railroads, rail unions rapidly grew in size and influence; so much so that, after the war, rail unions were able to obtain agreements from the rail owners that granted speech and association rights to rail workers. Congress soon ratified this labor-management compact by enacting the Railway Labor Act of 1926 giving a firm, legal footing to the right of railway union members to exercise a large voice in decisions regarding the terms and conditions of their employment.

Following the Railway Labor Act, Congress enacted several important labor laws that granted more industrial democracy to the industrial working class. Many provisions in these labor laws, along with the Railway Labor Act, were also First Amendment landmarks, but in a different way than we have seen thus far. While most, if not all, of the laws that we have examined thus far ran afoul of the First Amendment by restricting people's rights thereunder, many of the labor laws fulfill or at least seek to fulfill the spirit of the First Amendment by increasing the rights of workers (and later, employers) in an economic setting. For example, the 1934 amendment to the 1926 Railway Labor Act prohibited employers from placing limitations on workers' First Amendment freedom of association; the 1951 amendment to the Railway Labor Act permitted "union shops," which caused freedom of association problems for many workers who were reluctant to join unions; the National Labor Relations (Wagner) Act of 1935 established a general regime for all union elections that permitted workers to vote by secret ballot and outlawed certain practices (called unfair labor practices) that interfered with the rights of labor and management; the Labor Management Relations (Taft-Hartley) Act of 1947 amended the Wagner Act to protect the First Amendment rights of management; and, finally, Title I of the Labor-Management Reporting and Disclosure Act (Landrum-Griffin Act) of 1959 contained an economic "workers' bill of rights" that included freedom of speech and assembly similar to those provided by the First Amendment. To be sure, some labor laws have restricted rather than enhanced First Amendment freedoms, as we saw with the Labor Management Relations Act of 1947, which prohibited unions from making political expenditures. This act also restricted the ability of unions to engage in certain concerted or organizational activity, such as boycotts in certain situations.

Enhancing—as opposed to restricting—rights of expression and association for workers through legislation usually does not present a First Amendment problem. For one thing, Congress can deflect attention (and has done so) from the First Amendment by basing such laws on its regulatory power under the commerce clause in Article I, Section 8, of the U.S. Constitution. For another, and more precise, reason, the First Amendment operates as a negative, meaning that it prohibits congressional interference with its freedoms in the public realm, rather than requiring their positive enhancement in the private sector. Even so, some of the many labor statutes that seek to extend political rights to workers in an industrial setting have had some ironically negative results. The first instance is illustrated by an amendment to the Railway Labor Act of 1926, and the second by the National Labor Relations Act of 1935.

NOTES

1. The term *labor law* usually refers to the body of laws that are applied to employer–employee situations in which workers join together, or seek to join together, in unions to bargain collectively with their employers. *Employment law*, on the other hand, usually refers to employer–employee situations in which there are no unions.

2. As an example of how workers were viewed by the law, one can examine the contents of legal encyclopedias even as late as the second half of the twentieth century and discover employer–employee relations indexed under "master and servant."

3. The Sherman Antitrust Act of 1890 is the basic antimonopoly statute that prohibits "every contract, combination in the form of trust or otherwise, or conspiracy, in restraint of trade or commerce among the several States, or with foreign nations." The act provides criminal penalties and civil damages in an amount three times the losses suffered as a result of the violation. See *Loewe v. Lawlor* (1908), in which the Supreme Court applied the Sherman Act to a combination of workers—namely, unions.

4. The courts held that the anti-injunction provision of the Clayton Act did not extend to permit otherwise unlawful actions, meaning impeding interstate commerce or interfering with liberty of contract. For example, see *Duplex Printing Co. v. Deering* (1921). Other enactments that were also met by judicial antagonism include: the Act of October 1, 1888; the Erdman Act of June 1, 1898 (which, incidentally, grew out of the Pullman strike of 1894, and spawned the notable case of *In re Debs* [1895]); the Newlands Act of July 15, 1913; the Adamson Law of September 3, 1916; and the Transportation Act of 1920.

THE RAILWAY LABOR ACT OF 1926

The Railway Labor Act of 1926 was enacted after a successful surge in union activity during World War I, when the railroads were operated by the national government. In fact, union power was so great after the war, and the unions so emboldened, that they urged Congress to nationalize the railway system instead of returning it to the owners. Although nationalization was never a real possibility for the unions, reaching a basic agreement from a position of power was, and it provided the basic right for workers to associate in unions and bargain as a unit. The 1926 act also provided for an elaborate mechanism of arbitration and mediation to settle disputes, thus discouraging strikes and other economic disruptions in the railway industry. Although the Railway Labor Act has been amended several times, it still forms the basic regulatory regime for labor-management relations in the railway industry.

One of these amendments—the union shop provision—created freedom of speech and freedom of association problems for some workers while extending them to others. Section 2, Clause 11 of the Railway Labor Act as amended provided that a railway carrier and a labor organization could enter into an agreement that required all employees to become members of the labor organization within a stated time.[1] The "union shop" has a long and colorful history, beginning in 1908 when the Supreme Court invalidated the Erdman Act's ban of "yellow dog contracts" (contracts between employers and individual employees that provide for the immediate termination of employment for those employees who participate in any unionizing activity), on the grounds that the statute invaded the personal liberty and property rights of employers under the Fifth Amendment's due process clause. By the mid-1930s, the union shop was widely used by employers to establish and dominate so-called company unions.

Although company unions were formally outlawed by the 1935 Wagner Act, they continued for a time under the name of "independent unions." By 1951, when the union shop provision of the Railway Labor Act was written into the law, the situation had radically changed. Company, or independent, unions were practically nonexistent. Moreover, among the 75–80 percent of railroad employees who were dues-paying union members, resentment began to rise because it was felt that nonunion members were obtaining union benefits without bearing a fair share of union-related costs.[2] As Senator Lister Hill (D-AL), who sponsored the union shop provision, stated, "the question in this instance is whether those who enjoy the fruits and the benefits of the unions should make a fair contribution to the support of the unions."[3] Thus, Congress enacted the present amendment, which permitted union shops, this time under union domination.

The union shop provision confronted the First Amendment when a group of nonunion employees of a railroad brought suit in 1955 against a railroad company and several unions, alleging that the union contract provision deprived them of freedoms of speech and association guaranteed by the First Amendment. The complainants insisted that their First Amendment freedom of association included the freedom to refrain from belonging to a union. The U.S. Supreme Court upheld the validity of the union shop provision in *Railway Employees' Dept. v. Hanson* (1956).

The union shop provision of the Railway Labor Act is a good example of Congress enacting a narrowly drawn statute that pursues a compelling governmental function in a matter that impacts First Amendment rights. First, the combined goal of "establishing industrial peace through stabilized labor-management relations" is a compelling governmental function, even though pursuing it restricts First Amendment rights. Second, in light of the fact that the enactment does adversely impact First Amendment rights, the statute is narrowly drafted so that the restriction does not unduly limit an unwilling employee's rights any more than is necessary to achieve the statutory purpose. As the court stated in *Hanson*, "The only conditions to union membership . . . are the payment of 'periodic dues,' initiation fees, and assessments. . . . The financial support required relates, therefore, to the work of the union in the realm of collective bargaining. . . . If 'assessments' are in fact imposed for purposes not germane to collective bargaining, a different [result] would be presented" (p. 235).

The Railway Labor Act, Railway Labor Act of 1926 as amended

Chapter 347. An Act to provide for the prompt disposition of disputes between carriers and their employees, and for other purposes.

Definitions

Section 1. When used in this Act and for the purposes of this Act:

First. The term "carrier" includes any express company, sleeping-car company, and any carrier by railroad, subject to the Interstate Commerce Act, including all floating equipment such as boats, barges, tugs, bridges, and ferries; and other transportation facilities used by or operated in connection with any such carrier by railroad, and any receiver or any other individual or body, judicial or otherwise, when in the possession of the business of employers or carriers covered by this Act . . .

Fifth. The term "employee" as used herein includes every person in the service of a carrier (subject to its continuing authority to supervise and direct the manner of rendition of his service) who performs any work defined as that of an employee or subordinate official in the orders of the Interstate Commerce Commission . . .

General Duties

Section 2. First, it shall be the duty of all carriers, their officers, agents, and employees to exert every reasonable effort to make and maintain agreements concerning rates of pay, rules, and working conditions, and to settle all disputes, whether arising out of the application of such agreements or otherwise, in order to avoid any interruption to commerce or to the operation of any carrier growing out of any dispute between the carrier and the employees thereof.

Second. All disputes between a carrier and its employees shall be considered, and, if possible, decided, with all expedition, in conference between representatives designated, and authorized so to confer, respectively by the carriers and the employees thereof interested in the dispute.

Third. Representatives, for the purpose of this Act, shall be designated by the respective parties in such manner as may be provided in their corporate organization or unincorporated association, or by other means of collective action, without interference, influence, or coercion exercised by either party over the self-organization or designation of representatives by the other.

Approved May 20, 1926.

THE 1934 AMENDMENT TO THE RAILWAY LABOR ACT

Chapter 691. To amend the Railway Labor Act . . .

General Duties

Third. Representatives, for the purpose of this Act, shall be designated by the respective parties without interference, influence, or coercion by either party over the designation of representatives by the other; and neither party shall in any way interfere with, influence, or coerce the other in its choice of representatives. Representatives of employees for the purpose of this Act need not be persons in the employ of the carrier, and no carrier shall, by interference, influence, or coercion seek in any manner to prevent the designation by its employees as their representatives of those who or which are not employees of the carrier.

Fourth. Employees shall have the right to organize and bargain collectively through representatives of their own choosing. The majority of any craft or class of employees shall have the right to determine who shall be the representative of the craft or class for the purposes of this Act. No carrier, or its officers, or agents, shall deny or in any way question the right of its employees to join, organize, or assist in organizing the labor organization of their choice . . .

Approved June 21, 1934.

THE 1951 AMENDMENT TO THE RAILWAY LABOR ACT

Chapter 1220. To amend the Railway Labor Act and to authorize agreements providing for union membership and agreements for deductions from the wages of carriers' employees for certain purposes and under certain condition.

[Amending the Railway Labor Act by adding to Section 2 thereof, as paragraph "Eleventh" the following language.]

Eleventh. . . . [A]ny carrier or carriers as defined in this Act and a labor organization or labor organizations duly designated and authorized to represent employees in accordance with the requirements of this Act shall be permitted—

(a) to make agreements requiring as a condition of employment, that within sixty days following the beginning of such employment, or the effective date of such agreements, which ever is the later, all employees shall become members of the labor organization representing their craft or class. Provided, that no such agreement shall require such condition of employment with respect to employees to whom membership is not available upon the same terms and conditions as are generally applicable to any other member or with respect to employees to whom membership was denied or terminated for any reason other than the failure of the employee to tender the periodic dues, initiation fees, and assessments (not including fines and penalties) uniformly required as a condition of acquiring or retaining membership.

(b) to make agreements providing for the deduction by such carrier or carriers from the wages of its or their employees in a craft or class and payment to the labor organization representing the craft or class of such employees, of any periodic dues, initiation fees, and assessments (not including fines and penalties) uniformly required as a condition of acquiring or retaining membership; . . .

Approved January 10, 1951.

NOTES

1. A union shop is a business or industrial establishment whose employees are required to be union members or to agree to join the union (assuming that a majority of the employees have voted to be represented by a union) within a specified time after being hired. Sometimes the term *closed shop* is incorrectly used synonymously with the term *union shop*. The difference is that while union shop applicants have a specified time to join the union after employment, closed shop applicants must join before employment. A third type is the *agency shop*, one in which employees are not compelled to join the union but are required to pay union dues because they benefit from union activities. A statutory companion to the railway union shop provision that covers labor unions in a general way is § 14(b) of the Taft-Hartley Act of 1947. Section 14(b) permits each state the right to choose to "opt out" of the union shop requirement by enacting what are popularly known as "right-to-work" laws.

2. See S. Rep. No. 2262, 81st Cong., 2nd Sess., pp. 3–4.

3. 96 Cong. Rec., Pt. 12, p. 16279.

THE NATIONAL LABOR RELATIONS
ACT OF 1935

The National Labor Relations Act (NLRA) of 1935, known as the Wagner Act and hailed by labor leader Samuel Gompers as labor's magna carta, established collective bargaining between workers and employers as a national labor policy and created a firm legal basis for the operation of unions that affect interstate commerce by providing for union elections by secret ballot and protecting union members' speech and association rights from employers' intimidation and coercion. The NLRA, as amended in 1947 by the Taft-Hartley Act and in 1959 by the Landrum-Griffin Act, is still in force. The NLRA established the National Labor Relations Board (NLRB) to enforce these rights by conducting union elections and hearing and resolving disputes regarding violations of act. The NLRA as amended is not one-sided; it gives mutual rights and obligations to management and labor alike. Just as each side has free speech rights under the act, either can run afoul of the act by committing what are called unfair labor practices.

Just as extending rights to workers can create First Amendment tensions among workers, it can also create tension between workers and managers. Thus, while § 8(a)(1) of the National Labor Relations Act enhances workers' First Amendment rights by prohibiting the interference, restraint, or coercion of employees by employers in the exercise of the employees' rights to self-organization, the free speech rights of employers to communicate their (anti-union) views cannot be disregarded in the meantime. Recognizing the First Amendment rights of management, Congress amended the NLRA by enacting § 8(c), which provided that expressions of "any views, argument, or opinion" by management shall not be "evidence of an unfair labor practice," as long as such expression contained "no threat of reprisal or force or promise of benefit" to employees.

The First Amendment clash between sections 8(a)(1) and 8(c) of the NLRA came to a head in a case involving the Teamsters Union and a wire-weaving company in Holyoke, Massachusetts. In July 1952, the NLRB conducted an election among the company's journeymen and apprentice wire weavers. After the union lost the election, it petitioned the NLRB to set aside the election, alleging that Sinclair's managers had violated the employees' § 8(a)(1) rights by threatening to close the plant in retaliation if the workers voted for the union. The union alleged that this threat of reprisal caused the union to lose the election. Sinclair defended the speeches and written communications made by its officers during the election campaign on First Amendment grounds.

The U.S. Supreme Court upheld the First Amendment rights of management, declaring that Congress acted properly in implementing the First Amendment by enacting § 8(c). However, the Court found that Sinclair's managers had exceeded their free speech rights in this case by making speeches and distributing information that contained "threats of reprisal" against the workers. *National Labor Relations Board v. Gissel Packing Co.* (1969). In balancing the First Amendment rights of management against those of the workers, the Court used a standard that is reminiscent of the "clear and present danger" test it used in antisedition laws. The Court stated:

> Any assessment of the precise scope of employers' expression, of course, must be made in the context of its labor relations setting. Thus, an employer's rights cannot outweigh the equal rights of the employees to associate freely . . . any balancing of those rights must take into account the economic dependence of the employees on their employers, and the necessary tendency of the former, because of that relationship, to pick up intended implications of the latter that might be more readily dismissed by a more disinterested ear. (p. 617)

The National Labor Relations (Wagner) Act of 1935

Chapter 372. An Act to diminish the causes of labor disputes burdening or obstructing interstate and foreign commerce, to create a National Labor Relations Board, and for other purposes.

Findings and Policy

Section 1. The denial by employers of the right of employees to organize and the refusal by employers to accept the procedure of collective bargaining lead to strikes and other forms of industrial strife or unrest, which have the intent or the necessary effect of burdening or obstructing commerce . . .

The inequality of bargaining power between employees who do not possess full freedom of association or actual liberty of contract, and employers who are organized in the corporate or other forms of ownership association substantially burdens and affects the flow of commerce, and tends to aggravate recurrent business depressions, by depressing wage rates and the purchasing power of wage earners in industry and by preventing the stabilization of competitive wage rates and working conditions within and between industries.

Experience has proved that protection by law of the right of employees to organize and bargain collectively safeguards commerce from injury, impairment, or interruption, and promotes the flow of commerce by . . . restoring equality of bargaining power between employers and employees. . . .

Rights of Employees

Section 7. Employees shall have the right to self-organization, to form, join, or assist labor organizations, to bargain collectively through representatives of their own choosing, and to engage in concerted activities, for the purpose of collective bargaining or other mutual aid or protection.

Section 8. It shall be an unfair labor practice for an employer—

(1) To interfere with, restrain, or coerce employees in the exercise of the rights granted in section 7.

(2) To dominate or interfere with the formation or administration of any labor organization, or contribute financial or other support to it . . .

(3) By discrimination in regard to hire or tenure of employment or any term or condition of employment to encourage or discourage membership in any labor organization . . .

(4) To discharge or otherwise discriminate against an employee because he has filed charges or given testimony under this Act.

(5) To refuse to bargain collectively with the representatives of his employees . . .

The pertinent provisions of the Labor Management Reporting (Taft-Hartley) Act, 61 Stat. 136 provide:

TITLE I—AMENDMENT OF NATIONAL LABOR RELATIONS ACT

Section 101. The National Labor Relations Act is hereby amended to read as follows:

Unfair Labor Practices

Section 8. (c) The expressing of any views, arguments, or opinion, or the dissemination thereof, whether in written, printed, graphic, or visual form, shall not constitute or be evidence of an unfair practice under any of the provisions of this Act, if such expression contains no threat of reprisal or force or promise of benefit.

The pertinent provisions of the Labor-Management Reporting and Disclosure Act of 1959, 73 Stat. 519, provide:

Declaration of Findings, Purposes, and Policy

Section 2. (a) The Congress finds that, in the public interest, it continues to be the responsibility of the Federal Government to protect employees' right to organize, choose their own representatives, bargain collectively, and otherwise engage in concerted activities . . . and that in order to accomplish the objectives of a free flow of commerce, it is essential that labor organizations, employers, and their officials adhere to the highest standards of responsibility and ethical conduct in administering the affairs of their organizations, particularly as they affect labor-management relations. . . .

(c) The Congress, therefore, further finds and declares that the enactment of this Act is necessary to eliminate or prevent improper practices on the part of labor organizations, employers, labor relations consultants, and their officers and representatives which distort and defeat the policies of the Labor Management Relations Act of 1947, as amended, and the Railway Labor Act, as amended, and have the tendency or necessary effect of burdening or obstructing commerce. . . .

TITLE I—BILL OF RIGHTS OF LABOR ORGANIZATIONS

Section 101. (a)(1) Equal Rights. Every member of a labor organization shall have equal rights and privileges within such organization to nominate candidates, to vote in elections or referendums of the labor organization, to attend membership meetings, and to participate in the deliberations and voting upon the business of such meetings, subject to reasonable rules and regulations in such organization's constitution and bylaws.

(2) Freedom of Speech and Assembly. Every member of any labor organization shall have the right to meet and assemble freely with other members; and to express any views, arguments, or opinions; and to express at meetings of the labor organization his views, upon candidates in an election of the labor organization or upon any business properly

before the meeting, subject to the organization's established and reasonable rules pertaining to the conduct of meetings. . . .

(4) Protection of the Right To Sue. No labor organization shall limit the right of any member thereof to institute an action in any court, or in a proceeding before any administrative agency . . . [or] appear as a witness in any judicial, administrative, or legislative proceeding, or to petition any legislature or to communicate with any legislator . . .

(5) Safeguards against Improper Disciplinary Action. No member of any labor organization may be fined, suspended, expelled, or otherwise disciplined except for nonpayment of dues by such organization or by any officer thereof unless such member has been (A) served with written specific charges; (B) given a reasonable time to prepare his defense; [and (C)] afforded a full and fair hearing.

Approved July 5, 1935.

7

Federally Funded Programs

The landmark statutes examined in the preceding chapters constitute political-legal categories, such as obscenity, sedition, and campaign financing that typically raise First Amendment issues. There
are several statutes that are not included in these categories but still
deserve the status of landmarks in view of their collateral impact
on First Amendment rights. Three such enactments are the "anti-
abortion" provision of Title X of the Family Planning Services and
Population Research Act enacted in 1970, the "charitable organization exemption" provision of the Internal Revenue Code, and the
"decency and respect" clause of the 1990 Amendment to the National Foundation for the Arts and Humanities Act. These statutes
reveal the scope of First Amendment rights by illustrating how legislation in almost any area can potentially impact the rights.

FAMILY PLANNING SERVICES AND POPULATION RESEARCH ACT OF 1970

Congress enacted the Family Planning Services and Population Research Act of 1970 to provide funds for various family planning services.[1] While it was the declared purpose of Congress "to make comprehensive, voluntary family planning services, and information relating thereto, readily available to all persons," Section 1008 warns that "none of the funds appropriated under this subchapter shall be used in programs where abortion is a method of family planning."[2] During the next eighteen years, federal grantees that performed abortions were denied funds under the 1970 act. During the height of anti-abortion activity in the country, the Department of Health and Human Services issued a set of revised regulations in 1988 that defined "family planning" as excluding abortion as a method of family planning, which meant that federal grant recipients could not counsel or refer their clients for abortion as a family planning option. Moreover, grant recipients could not encourage, promote, or advocate abortion as a method of family planning (53 Fed. Reg. 2922 *et seq.*, (Feb. 2, 1988).[3]

Dr. Irving Rust was an obstetrician and gynecologist who supervised a Title X–funded health care program at the Bronx Center (part of Planned Parenthood of New York City). He and others, including the state of New York, sued Otis R. Bowen, the secretary of the U.S. Department of Health and Human Services, for violating their First Amendment rights. The simple one-line provision in Section 1008 does not contain the "counseling and referral" clause that is used by the regulation. In fact, the legislative history contained in the joint House and Senate conference report mentions "prohibit[ing] the use of such funds for abortion," which seems to indicate that the prohibition applied only to abortion itself.[4] Nonetheless, the secretary's regulations did contain a clear prohibition of "counseling and referral," commonly referred to as the "gag rule," which the plaintiffs claimed violated their First Amendment rights.

The plaintiffs in *Rust v. Sullivan* (1991) claimed that the statute— and, in particular, the implementing regulation containing the gag rule—discriminated against them on the basis of their viewpoint and that it unlawfully prohibited all discussion about abortion as a legally approved family planning option. After all, abortion under certain circumstances had been not only a lawful right since *Roe v. Wade* (1973), but also a constitutionally protected right. Even so, the U.S. Supreme Court held that the government may "make a value judgment favoring childbirth over abortion, and implement that judgment by the allocation of public funds." In short, the "Government can, without violating the Constitution, selectively fund a program to encourage certain activities it believes to be in the public interest, without at the same time funding an alternative program which seeks to deal with the problem in another way" (*Rust v. Sullivan*, 1991, pp. 192–193). The Court also distinguished between "grantees" and "projects," holding that the statute and regulation limited activity related only to the use of project funds, not the grantee's activities in general. Recipients are not limited in the way they may choose to use other or wholly private funds. Finally, the Court held that by accepting Title X funds, recipients voluntarily consent to the attached restrictions without impacting their First Amendment rights.

After *Rust*, the Supreme Court invalidated a funding restriction by drawing a distinction between a funding program that is designed to "facilitate private speech and one that seeks to promote a governmental message." In *Legal Services Corporation v. Velazquez* (2001), the Court struck down a statutory restriction contained in the Legal Services Corporation Act that prohibited grantees from representing any client who challenges existing welfare law, even if the statutory validity challenge becomes apparent after representation is well under way. The Court distinguished *Rust* and *Velazquez* on the grounds that the funding mechanism under the Family Planning Services and Population Research Act of 1970 "used private speakers to transmit information pertaining to its own programs," whereas the Legal Services Corporation Act of 1974 was "designed to facilitate private speech [namely, the interests of indigent clients], not to represent a governmental message" (pp. 15–17).[5]

The Family Planning Services and Population Research Act of 1970

Section 300. Project grants and contracts for family planning services[6]

(a) Authority of Secretary: The Secretary is authorized to make grants to and enter into contracts with public or nonprofit private entities to assist in the establishment and operation of voluntary family planning projects which shall offer a broad range of acceptable and effective family planning methods and services (including natural family planning methods, infertility services, and services for adolescents). . . .

(b) Factors determining awards: Establishment and preservation of rights of local and regional entities. In making grants and contracts under this section the Secretary shall take into account the number of patients to be served, the extent to which family planning services are needed locally, the relative need of the applicant, and its capacity to make rapid and effective use of such assistance. Local and regional entities shall be assured the right to apply for direct grants and contracts under this section, and the Secretary shall by regulation fully provide for and protect such right. . . .

Section 300a. Formula grants to States for family planning services

(a) Authority of Secretary; prerequisites: The Secretary is authorized to make grants, from allotments made under subsection (b) of this section, to State health authorities to assist in planning, establishing, maintaining, coordinating, and evaluating family planning services. . . .

(b) Factors determining amount of State allotments: The sums appropriated to carry out the provisions of this section shall be allotted to the States by the Secretary on the basis of the population and the financial need of the respective States. . . .

Section 300a-1. Training grants and contracts; authorization of appropriations

(a) The Secretary is authorized to make grants to public or nonprofit private entities and to enter into contract with public or private entities and individuals to provide the training for personnel to carry out family planning service programs described in section 300 or 300a of this title. . . .

Section 300a-2. Conduct, etc., of research activities

The Secretary may—

(1) conduct, and

(2) make grants to public or nonprofit private entities and enter into contracts with public or private entities and individuals for projects for, research in the biomedical, contraceptive development, behavioral, and program implementation fields related to family planning and population. . . .

Section 300a-4. Grants and contracts

(a) Promulgation of regulations governing execution; amount of grants. Grants and contracts made under this subchapter shall be made in accordance with such regulations as the Secretary may promulgate . . .

(b) Payment of grants: Grants under this subchapter shall be payable in such installments and subject to such conditions as the Secretary may determine to be appropriate to assure that such grants will be effectively utilized for the purposes for which made. . . .

Section 300a-6. Prohibition against funding programs using abortion as family planning method

None of the funds appropriated under this subchapter shall be used in programs where abortion is a method of family planning.

Approved December 24, 1970.

NOTES

1. Codified at 42 U.S.C. §§ 300–300a-8. The Family Planning Services and Population Research Act is Subchapter VIII of the Public Health and Welfare laws and is commonly referred to as Title X of Chapter 373 of Pub. L. 91–572.

2. 116 Cong. Rec. 24094 (1970).

3. Codified at 42 C.F.R. §§ 59.2, 59.8, 59.9, and 59.10 (1988). Following his inauguration in 1993, President Clinton ordered the Department of Health and Human Services to suspend the rules and initiate a new rulemaking process (Presidential Memorandum of January 22, 1993, published at 58 FR 7455, February 5, 1993). The secretary subsequently suspended the 1988 rules on February 5, 1993 (58 FR 7462) and issued proposed rules for public comment (58 FR 7464). New rules became effective July 3, 2000, that revised the regulations that apply to grantees under the federal family planning program by readopting the regulations with one revision—namely, omitting the "Gag Rule" that restricted family planning grantees from providing abortion-related information in their grant-funded projects (*Federal Register* 65, no. 128, July 3, 2000, pp. 41269–41280). On his third day in office, President George W. Bush restored his Republican predecessors' approach by reinstating the "Mexico City Policy," which was named for the 1984 population conference where the Reagan administration initially announced it. On January 22, 2001, President Bush signed the order that denies U.S. funds to overseas groups that use their own money to promote or perform abortions. See News Release by the Office of the Press Secretary, The White House, June 22, 2001 (at http://www.whitehouse.gov/news/releases/20010123-5.html).

4. H. R. Conf. Rep. No. 91–1667 (1970), p. 8.

5. The restrictions at issue in *Velazquez* were part of a set of restrictions enacted in the Omnibus Consolidated Rescissions and Appropriations Act of 1996, and continued in each subsequent annual appropriations act. The relevant portion of § 504(a)(16) prohibits funding of any organization "that initiates legal representation or participates in any other way, in litigation, lobbying, or rulemaking, involving an effort to reform a Federal or State welfare system, except that this paragraph shall not be construed to preclude a recipient from representing an individual eligible client who is seeking specific relief from a welfare agency if such relief does not involve an effort to amend or otherwise challenge existing law in effect on the date of the initiation of the representation."

6. Sec. 300a-41. Repealed. Pub. L. 97–35, Title IX, Sec. 955(b), Title XXI, Sec. 2193(f), Aug. 13, 1981, 95 Stat. 592, 828.

THE TAX REFORM ACT OF 1976

Section 501 of the federal Internal Revenue Code, which provides tax-exempt status to nonprofit organizations and their donors, is the "linchpin of the statutory benefit system" (*Simon v. Eastern Kentucky Welfare Rights Organization*, 1976, p. 29, n.1). Section 501(c)(3) of the Internal Revenue code provides for the types of organizations that are exempt from federal taxation on the income they receive.[1] Most of the covered organizations are charitable corporations or organizations. All such organizations are operated on a nonprofit basis, which is the principal reason that Congress grants them an exemption from income taxation. Moreover, since most of their income is derived from private contributions, Congress has granted many organizations an additional benefit under I.R.C. 170(c)(2), whereby their contributors are permitted to receive tax deductions for all contributions they make to the organizations.

Section 501(c)(3) organizations are restricted in their activities. They must be exclusively devoted to religious, charitable, scientific, literary, or educational activities. These organizations are not permitted to engage in lobbying the government or political campaign activities on behalf of any candidate for public office that brings the First Amendment into play. An organization that otherwise complies with Section 501 but engages in lobbying will be treated as 501(c)(4) organizations. The income of Section 501(c)(4) organizations or lobbying organizations are exempt from taxation, but their contributors may not take a deduction for their contributions.

Many Section 501 organizations claim, among other things, that 501(c)(3)'s restriction on political activity interferes with freedom of expression. One such organization was Taxation with Representation of Washington (TRW), a nonprofit corporation organized in 1977 to lobby the three branches of government in matters concerning federal taxation. Although TRW's 501(c)(4) status was not in jeopardy, the Internal Revenue Service denied it 501(c)(3) status in 1978 on the basis of its lobbying activities. Without 501(c)(3) status, TRW lost the benefit of receiving contributions that were tax deductible for its donors. After exhausting its administrative remedies, TRW sued Secretary of the Treasury Donald Regan in federal court, asking for a declaration that the antilobbying provision of 503(c)(3) violated its First Amendment right of free expression.

TRW's claim appeared to have merit, based on an earlier Supreme Court decision that declared that

> even though a person has no "right" to a valuable governmental benefit and even though the government may deny him the benefit for any number of reasons, there are some reasons upon which the government may not rely. It may not deny a benefit to a person on a basis that infringes his constitutionally protected interests—especially his interest in freedom of speech. . . . Such interference with constitutional rights is impermissible. (*Perry v. Sindermann*, 1972, p. 597)

Yet, when the TRW case reached the U.S. Supreme Court, it held against the First Amendment claim. The Court distinguished between the First Amendment right of TRW to lobby the government on the one hand and tax deductions or exemptions on the other. In short, the Court saw TRW's tax benefit as a governmental subsidy. Declaring that "Congress has not infringed any First Amendment rights or regulated any First Amendment activity[;] Congress has simply chosen not to pay for TRW's lobbying," the Court went on to "reject the notion that First Amendment rights are somehow not fully realized unless they are subsidized by the State" (*Regan v. Taxation With Representation of Washington*, 1983, p. 546).

The Tax Reform Act of 1976

Section 501. Exemption from tax on corporations, certain trusts, etc.

(a) Exemption from taxation. An organization described in subsection (c) or (d) or section 401(a) shall be exempt from taxation under this subtitle unless such exemption is denied under section 502 or 503.

(b) Tax on unrelated business income and certain other activities. An organization exempt from taxation under subsection (a) shall be subject to tax to the extent provided in parts II, III, and VI of this subchapter, but (notwithstanding parts II, III, and VI of this subchapter) shall be considered an organization exempt from income taxes for the purpose of any law which refers to organizations exempt from income taxes.

(c) List of exempt organizations. The following organizations are referred to in subsection (a):

(1) Any corporation organized under Act of Congress which is an instrumentality of the United States but only if such corporation—

(A) is exempt from Federal income taxes—

(i) under such Act as amended and supplemented before July 18, 1984, or (ii) under this title without regard to any provision of law which is not contained in this title and which is not contained in a revenue Act, or

(B) is described in subsection (1).

(2) Corporations organized for the exclusive purpose of holding title to property, collecting income therefrom, and turning over the entire amount thereof, less expenses, to an organization which itself is exempt under this section. Rules similar to the rules of subparagraph (G) of paragraph (25) shall apply for purposes of this paragraph.

(3) Corporations, and any community chest, fund, or foundation, organized and operated exclusively for religious, charitable, scientific, testing for public safety, literary, or educational purposes, or to foster national or international amateur sports competition (but only if no part of its activities involve the provision of athletic facilities or equipment), or for the prevention of cruelty to children or animals, no part of the net earnings of which inures to the benefit of any private shareholder or individual, no substantial part of the activities of which is carrying on propaganda, or otherwise attempting, to influence legislation (except as otherwise provided in subsection (h)), and which does not participate in, or intervene in (including the publishing or distributing of statements), any political campaign on behalf of (or in opposition to) any candidate for public office.

(4)—

(A) Civic leagues or organizations not organized for profit but operated exclusively for the promotion of social welfare, or local associations of employees, the membership of which is   limited to the employees of a designated person or persons in a particular municipality, and the net earnings of which are devoted exclusively to charitable, educational, or recreational purposes.

(B) Subparagraph (A) shall not apply to an entity unless no part of the net earnings of such entity inures to the benefit of any private shareholder or individual.

Approved October 4, 1976.

NOTE

1. Congress enacted this section of the code as part of the Tax Reform Act of 1976.

NATIONAL FOUNDATION ON THE ARTS AND HUMANITIES ACT (1990)

In 1965 Congress established the National Endowment for the Arts (NEA) for the "encouragement and support of national progress and scholarship in the humanities and the arts," by promoting "free inquiry and expression [and at the same time ensuring that] conformity for its own sake is not to be encouraged."[1] The National Foundation on the Arts and Humanities Act[2] vested the NEA with the responsibility to distribute federal funds to applicants who advance and support the arts, such as art museums, stage productions, and musical organizations. According to the Senate report that accompanied the legislation, it is

> the intent of the committee that in the administration of this act there be given the fullest attention to freedom of artistic and humanistic expression. One of the artist's and humanist's great values to society is the mirror of self-examination which they raise so that society can become aware of its shortcomings as well as its strengths. ... Countless times in history artists and humanists who were vilified by their contemporaries because of their innovations in style or mode of expression have become prophets to a later age. Therefore, the committee affirms that the intent of this act should be the encouragement of free inquiry and expression. ... [C]onformity for its own sake is not to be encouraged, and ... no undue preference should be given to any particular style or school of thought or expression.[3]

By the 1980s the NEA began to receive criticism as it became surrounded in controversies over quarrels about some of its funding decisions. One member of Congress was highly critical for NEA's support of a production of Giuseppe Verdi's *Rigoletto* that portrayed several characters as members of the Mafia. The member of Congress, Representative Mario Biaggi (D-NY) took the characterization as demeaning to Italian Americans. In 1989 many members of Congress were incensed by the NEA's support of an exhibition of the photographer Robert Mapplethorpe's work that included homoerotic photographs. More controversy surrounded the exhibit of Andres Serrano's work entitled *Piss Christ*, which was a photograph of a crucifix immersed in urine.[4]

As a reaction to the controversies surrounding the Mapplethorpe-Serrano exhibits and others, Congress first acted by eliminating $45,000—the exact amount received by Mapplethorpe and Serrano—from NEA's budget. Congress then placed a restriction on NEA's funding discretion with Section 304(a) of the Department of the Interior and Related Agencies Appropriation Act of 1990, which provided that no funds could be used to promote, disseminate, or produce materials that, in the judgment of the NEA, are considered obscene, including but not limited to depictions of sadomasochism, homoeroticism, sexual exploitation of children, or individuals engaged in sex acts and which, when taken as a whole, do not have serious literary, artistic, political, or scientific value.[5]

Congress enacted another amendment to the National Foundation on the Arts and Humanities Act in 1990 that required the NEA to ensure that "artistic excellence and artistic merit are the criteria by which [grant] applications are judged, taking into consideration general standards of decency and respect for the diverse beliefs of the American public."[6] Some members of Congress supported this "decency and respect clause" on grounds similar to those who supported the constitutional rationale in the abortion "gag rule" and the "lobbying provision" of 501(c)(3). For example, one of the sponsors, Representative Thomas Coleman (R-MO), stated that "works which deeply offend the sensibilities of significant portions of the public ought not to be supported with public funds."[7] As might be expected, the "decency and respect clause" was soon the subject of litigation in a case that actually commenced before the "decency and respect" amendment was enacted. The case involved Karen Finley and three other performing artists whose works addressed political and sexual issues such as homosexuality, AIDS, and violence against women.

A panel of experts in the relevant artistic field reviews each application for funding and makes a recommendation to the NEA chairperson, who has the final authority to award grants but may not award grants to any applicant that received a negative recommendation from the panel. Although the advisory panel of experts had recommended approval of Karen Finley's application, NEA chair John Frohnmayer rejected it, and a trial over the "decency and respect" clause ensued.

Finley's group brought suit and contended that the "decency and respect" clause violated the First Amendment because it restricts artistic expression—particularly if the expression fails to conform to mainstream values or ill-defined standards of decency. Moreover, the clause permits NEA to discriminate on the basis of viewpoints. The U.S. Supreme Court upheld the statute containing the decency and respect clause, declaring that "it seems unlikely that [the clause] will introduce any greater element of selectivity than the determination of 'artistic excellence' itself." Moreover, the Court noted that "any content-based considerations that may be taken into account in the grant-making process are a consequence of the nature of arts funding." Recognizing that education was a critical component of NEA's mission, the court went on to note that "it is well established that 'decency' is a permissible factor where 'educational suitability' motivates its consideration" (*National Endowment for the Arts v. Finley*, 1998, pp. 584–585).[8]

The principal leg upon which the *Finley* court stood to uphold the decency and respect clause was the fact that the enactment involved the use of public funds rather than the outright prohibition of expression, as can be seen by the following statements. "Although the First Amendment certainly has application in the subsidy context, we note that the Government may allocate competitive funding according to criteria that would be impermissible were direct regulation of speech or a criminal penalty at stake." Quoting *Mather v. Roe* (1977), the court reaffirmed that Congress may selectively fund some programs to the exclusion of others on the basis that there is a "basic difference between direct state interference with a protected activity and state encouragement of an alternative activity consonant with legislative policy" (*Finley*, 1998, pp. 584–588).

The National Foundation on the Arts and Humanities Act (1990)

TITLE 20 EDUCATION

Section 951. Declaration of findings and purposes.
The Congress finds and declares the following:

(1) The arts and the humanities belong to all the people of the United States.

(2) The encouragement and support of national progress and scholarship in the humanities and the arts, while primarily a matter for private and local initiative, are also appropriate matters of concern to the Federal Government.

(3) An advanced civilization must not limit its efforts to science and technology alone, but must give full value and support to the other great branches of scholarly and cultural activity in order to achieve a better understanding of the past, a better analysis of the present, and a better view of the future.

(4) Democracy demands wisdom and vision in its citizens. It must therefore foster and support a form of education, and access to the arts and the humanities, designed to make people of all backgrounds and wherever located masters of their technology and not its unthinking servants.

(5) It is necessary and appropriate for the Federal Government to complement, assist, and add to programs for the advancement of the humanities and the arts by local, State, regional, and private agencies and their organizations. In doing so, the Government must be sensitive to the nature of public sponsorship. Public funding of the arts and humanities is subject to the conditions that traditionally govern the use of public money. Such funding should contribute to public support and confidence in the use of taxpayer funds. Public funds provided by the Federal Government must ultimately serve public purposes the Congress defines. . . .

Section 953. National Foundation on the Arts and the Humanities.

(a) Establishment; composition. There is established a National Foundation on the Arts and the Humanities. . . .

(b) Purpose. The purpose of the Foundation shall be to develop and promote a broadly conceived national policy of support for the humanities and the arts in the United States, and for institutions which preserve the cultural heritage of the United States pursuant to this subchapter.

(c) Prohibition against Federal supervision over policy determination, personnel, or curriculum, or administration or operation of any school or other non-Federal body. In the administration of this subchapter no department, agency, officer, or employee of the United States shall exercise any direction, supervision, or control over the policy determination, personnel, or curriculum, or the administration or operation of any school or other non-Federal agency, institution, organization, or association.

Section 954. National Endowment for the Arts.

(a) Establishment. There is established within the Foundation a National Endowment for the Arts. . . .

(c) Program of contracts, grants-in-aid, or loans to groups and individuals for projects and productions; traditionally under represented recipients of financial assistance. The Chairperson, with the advice of the National Council on the Arts, is authorized to establish and carry out a program of contracts with, or grants-in-aid or loans to, groups or, in appropriate cases, individuals of exceptional talent engaged in or concerned with the arts. . . .

(d) Application for payment: regulations and procedures. No payment shall be made under this section except upon application therefore which is submitted to the National Endowment for the Arts in accordance with regulations issued and procedures established by the Chairperson. In establishing such regulations and procedures, the Chairperson shall ensure that—

(1) artistic excellence and artistic merit are the criteria by which applications are judged, taking into consideration general standards of decency and respect for the diverse beliefs and values of the American public; and

(2) applications are consistent with the purposes of this section. Such regulations and procedures shall clearly indicate that obscenity is without artistic merit, is not protected speech, and shall not be funded. Projects, productions, workshops, and programs that are determined to be obscene are prohibited from receiving financial assistance under this subchapter from the National Endowment for the Arts. The disapproval or approval of an application by the Chairperson shall not be construed to mean, and shall not be considered as evidence that, the project, production, workshop, or program for which the applicant requested financial assistance is or is not obscene.

Approved November 5, 1990.

NOTES

1. 111 Cong. Rec. 13108 (1965), 20 U.S.C. § 952(2).

2. Although this landmark statute deals with issues related to obscenity and decency, it is included in this section rather than the section dealing with obscenity because, in the typical case of obscenity and decency, Congress flatly prohibits particular types of expression; in this case, however, Congress is not prohibiting any activity, it is simply refusing to support certain lawful types of expression with public funds.

3. S. Rep. 300, 89th Cong., 1st Sess., p. 4 (1965).

4. See 135 Cong. Rec. 22372, H3637, H3640, S5594, S5805 (1989).

5. The NEA implemented 304(a) by requiring grantees to certify in advance that none of the funds awarded would be used "to promote, disseminate, or produce materials which in the judgment of the NEA . . . may be considered obscene." The administration of 304(a) by NEA—not 304(a) itself—was declared to violate the First Amendment rights of NEA grantees in *Bella Lewitzsky Dance Foundation v. Frohnmayer*, 754 F. Supp. 774 (C.D. Cal. 1991). No appeal was taken in this case.

6. Codified at 20 U.S.C. § 954(d).

7. 136 Cong. Rec. 28631 (1990).

8. It might be noted, as we saw in the chapter on obscenity, that the First Amendment restriction does not permit Congress to enact a general prohibition of indecent material.

8

Freedom of Religion

The First Amendment in part provides that Congress "shall make no law respecting an establishment of religion, or prohibiting the free exercise thereof." Understanding the scope and depth of religious freedom under this provision is not a simple matter.[1] As Associate Supreme Court Justice Byron White stated, "candor compels the acknowledgment that we can only dimly perceive the boundaries of permissible governmental activity in this sensitive area" (*Tilton v. Richardson*, 1971, p. 678). For one thing, the First Amendment actually contains two provisions, or clauses as we have commonly called them, that govern the relationship between government and religion: the Establishment Clause and the Free Exercise Clause. For another, the constitutional standard by which Congress and the courts have applied each clause in each situation is different. Not only do the constitutional standards differ, each has changed over time and continues to be in a state of flux. Finally, Congress and the Supreme Court have very different, even antagonistic, ideas regarding the proper constitutional standard in many situations and which branch of government should have the last say.

The freedom of religion provision "embraces two concepts—freedom to believe and the freedom to act" (*Cantwell v. State of Connecticut*, 1940, p. 303). A useful explanation of the relationship between the clauses is one that a South Carolina chancellor wrote in 1843 that the U.S. Supreme Court has approved.[2] Chancellor David Johnson stated that, on the one hand, the "structure of our government has, for the preservation of civil liberty, rescued the temporal institutions from religious interference. On the other hand, it has secured religious liberty from the invasion of the civil authority."[3] In short, civil authority and religious liberty are deemed to have different concerns that cause each to be suspicious of the other. A look at some efforts by Congress to act for the public good while allowing for these concerns—which has been no easy task— is the goal of this section. Before we examine the landmark statutes regarding religious freedom, it is good to bear in mind that the interplay between the federal courts and state governments dominates the substance of First Amendment law, and this holds true for religious liberties as much as any aspect of the First Amendment. Indeed, most texts on the subject of religious freedom and the First Amendment mention Congress rarely if at all. Nonetheless, over the years, Congress has enacted several statutes that significantly affect religious issues, and its role as a meaningful player in this area is becoming more crucial year by year.

Nine congressional landmarks are important because they illustrate the impact of the First Amendment on legislation affecting religious issues in significant ways. They illustrate the complex relationship between governmental action and the two religious freedom clauses, showing how at times Congress seeks to enhance religious freedom directly, and at other times it simply strives to avoid a clash with the First Amendment. Examination of these statutes will also reveal the patchwork and transient nature of the constitutional standards that courts have applied to congressional enactments in this area, and the battle between Congress and the Supreme Court over which branch will have the last word in establishing those standards. In short, these landmark statutes illustrate the wisdom of Justice White's caution that the "boundaries of permissible governmental activity in this sensitive area" are difficult at best. We will see that, although congressional enactments created a wall of separation between religion and governmental action quite early, a twofold pattern has evolved by which Congress has taken different approaches to situations involving the Free Exercise Clause and those that involve the Establishment Clause. On the one hand, Congress has sought to maintain a firm wall of separation between an individual's right to exercise religion and the ability of government to interfere with such activity. On the other hand, Congress has been much more willing to overstep the wall of separation in Establishment Clause situations by providing financial assistance to sectarian schools and permitting religious organizations to receive public funds on an equal footing with public and secular organizations.

Three landmark congressional enactments relating to the Free Exercise Clause will be examined. The first enactment, the Morrill Anti-Bigamy Law of 1862, established the principle of separation of government and religion that came to be portrayed as "a wall of separation." The wall analogy dates to Roger Williams (1603–1683), the English cleric who founded a community in Providence, Rhode Island, in 1636 based on religious freedom and democratic ideals after he was expelled from Massachusetts for his criticism of Puritanism, and Thomas Jefferson. It rested on a distinction between belief and action, with individuals at liberty to hold whatever beliefs they chose, and government at liberty to regulate some action that unduly interfered with the liberty of others.

The second enactment, the Religious Freedom Restoration Act (RFRA) of 1993, was a reaction to a Supreme Court decision that relaxed the strict scrutiny standard that had for some time been applied by the courts in Free Exercise cases to determine if governmental action had penetrated the "wall." In 1990, the Court began to relax the strict scrutiny standard in favor of a "neutrality" standard. Congress enacted RFRA as a direct response to that judicial change by reinstituting the strict scrutiny test.

The third landmark enactment regarding the Free Exercise Clause is the Religious Land Use and Institutionalized Persons Act of 2000, which was another effort to overrule a decision of the Supreme Court, this one being the decision that invalidated the RFRA.

Congress enacted three congressional landmarks in situations involving the Establishment Clause. The Indian Appropriations Act of 1895 established the notion of a wall of separation between government and religion in Establishment Clause cases—much like the one created by the Anti-Bigamy Law of 1862—by ending a long tradition of providing federal funds for sectarian schools that sought to teach Native American students.

Less than a century later, following the lead of the Supreme Court's approval of public financing for certain aspects of sectarian education, Congress enacted Title I of the Elementary and Secondary Education Act of 1965 that distributed federal funds in some cases on an "in kind" basis to sectarian schools, and in other situations directly to students and parents of students who attend sectarian schools, who were in turn able to defray some of their costs associated with attending sectarian schools.

In 1996, Congress enacted the third landmark statute by providing for the distribution of public funds directly to religious organizations in certain situations. Section 104 of the Personal Responsibility and Work Opportunity Reconciliation Act of 1996 requires that federal funds be distributed to religious organizations on the same basis as they are distributed to secular organizations that perform similar types of publicly funded community and public services.

A look at two other congressional landmarks is interesting in that they implicate the Free Exercise and Establishment clauses simultaneously. The first is the American Indian Religious Freedom Act Amendment of 1994, which sought to enhance the Free Exercise rights of members of the Native American Church by exempting their ceremonial use of peyote from criminal prosecution under the antidrug laws. While the statute does enhance the Free Exercise rights of members of the Native American Church, some claim that it violates the Establishment Clause by refusing to extend such a right to peyote users who are not members of the Native American Church, thus promoting one religious group over others.

The second is the Equal Access Act of 1984, which essentially declared it unlawful for any public high school that receives federal funds to discriminate against students because of the content of their speech, including religious and philosophical content.

Finally, legislation concerning the national motto is examined.

NOTES

1. Nor is the scope of this work to be a composite examination of the constitutional law of religious freedom under the First Amendment. Rather, the goal is much more modest, intending to convey the general contours of this area to the extent that the role of Congress will become both evident and appreciated.

2. The explanation was first approved as early as *Watson v. Jones*, 1871, p. 730, and as late as *Larkin v. Grendel's Den, Inc.*, 1982, p. 126.

3. See *Harmon v. Dreher*, 2 Speer's Equity Reports, 1843, p. 120.

THE FREE EXERCISE CLAUSE

THE MORRILL ANTI-BIGAMY LAW OF 1862

The standard for determining whether a statute violates the Free Exercise Clause revolves around a "belief-action" distinction that is much like the "speech-action" distinction used in the clear-and-present-danger test associated with freedom of speech. The belief-action standard was first applied in a case, *Reynolds v. United States* (1879), that upheld the Morrill Anti-Bigamy Law of 1862, Section 5352 of the Revised Statutes, which made polygamy a crime. Although the statute was applicable to all federal territories, Congress aimed it primarily at members of the Church of Jesus Christ of Latter-Day Saints (the Mormons), who were the dominant religious group in the Utah Territory and the only major religious group to practice polygamy (for men) as part of its religious belief system. Thus, the statute immediately brought the Free Exercise Clause into play.

The *Reynolds* case began when George Reynolds, secretary at the time to Brigham Young, leader of the Church of Jesus Christ of Latter-Day Saints, agreed to become a defendant to test the Anti-Bigamy Law's constitutionality. Writing for the Court in *Reynolds*, Chief Justice Morrison Waite quoted and adopted Thomas Jefferson's now famous description of government's relationship with religion as "a wall of separation between church and state." The chief justice understood this "wall" to mean that "Congress was deprived of all legislative power over mere opinion, but was left free to reach actions that were in violation of social duties or subversive of good order" (p. 164). Thus, the Court upheld the statute against a First Amendment attack because polygamy itself is "an offense against society"—relating to Reynolds's actions rather than his beliefs (p. 166). In short, the Anti-Bigamy Law applied to everyone's action in a neutral way, whether or not it stemmed from or affected a religious belief.

The Morrill Anti-Bigamy Law of 1862

Every person having a husband or wife living, who marries another, whether married or single, in a Territory, or other place over which the United States have exclusive jurisdiction, is guilty of bigamy, and shall be punished by a fine of not more than $500, and by imprisonment for a term of not more than five years.

THE RELIGIOUS FREEDOM RESTORATION
ACT OF 1993

After *Reynolds*, the Supreme Court developed a test by applying the Free Exercise Clause to a line of cases involving state government, which became commonly known as the Sherbert-Yoder doctrine.[1] The Sherbert-Yoder standard did not depart so much from the *Reynolds* belief-action standard as it gave it structure: it required the application of a strict scrutiny examination in contested cases. In other words, in order for a statute to affect religious actions, it had to satisfy strict scrutiny's three-pronged test. First, does the statute substantially burden a religious practice? Second, if it does, can the burden be justified by a compelling governmental interest? Third, does the statute in question use the least restrictive means to achieve the compelling governmental interest?

By the end of the next three decades, the Supreme Court had changed the Sherbert-Yoder standard in a ruling that approved a state's statutory burden on a religious practice even without proof of a compelling governmental interest because the law was a "neutral law of general applicability" (*Employment Division v. Smith*, 1990, p. 879). In *Smith*, the Court upheld Oregon's denial of unemployment compensation to two Native American workers because their dismissal at work was based on their use of peyote, which was illegal under the state's penal code. Although Smith and his co-worker claimed that they were exercising a right to smoke peyote as part of their religious belief, the Court found that "generally applicable, religion-neutral laws that have the effect of burdening a particular religious practice need not be justified by a compelling governmental interest" (p. 886).

Congress, responding to the *Smith* decision, began a direct confrontation with the Supreme Court that continues to this day. The Religious Freedom Restoration Act (RFRA) of 1993 became effective on November 16, 1993, with widespread public support and overwhelming congressional majorities. It reinstituted the Sherbert-Yoder standard by requiring that governments cannot substantially burden religious exercise without a compelling public interest to justify the burden, and then only by using the least restrictive means to achieve the compelling interest. Congress found that even laws that are supposedly "neutral toward religion may burden religious exercise as surely as laws intended to interfere with religious exercise" (Section 2(a)(2)), and it forthrightly declared that the purpose of the RFRA was to overturn the *Smith* decision by reinstating the Sherbert-Yoder standard.

Nevertheless, the RFRA was short-lived. Little more than a year later, the Supreme Court answered the congressional challenge by upholding a lower court's declaration that the RFRA was a "violation of the United States Constitution . . . by unconstitutionally changing the burden of proof as established under *Employment Division v. Smith*" (*Flores v. Boerne*, 877 F. Supp. 355, 358, WD Tex. Mar. 1995). In an opinion written by Justice Anthony Kennedy, the Supreme Court found that the RFRA was an illegitimate "attempt [to make] a substantive change in constitutional protections" that the court had determined (*Boerne v. Flores*, 1997, p. 532).[2]

The Religious Freedom Restoration
Act of 1993[3]

Section 2. Congressional Findings and Declaration of Purposes.

(a) Findings: The Congress finds that—

(1) the framers of the Constitution, recognizing free exercise of religion as an unalienable right, secured its protection in the First Amendment to the Constitution;

(2) laws "neutral" toward religion may burden religious exercise as surely as laws intended to interfere with religious exercise;

(3) governments should not substantially burden religious exercise without compelling justification;

(4) in *Employment Division v. Smith*, 494 U.S. 872 (1990) the Supreme Court virtually eliminated the requirement that the government justify burdens on religious exercise imposed by laws neutral toward religion; and

(5) the compelling interest test as set forth in prior Federal court rulings is a workable test for striking sensible balances between religious liberty and competing prior governmental interests.

(b) Purposes: The purposes of this Act are—

(1) to restore the compelling interest test as set forth in *Sherbert v. Verner*, 374 U.S. 398 (1963) and *Wisconsin v. Yoder*, 406 U.S. 205 (1972)

and to guarantee its application in all cases where free exercise of religion is substantially burdened; and

(2) to provide a claim or defense to persons whose religious exercise
is substantially burdened by government.

Section 3. Free Exercise of Religion Protected.

(a) In General: Government shall not substantially burden a person's exercise of religion even if the burden results from a rule of general applicability, except as provided in subsection (b).

(b) Exception: Government may substantially burden a person's exercise
of religion only if it demonstrates that application of the burden to the
person—

(1) is in furtherance of a compelling governmental interest; and

(2) is the least restrictive means of furthering that compelling governmental interest.

(c) Judicial Relief: A person whose religious exercise has been burdened
in violation of this section may assert that violation as a claim or defense
in a judicial proceeding and obtain appropriate relief against a government. Standing to assert a claim or defense under this section shall be
governed by the general rules of standing under Article III of the Constitution. . . .

Section 6. Applicability.

(a) In General.—This Act applies to all Federal and State law, and the
implementation of that law, whether statutory or otherwise, and whether
adopted before or after the enactment of this Act. . . .

(c) Religious Belief Unaffected.—Nothing in this Act shall be construed
to authorize any government to burden any religious belief.

Section 7. Establishment Clause Unaffected.

Nothing in this Act shall be construed to affect, interpret, or in any way
address that portion of the First Amendment prohibiting laws respecting
the establishment of religion (referred to in this section as the "Establishment Clause"). Granting government funding, benefits, or exemptions, to
the extent permissible under the Establishment Clause, shall not constitute a violation of this Act. As used in this section, the term 'granting,'
used with respect to government funding, benefits, or exemptions, does
not include the denial of government funding, benefits, or exemptions.
Approved November 16, 1993.

NOTES

1. So named after two of the most notable cases in this line: *Sherbert v. Verner*
(1963) and *Wisconsin v. Yoder* (1972). The first dealt with whether a state could

deny unemployment compensation to a member of the Seventh-Day Adventist Church who lost a job for refusing to work on Saturday; the second dealt with whether Amish parents could be required to educate their children in public schools beyond the eighth grade.

2. The RFRA-Boerne confrontation is not the first time that Congress and the Supreme Court have battled over different interpretations of the First Amendment. On an earlier occasion, Congress enacted Section 508 of the National Defense Authorization Act for Fiscal Years 1988 and 1989 to overturn the Supreme Court's decision in *Goldman v. Weinberger*, 475 U.S. 503 (1986), which had upheld the constitutionality of an Air Force regulation that prohibited Captain Simcha Goldman, a commissioned clinical psychologist who was an Orthodox Jew and a rabbi, from wearing his yarmulke indoors while on duty. Congress disagreed with both the Supreme Court and the Air Force that the military's perceived need for uniformity of dress and for discipline, overrode the First Amendment right of an Orthodox Jewish serviceman such as Dr. Goldman to fulfill his traditional Jewish obligation by wearing a yarmulke. (See Public Law 100–180, section 508, Department of Defense Authorization Act, 1988–89, December 4, 1987.)

3. Legislative History—H. R. 1308 (S. 578). H. R. Rep. No. 103–88 (Comm. on the Judiciary), S. Rep. No. 103–111 (accompanying S. 578 [Comm. on the Judiciary]), Cong. Rec. Vol. 139 (1993): May 11; 1308 passed the house, Oct. 26, 27, S. 578 amended, passed in lieu; Nov. 3, House concurred in Senate amendment; Nov. 16, Presidential remarks, Weekly Compilation of Presidential Documents, Vol. 29 (1993).

RELIGIOUS LAND USE AND
INSTITUTIONALIZED PERSONS ACT OF 2000

After *Boerne*, some members of Congress responded immediately by introducing a bill entitled the Religious Liberty Protection Act (RLPA) in the House of Representatives as H. R. 4019 and in the Senate as S. 2148. The proposed legislation, which had bipartisan support, would have effectively reinstituted the RFRA with very broad language, much like the language used in the RFRA. Section 2(a) and 2(b) of the RLPA, as reported by the Senate Judiciary Committee's Constitution Subcommittee, provided that

> a government shall not substantially burden a person's religious exercise in a program or activity, operated by a government, that receives federal financial assistance, even if the burden results from a rule of general applicability . . . [unless the] government demonstrates that application of the burden to the person (1) is in furtherance of a compelling governmental interest; and (2) is the least restrictive means of furthering that compelling governmental interest.

Although the House of Representatives passed H. R. 4019 in 1999, the Senate failed to act on the proposed legislation. However, Congress soon followed with a statute that, as its title indicates, was somewhat more limited in scope than the RFRA. The Religious Land Use and Institutionalized Persons Act (RLUIPA) of 2000 reinstituted the "compelling interest-least restrictive means" test in four areas, which, when combined, give the statute great latitude over a wide range of subject matter. The legislation (S. 2869) was introduced by Senator Orrin G. Hatch (R-UT) and Edward M. Kennedy (D-MA) in the Senate on July 13, 2000, and was passed by the Senate two weeks later on July 27, 2000, with little discussion. Congressman Charles T. Canady (R-FL) introduced S. 2869 the same day, and it passed by voice vote.[1] The concerns that caused the legislation to undertake a more limited scope than the RFRA included a fear that a broad-based law would unintentionally restrict the ability of states and localities to protect the health and safety of children and would also hamper enforcement of civil rights laws, including those that prohibit discrimination based upon sexual orientation.[2]

When governments create a substantial burden on a religious practice in these areas, RLUIPA requires them to establish that the burden promotes a compelling public interest and is the least restrictive means of achieving that compelling interest. The four situations are those in which (1) the action imposes a substantial burden in a program that receives federal funds; (2) a substantial burden would affect commerce with foreign nations, among the states, or with Indian tribes; (3) the action imposes a substantial burden in the implementation of a land use regulation such as zoning laws; and (4) the action imposes a substantial burden on the religious exercise of persons residing in or confined to certain public institutions such as government hospitals and prisons. RLUIPA also provides that no government can impose a substantial burden on the religious exercise of a person residing in or confined to such institutions as public hospitals and prisons, even if the burden results from a rule of general applicability, unless the action can satisfy the strict scrutiny standard.

Religious Land Use and Institutionalized Persons Act (RLUIPA) of 2000[3]

Section 2. Protection of Land Use as Religious Exercise.
(a) Substantial Burdens.—

(1) General rules.—No government shall impose or implement a land use regulation in a manner that imposes a substantial burden on the religious exercise of a person, including a religious assembly or institution, unless the government demonstrates that imposition of the burden on that person, assembly, or institution—

(A) is in furtherance of a compelling governmental interest; and

(B) is the least restrictive means of furthering that compelling governmental interest.

(2) Scope of application.—This subsection applies in any case in which—

(A) the substantial burden is imposed in a program or activity that receives Federal financial assistance, even if the burden results from a rule of general applicability;

(B) the substantial burden affects, or removal of that substantial burden would affect, commerce with foreign nations, among the several States, or with Indian tribes, even if the burden results from a rule of general applicability; or

(C) the substantial burden is imposed in the implementation of a land use regulation or system of land use regulations, under which a government makes, or has in place formal or informal procedures or practices that permit the government to make, individualized assessments of the proposed uses for the property involved.

(b) Discrimination and Exclusion.—

(1) Equal terms.—No government shall impose or implement a land use regulation in a manner that treats a religious assembly or institution on less than equal terms with a nonreligious assembly or institution.

(2) Nondiscrimination.—No government shall impose or implement a land use regulation that discriminates against any assembly or institution on the basis of religion or religious denomination.

(3) Exclusions and limits.—No government shall impose or implement a land use regulation that—

(A) totally excludes religious assemblies from a jurisdiction; or

(B) unreasonably limits religious assemblies, institutions, or structures within a jurisdiction.

Section 3. Protection of Religious Exercise of Institutionalized Persons.

(a) General Rule.—No government shall impose a substantial burden on the religious exercise of a person residing in or confined to an institution, as defined in section 2 of the Civil Rights of Institutionalized Persons Act (42 U.S.C. 1997), even if the burden results from a rule of general applicability, unless the government demonstrates that imposition of the burden on that person—

(1) is in furtherance of a compelling governmental interest; and

(2) is the least restrictive means of furthering that compelling governmental interest.

(b) Scope of Application.—This section applies in any case in which—

(1) the substantial burden is imposed in a program or activity that receives Federal financial assistance; or

(2) the substantial burden affects, or removal of that substantial burden would affect, commerce with foreign nations, among the several States, or with Indian tribes.

Section 4. Judicial Relief.

(a) Cause of Action.—A person may assert a violation of this Act as a claim or defense in a judicial proceeding and obtain appropriate relief against a government. Standing to assert a claim or defense under this section shall be governed by the general rules of standing under Article III of the Constitution. . . .

Section 5. Rules of Construction.

(a) Religious Belief Unaffected.—Nothing in this Act shall be construed to authorize any government to burden any religious belief.

(b) Religious Exercise Not Regulated.—Nothing in this Act shall create any basis for restricting or burdening religious exercise or for claims against a religious organization including any religiously affiliated school or university, not acting under color of law.

(c) Claims to Funding Unaffected.—Nothing in this Act shall create or preclude a right of any religious organization to receive funding or other assistance from a government, or of any person to receive government funding for a religious activity, but this Act may require a government to incur expenses in its own operations to avoid imposing a substantial burden on religious exercise. . . .

Section 6. Establishment Clause Unaffected.

Nothing in this Act shall be construed to affect, interpret, or in any way address that portion of the First Amendment to the Constitution prohibiting laws respecting an establishment of religion (referred to in this section as the "Establishment Clause"). Granting government funding, benefits, or exemptions, to the extent permissible under the Establishment Clause, shall not constitute a violation of this Act. In this section, the term "granting," used with respect to government funding, benefits, or exemptions, does not include the denial of government funding, benefits, or exemptions. . . .

Section 8. Definitions.

    (5) Land use regulation.—The term "land use regulation" means a zoning or land marking law, or the application of such a law, that limits or restricts a claimant's use or development of land (including a structure affixed to land), if the claimant has an ownership, leasehold, easement, servitude, or other property interest in the regulated land or a contract or option to acquire such an interest.

    (6) Program or activity.—The term "program or activity" means all of the operations of any entity as described in paragraph (1) or (2) of section 606 of the Civil Rights Act of 1964 (42 U.S.C. 2000d-4a).

    (7) Religious exercise.—

(A) In general.—The term "religious exercise" includes any exercise of religion, whether or not compelled by, or central to, a system of religious belief.

(B) Rules the use, building, or conversion of real property for the purpose of religious exercise will be considered to be religious exercise of the person or entity that uses or intends to use the property for that purpose.

Approved September 22, 2000.

NOTES

1. See 146 Cong. Rec. S. 7774, and 146 Cong. Rec. H. 7190.
2. See 146 Cong. Rec. S. 7774–7781, July 27, 2000.
3. Legislative History—S. 2869. Cong. Rec., Vol. 146 (2000): July 27, considered and passed Senate and House.

THE ESTABLISHMENT CLAUSE

An early, if not the first, federal enactment concerning religion was Article 3 of the Northwest Ordinance of 1787, passed on July 13, 1787, by Congress, which was then serving under the Articles of Confederation (1781–1789). The Article—which concerned the area lying west of Pennsylvania, north of the Ohio River, east of the Mississippi River, and south of the Great Lakes—provided that

> religion, morality, and knowledge, being necessary to good govern-
> ment and the happiness of mankind, schools and the means of ed-
> ucation shall forever be encouraged. The utmost good faith shall
> always be observed towards the Indians; their lands and property
> shall never be taken from them without their consent; and, in their
> property, rights, and liberty, they shall never be invaded or dis-
> turbed, unless in just and lawful wars authorized by Congress; but
> laws founded in justice and humanity, shall from time to time be
> made for preventing wrongs being done to them, and for preserving
> peace and friendship with them.[1]

Although most of the Establishment Clause cases have involved public aid to sectarian schools by state governments, Congress was actively engaged in distributing public revenue to religious mission-aries for schools for Indian children throughout the nineteenth century. It has become ever more involved in aid to education—including aid to private and sectarian schools—during the past several years. For example, between 1820 and 1896, direct financial aid by Congress to nonpublic schools—most of which were Christian schools for Native Americans—grew from $12,000 to

$1,235,000. Between 1970 and 1995, direct aid to education increased from $4.6 million to $55.8 million—a rise of more than 1,100 percent.[2] In 1803, the governor of the Indiana Territory, William Henry Harrison—later the ninth president of the United States—concluded a treaty with the Kaskaskia Indians that included a provision for the federal government to contribute to the construction of a church and the annual salary of a Catholic priest.[3]

NOTES

1. See "Documents Illustrative of the Formation of the Union of the American States," U.S. Government Printing Office, 1927. House Document No. 398. Selected, Arranged and Indexed by Charles C. Tansill.

2. The 1820 funding of Native American schools is discussed in Fredric Mitchell, "Church-State Conflict," *Journal of American Indian Education* 2, no. 3 (October 1962) (http://jaie.asu.edu/v2/V2S3stat.htm) [accessed February 22, 2001]. The 1896 figure is discussed in *Reuben Quick Bear v. Leupp*, 210 U.S. 50, 79. Current educational financing by the federal government is found at *Digest of Education Statistics, 1999*, Department of Education, Washington, D.C. (http://nces.ed.gov/pubs2000/digest99/d99t034.html) [accessed February 28, 2001].

3. Mitchell, "Church-State Conflict."

THE ESTABLISHMENT CLAUSE

THE INDIAN APPROPRIATIONS ACTS OF
1895 AND 1896

The relationship between Congress and the Establishment Clause became an issue of some importance toward the end of the nineteenth century. President Ulysses S. Grant proposed an amendment in 1875 that would finance a system of free public education while prohibiting public funds to sectarian schools.[1] In the same year, Senator James G. Blaine (R-ME)—a former Speaker of the U.S. House of Representatives, a former secretary of state, and the 1884 Republican candidate for president—introduced an amendment in the House of Representatives that provided that "no State shall make any law respecting an establishment of religion or prohibiting the free exercise thereof; and no money raised by taxation in any State, for the support of public schools, or derived from any public fund therefor, nor any public lands devoted thereto, shall ever be under the control of any religious sect, nor shall any money so raised, or lands so devoted be divided between religious sects or denominations." The amendment earned the necessary two-thirds vote in the House (180 to 70), but failed in the Senate by a vote of 28 to 16.[2]

Although the Blaine proposal was unsuccessful, Congress inserted, for the first time, a provision in the Indian Appropriations Act of 1895 that required a gradual elimination of appropriations of public money for sectarian education. Each year after 1895, Congress was to provide less financial aid to sectarian schools, until such aid ceased completely. The 1895 enactment required the Department of the Interior to contract with the missionary schools for Indians "to an extent not exceeding 80 percent of the amount so used in the fiscal year 1895, and the Government shall as early as practicable make provision for the education of the Indians in Government Schools."[3] The provision contained two significant features. It embodied a congressional assumption that the public was responsible for basic education, and although it did not suggest that education was an exclusively public enterprise, it did represent a policy statement that sectarian schools should not receive public financial aid.

The 1896 Indian Appropriations Act contained another equally important provision, which related to the new congressional policy of governmental support for sectarian education. This provision stipulated that "it is hereby declared to be the settled policy of the Government to hereafter make no appropriation whatever to education in any sectarian school." Thus, while Congress sought to end all programs of financial aid to missionary schools for Native Americans, it did undertake simultaneously a public responsibility for providing secular education to Native American children. An 1897 statute that declared the settled policy of the government to be opposed to making any appropriations whatever solidified this policy of separating government from sectarian schools out of the Treasury of the United States.[4] The 1897 act was replaced by a statute in 1968 that provided that

> funds appropriated on and after March 30, 1968, to the Secretary of the Interior for the education of Indian children shall not be used for the education of such children in elementary and secondary education programs in sectarian schools. This prohibition shall not apply to the education of Indians in accredited institutions of higher education and in other accredited schools offering vocational and technical training, but no scholarship aid provided for an Indian student shall require him to attend an institution or school that is not of his own free choice, and such aid shall be, to the extent consistent with sound administration, extended to the student individually rather than to the institution or school.[5]

Nevertheless, the dual policy of the government assuming the responsibility for the public's education while doing it exclusively through public schools has not been an easy task. Part of the reason is the fact that many children attend private and sectarian schools, and in the minds of many they require and deserve financial assistance from the public along with their public school counterparts.[6] As we will see, Congress has resumed the policy of providing some financial assistance to sectarian schools.

The Indian Appropriations Act of 1895

Support of Schools:

For the support of Indian day and industrial schools and for other purposes . . . $1,164,350 . . . Provided, that the Secretary of the Interior shall
make contracts, but only with the present contract schools, for the education of Indian pupils during the fiscal year ending June 30, 1896, to an
extent not exceeding 80% of the amount so used in the fiscal year 1895,
and the Government shall, as early as practicable, make provision for the
education of Indians in Government schools.

The Indian Appropriations Act of 1896

Support of Schools:

For support of Indian day and industrial schools and for other educational
purposes, . . . $1,235,000, . . .

And it is hereby declared to be the settled policy of the Government to
hereafter make no appropriation whatever for education in any sectarian
school. Provided, that the Secretary of the Interior may make contracts
with contract schools and apportioning, as near as may be, the amount
so contracted for among schools of various denominations for the education of Indian pupils during the fiscal year 1897, but shall only make
such contracts at places where non-sectarian schools cannot be provided
for such Indian children, and to an amount not exceeding 50% of the
amount so used for the fiscal year 1895.

NOTES

1. See John R. Vile, *Encyclopedia of Constitutional Amendments, Proposed Amendments, and Amending Issues, 1789–1995* (Santa Barbara, CA: ABC-CLIO, 1996),
pp. 35–36.

2. See Cong. Rec. 44th Cong., 1st Sess., December 14, 1875. Although the Blaine
amendment was unsuccessful, as many as thirty-eight states have—some before and
some afterward—included similar provisions in their constitutions. Ironically, just
as President George W. Bush is planning to increase the flow of public money to
faith-based organizations on the federal level, an 1885 constitutional provision that
Florida patterned after Blaine's amendment is frustrating a school voucher plan
pursued by his brother, Florida Governor Jeb Bush. See Jo Becker, "Voucher Debate Entwined with a Century-Old Fight," *St. Petersburg Times*, July 6, 1999.

3. See *Reuben Quick Bear v. Leupp*, 1908, p. 78 (1908).

4. See Act of June 7, 1897, ch. 3, § 1, 30 Stat. 79.

5. See Pub. L. 90–280, Sec. 2, Mar. 30, 1968, 82 Stat. 71.

6. Although 25 percent of all schools in the United States are private, 15 percent are nonsectarian. Thus one in ten U.S. students attends a sectarian school. See http://www.capenet.org/facts.html [accessed March 4, 2001].

ELEMENTARY AND SECONDARY
EDUCATION ACT OF 1965, TITLE I

Up until the middle of the twentieth century, courts were prone to invalidate practically all governmental efforts to provide public money to sectarian schools. Courts utilized a standard that was summarized by Associate Justice Hugo Black in *Everson v. Board of Education of Ewing* (1947), who stated the following:

> The "establishment of religion" clause of the First Amendment means at least this: Neither a state nor the Federal Government can set up a church. Neither can pass laws which aid one religion, aid all religions, or prefer one religion over another. Neither can force nor influence a person to go to or to remain away from church against his will or force him to profess a belief or disbelief in any religion. No person can be punished for entertaining or professing religious beliefs or disbeliefs, for church attendance or non-attendance. No tax in any amount, large or small, can be levied to support any religious activities or institutions, whatever they may be called, or whatever form they may adopt to teach or practice religion. Neither a state nor the Federal Government can, openly or secretly, participate in the affairs of any religious organizations or groups and *vice versa*. In the words of Jefferson, the clause against establishment of religion by law was intended to erect "a wall of separation between church and State." (pp. 16–17)

Be that as it may, beginning with *Everson*, as far as both the Supreme Court and Congress were concerned, the relationship between Congress and the First Amendment began to change in favor of governmental assistance to sectarian education and other religious organizations and activities.

The *Everson* decision validated a program that provided financial reimbursement to parents for the costs of bussing their children to religious as well as to public schools. Since this time, various financial programs, including direct financial aid to religious schools, have become an appropriate and permissible method of educational assistance to many members of Congress. In a matter of years, the Supreme Court had developed a three-pronged standard by which governmental enactments would be judged against the Establishment Clause. The standard, commonly referred to as the Lemon test, comes from the case that played a major role in its development—*Lemon v. Kurtzman* (1971). The Lemon test required that a statute in question must (1) have a secular (nonreligious) purpose, (2) have a primary effect that neither advances nor inhibits religion, and (3) not create excessive governmental entanglement with religion. As long as a public assistance program could satisfy the Lemon test, it could pass constitutional scrutiny.

After *Lemon*, the relationship between Congress and sectarian education began to change in earnest, starting with the 89th Congress, which enacted Title I of the Elementary and Secondary Education (ESEA) Act of 1965 as part of President Lyndon Johnson's War on Poverty.[1] ESEA quickly became the largest source of federal financial support for K–12 education, sending billions of dollars into poor communities for more than thirty years. The purpose of ESEA was to "provide full educational opportunity to every child regardless of economic background."[2] To achieve that goal, Title I provided federal funds to "local educational agencies" (LEAs), which spent the funds for remedial education, guidance counseling, and job counseling to students who resided within the attendance boundaries of public schools in low-income areas and who were failing, or were at risk of failing, their state's student performance standards. Title I funds had to be made available to all eligible children, regardless of whether they attended public or private (religious) schools, and the services provided to children attending private (and implicitly sectarian) schools were required to be "equitable in comparison to services and other benefits for public school children." Title I funds were not distributed directly to sectarian schools. Rather, the funds were distributed either to students or to the parents of students who attended sectarian schools, who could then in turn defray some of the costs of attending sectarian schools. Title I funds also went to sectarian schools as "in kind" contributions to educational costs.

A group of citizens sued in a New York federal district court, contesting the validity of Title I (as amended in 1994) under the Establishment Clause. Approximately 9 percent of the Title I funds administered in New York City directly benefited students in sectarian schools. Claiming that the statute and the board's program violated the Establishment Clause, six federal taxpayers sued when the city school board began furnishing Title I services to sectarian students on their school premises rather than at a neutral site, as had been the practice in the past. In *Aguilar v. Felton* (1985) the Supreme Court disapproved of the city's new program of providing on-site services at sectarian schools because it violated the First Amendment by requiring an excessive entanglement of church and state. However, the court reversed itself when it reopened the same case a decade later under an unusual legal procedure. The second case, *Agostini v. Felton* (1997), upheld the statute and the city's administrative implementation plan, and in doing so revised the Lemon test. The *Agostini* decision did not actually discard any of the Lemon test's three-pronged "purpose, effect, and excessive entanglement" criteria. Rather, it moved the elements around by making the "entanglement" inquiry part of the "effect on religion" test, so that now the "no effect on religion" test included the requirement that a program (1) must not result in governmental indoctrination, (2) must not define its recipients by reference to religion, and (3) must not create excessive entanglement between government and religion (*Agostini v. Felton*, 1997, p. 235).

Title I of the Elementary and Secondary Education (ESEA) Act of 1965 as Amended[3]

Section 6301. Declaration of policy and statement of purpose.
(a) Statement of policy.
   (1) In general U.S.C. The Congress declares it to be the policy of the United States U.S.C. that a high-quality education for all individuals and a fair and U.S.C. equal opportunity to obtain that education are a societal good, U.S.C. are a moral imperative, and improve the life of every individual, U.S.C. because the quality of our individual lives ultimately depends on U.S.C. the quality of the lives of others. . . .
Section 6321. Participation of children enrolled in private schools.
(a) General requirement.
   (1) In general. To the extent consistent with the number of eligible children identified under section 1115(b) [20 U.S.C. § 6315(b)] in a local educational agency who are enrolled in private elementary and secondary schools, a local educational agency shall, after timely and meaningful consultation with appropriate private school officials, provide such children, on an equitable basis, special educational services or other benefits under this part [20 U.S.C. § 6311 et seq.] (such as

dual enrollment, educational radio and television, computer equipment and materials, other technology, and mobile educational services and equipment).

(2) Secular, neutral, nonideological. Such educational services or other benefits, including materials and equipment, shall be secular, neutral, and nonideological.

(3) Equity. Educational services and other benefits for such private school children shall be equitable in comparison to services and other benefits for public school children participating under this part [20 U.S.C. § 6311 et seq.].

(4) Expenditures. Expenditures for educational services and other benefits to eligible private school children shall be equal to the proportion of funds allocated to participating school attendance areas based on the number of children from low-income families who attend private schools.

(5) Provision of services. The local educational agency may provide such services directly or through contracts with public and private agencies, organizations, and institutions. . . .

(c) Public control of funds.

(1) In general. The control of funds provided under this part [20 U.S.C. § 6311 et seq.], and title to materials, equipment, and property purchased with such funds, shall be in a public agency, and a public agency shall administer such funds and property.

Approved April 11, 1965, and October 20, 1994, respectively.

NOTES

1. Although Title I was reenacted, in varying forms, over the years, most recently in the Improving America's Schools Act of 1994, it was permitted to expire in 2000. The Student Results Act of 1999 (H. R. 2), which would have continued many of Title I's programs, passed the House of Representatives on October 21, 1999, by a comfortable margin of 358 to 67. The companion bill in the Senate, the Educational Opportunities Act (S. 2), was never brought to a vote. Nonetheless, the 1965 ESEA established a landmark not only in the relationship between government and education but also between the government and religion.

2. See S. Rep. No. 146, 89th Cong., 1st Sess. 5 (1965).

3. An important statutory enactment that grew out of ESEA is Chapter 2 of the Education Consolidation and Improvement Act of 1981, 95 Stat. 469, Pub. L. 97–35, as amended, 20 U.S.C. §§ 7301–7373, which provided federal funds through state educational agencies to local public and private educational agencies, which in turn lend educational materials such as computer and library materials to public and private (including sectarian) elementary and secondary schools. The Chapter 2 program was upheld by the Supreme Court in *Mitchell v. Helms* (2000).

THE PERSONAL RESPONSIBILITY AND WORK OPPORTUNITY RECONCILIATION ACT OF 1996

As shown in the previous section, governmental assistance to religious organizations has traditionally taken the form of direct financial aid to sectarian students or their parents, who have a free choice to use it, or by providing "in kind" aid sectarian schools, such as furnishing products or services rather than money.[1] Section 104 of Title I of the Personal Responsibility and Work Opportunity Reconciliation Act (PRWORA) of 1996 is notable in that it moves the government's relationship with religious organizations a step further by expressly requiring states to contract directly with private organizations, including charitable and religious organizations, whenever the states are disbursing federal funds under any of the programs covered by the Welfare Reform Act of 1996.[2]

The Welfare Reform Act of 1996 was a comprehensive redefinition of a wide range of programs designed to assist low-income families. The 1996 reform act eliminated the Aid to Families with Dependent Children (AFDC) program and replaced it with one called Temporary Assistance to Needy Families (TANF). TANF also replaced the Job Opportunities and Basic Skills training (JOBS) program. TANF provided federal funds and work opportunities to low-income families by granting states the funds and the flexibility under certain guidelines to develop and implement their own distribution programs, subject to certain guidelines and restrictions, such as those contained in Section 104.

One of the restrictions in Section 104 established what has come to be called "charitable choice," by specifically extending religious organizations the right to participate in many governmental programs to religious organizations.[3] Under the act, religious organizations have the right to accept certificates, vouchers, or other forms of disbursement on the same basis as all other nongovernmental organizations that participate in a TANF-financed program. The law specifically prohibits discrimination against any religious organization, and it contains other safeguards, such as the right of religious organizations to maintain their internal form of governance without interference, as well as preserving the right to retain religious art, icons, scripture, or other religious symbols while participating in the programs.[4]

The Personal Responsibility and Work Opportunity Reconciliation Act of 1996

Section 104. 42 U.S.C. 604a. Services Provided by Charitable, Religious, or Private Organizations.

(a) In General.—

    (1) State options.—A State may—

(A) administer and provide services under the programs described in subparagraphs (A) and (B)(i) of paragraph (2) through contracts with charitable, religious, or private organizations; and

(B) provide beneficiaries of assistance under the programs described in subparagraphs (A) and (B)(ii) of paragraph (2) with certificates, vouchers, or other forms of disbursement which are redeemable with such organizations. [Page 110 STAT. 2162]

    (2) Programs described.—The programs described in this paragraph are the following programs:

(A) A State program funded under part A of title IV of the Social Security Act (as amended by section 103(a) of this Act).

(B) Any other program established or modified under title I or II of this Act, that—

    (i) permits contracts with organizations; or

    (ii) permits certificates, vouchers, or other forms of disbursement to be provided to beneficiaries, as a means of providing assistance.

(b) Religious Organizations—The purpose of this section is to allow States to contract with religious organizations, or to allow religious organizations to accept certificates, vouchers, or other forms of disbursement under any program described in subsection (a)(2), on the same basis as any other nongovernmental provider without impairing the religious character of such organizations, and without diminishing the religious freedom of beneficiaries of assistance funded under such program.

(c) Nondiscrimination Against Religious Organizations.—In the event a State exercises its authority under subsection (a), religious organizations are eligible, on the same basis as any other private organization, as contractors to provide assistance, or to accept certificates, vouchers, or other forms of disbursement, under any program described in subsection (a)(2) so long as the programs are implemented consistent with the Establishment Clause of the United States Constitution. Except as provided in subsection (k), neither the Federal Government nor a State receiving funds under such programs shall discriminate against an organization which is or applies to be a contractor to provide assistance, or which accepts certificates, vouchers, or other forms of disbursement, on the basis that the organization has a religious character.

(d) Religious Character and Freedom.—

(1) Religious organizations.—A religious organization with a contract described in subsection (a)(1)(A), or which accepts certificates, vouchers, or other forms of disbursement under subsection (a)(1)(B), shall retain its independence from Federal, State, and local governments, including such organization's control over the definition, development, practice, and expression of its religious beliefs.

(2) Additional safeguards.—Neither the Federal Government nor a State shall require a religious organization to—

(A) alter its form of internal governance; or

(B) remove religious art, icons, scripture, or other symbols; in order to be eligible to contract to provide assistance, or to accept certificates, vouchers, or other forms of disbursement, funded under a program described in subsection (a)(2).

(e) Rights of Beneficiaries of Assistance.—

(1) In general.—If an individual described in paragraph (2) has an objection to the religious character of the organization or institution from which the individual receives, or would receive, assistance funded under any program described in subsection (a)(2), the State in which the individual resides shall provide such individual (if otherwise eligible for such assistance) within a reasonable period of time after the date of such objection with assistance from an alternative provider [Page 110 STAT. 2163] that is accessible to the individual and the value of which is not less than the value of the assistance which the individual would have received from such organization.

(2) Individual described.—An individual described in this paragraph is an individual who receives, applies for, or requests to apply for, assistance under a program described in subsection (a)(2).

(f) Employment Practices.—A religious organization's exemption provided under section 702 of the Civil Rights Act of 1964 (42 U.S.C. 2000e-1a) regarding employment practices shall not be affected by its participation in, or receipt of funds from, programs described in subsection (a)(2).

(g) Nondiscrimination Against Beneficiaries.—Except as otherwise provided in law, a religious organization shall not discriminate against an individual in regard to rendering assistance funded under any program described in subsection (a)(2) on the basis of religion, a religious belief, or refusal to actively participate in a religious practice.

(h) Fiscal Accountability.—

(1) In general.—Except as provided in paragraph (2), any religious organization contracting to provide assistance funded under any program described in subsection (a)(2) shall be subject to the same regulations as other contractors to account in accord with generally accepted auditing principles for the use of such funds provided under such programs.

(2) Limited audit.—If such organization segregates Federal funds provided under such programs into separate accounts, then only the financial assistance provided with such funds shall be subject to audit.

(i) Compliance.—Any party which seeks to enforce its rights under this section may assert a civil action for injunctive relief exclusively in an appropriate State court against the entity or agency that allegedly commits such violation.

(j) Limitations on Use of Funds for Certain Purposes.—No funds provided directly to institutions or organizations to provide services and administer programs under subsection (a)(1)(A) shall be expended for sectarian worship, instruction, or proselytization.

(k) Preemption.—Nothing in this section shall be construed to preempt any provision of a State constitution or State statute that prohibits or restricts the expenditure of State funds in or by religious organizations.

Approved August 22, 1996.

NOTES

1. Other examples of financial aid to recipients who have the choice of how to use the assistance, including using it with sectarian organizations, are the Federal Pell Grant program, 20 U.S.C. § 107a *et. seq.*, the GI Bill, 68 U.S.C. §§ 3201–3243, and the Child Care and Development Block Grant Act of 1990, 42 U.S.C. §§ 9858–9858q, which permits parents to use financial certificates for child care at sectarian child centers.

2. Congress has actually enacted legislation in the past that directly affects religious organizations, although in a different context. For example, Section 702 of Title VII of the Civil Rights Act of 1964 as amended exempts religious organizations from the prohibition of employment discrimination based on religion, to which other organizations are subject, along with race, sex, color, and national origin.

3. "Charitable choice" has become the name for statutory provisions that allow faith-based organizations to receive federal funding. The term came into vogue when Senator John Ashcroft (R-MO), now attorney general of the United States,

introduced various pieces of legislation—beginning with Section 104 in 1996—that contained such provisions. An example of other enactments that include a charitable choice provision is the 1998 amendment to the Community Services Block Grant Act, which requires states that participate in the Community Services Block Grant program to furnish "an assurance that the State and eligible entities in the State will, to the maximum extent possible, coordinate programs with and form partnerships with other organizations serving low-income residents of the communities and members of the groups served by the State, including religious organizations, charitable groups, and community organizations." On January 29, 2001, President George W. Bush issued two Executive Orders that established a White House Office of Faith-Based and Community Initiatives "to establish policies, priorities, and objectives for the Federal Government's comprehensive effort to enlist, enable, equip, empower, and expand the work of faith-based and other community organizations," and five Executive Department Centers for Faith-Based and Community Initiatives within the Departments of Health and Human Services, Housing and Urban Development, Justice, Education, and Labor "to eliminate regulatory, contracting, and other programmatic obstacles to the participation of faith-based and other community organizations in the provision of social services."

4. An earlier enactment had provided much the same thing as Section 104 on a smaller scale. The Adolescent Family Life Act of 1981 authorized direct financial grants to public or nonprofit private organizations for services and research in the area of premarital adolescent sexual relations and pregnancy. It required that the counseling and educational services should promote the involvement of religious organizations (along with other charitable and voluntary organizations). Moreover, grant applicants were required to describe how they would involve such nongovernmental organizations. The Adolescent Family Life Act was upheld against an Establishment Clause attack in *Bowen v. Kendrick* (1988).

BOTH CLAUSES SIMULTANEOUSLY

THE AMERICAN INDIAN RELIGIOUS
FREEDOM ACT OF 1978 AS AMENDED
IN 1994

Although we have examined various landmark statutes and some associated judicial decisions regarding the Free Exercise Clause and the Establishment Clause as two rather distinct provisions, it is well to bear in mind that they are also opposite sides of the same coin, and as such can create very interesting situations. While the Free Exercise Clause is usually drawn into play when Congress enacts a law that restricts a religious practice, and the Establishment Clause is drawn into play when Congress enacts a law that promotes a religious practice, a law can also seek to protect a religious practice that is otherwise being restricted while becoming entangled with the Establishment Clause. The American Indian Religious Freedom Act (AIRFA) of 1978 and its 1994 amendment, which exempted members of the Native American Church from being prosecuted under the Drug Abuse Control Act for using peyote, is a good example of the symbiotic relationship of the two sides.

The relationship of freedom of religion and the use of peyote by members of the Native American Church has a long and colorful history. Peyote is a spineless, dome-shaped cactus *(Lophophora williamsii)* native to Mexico and the southwest United States, having buttonlike tubercles that are chewed fresh or dry as a hallucinogenic drug by certain Native American peoples. Its use is one of the oldest religious traditions in the Western Hemisphere. Members of fifty Native American tribes use peyote as a sacrament in religious ceremonies, believing that it is a medicine, a protector, and a teacher that gives one an awareness of God.[1]

In 1965 Congress enacted the Drug Abuse Control Act Amendments, which prohibited the use of many then-popular psychedelic drugs (now called Schedule I drugs). Schedule I drugs generate hallucinations, distortions of perception, altered states of awareness, and conditions that resemble a psychosis.[2] Although Congress included peyote in the list of Schedule I drugs, there was concern that the prohibition should not include the ceremonial use of peyote by members of the Native American Church.[3] The Native American Church did not become an officially incorporated organization until 1918 (in Oklahoma), but it is one of the oldest religious traditions in North America. The church restricts membership to persons whose ethnic descent is at least 25 percent American Indian, and to the spouses of such persons. Claiming membership among fifty Native American tribes in North America, the Native American Church has used peyote since time immemorial. After the passage of the 1965 drug law amendment, the Drug Enforcement Administration included peyote in its Schedule I classification but issued a regulation that gave an exemption to members of the Native American Church. The federal regulation provided that the "listing of peyote as a controlled substance [under federal law] does not apply to the non-drug use of peyote in bona fide religious ceremonies of the Native American Church."[4]

Notwithstanding the position of Congress and the Drug Enforcement Administration, many state jurisdictions also considered peyote to be a Schedule I drug but did not provide a similar exemption for its use in the Native American Church. Then along came the Supreme Court's peyote decision in *Employment Division (Oregon) v. Smith* (1990) that held that "the government's ability to enforce generally applicable prohibitions of socially harmful conduct, like its ability to carry out other aspects of public policy, 'cannot depend on measuring the effects of a governmental action on a religious objector's spiritual development' " (p. 885). Congress responded to the *Smith* decision in 1994 by amending AIRFA.[5] The amendment provided a specific exemption from criminal prosecution for any member of the Native American Church who used peyote for religious purposes.

Thus, with the Supreme Court holding that a law of general application that criminalizes peyote is permissible under the Free Exercise Clause, and Congress declaring it an exemption when used by members of the Native American Church, the stage is set for a potential catch-22 situation. If the Free Exercise Clause, on the one hand, does not protect the use of peyote by anyone, then a statute that exempts its use by a religious group from criminal prosecution might appear, on the other, to violate the Establishment Clause. This predicament has presented itself in at least one case that has gone before a U.S. appellate court.

The case is *Peyote Way Church of God v. Thornburgh*, 922 F.2d 1210 (5th Cir. 1991). The Peyote Way Church of God was incorporated in 1979 in Arizona. The church, which has religious tenets much like those of the Native American Church, was founded by former members of the Native American Church who disagreed with the Native American Church's ancestry restrictions, preferring instead to accept anyone as a member who otherwise qualified, with similar beliefs. At the time they began the lawsuit, the Peyote Way Church of God had approximately 150 members, of whom 50 were active. Peyote Way Church members in Texas sought to prevent a prosecution under the Controlled Substance Act, 21 U.S.C. § 841, on the grounds that such prosecution would interfere with their rights under the Free Exercise Clause. They also asked for a judicial determination that the exemption granted only to the Native American Church was unfair to them and therefore a violation of the Establishment Clause by promoting one religious group over another. Regarding the Peyote Way Church of God's first claim, the Fifth Circuit Court of Appeals, quoting the *Smith* decision, held that the state did not violate the Free Exercise Clause "because it is 'a generally applicable [criminal prosecution] of socially harmful conduct,' and does not have as its purpose the proscription of religious conduct" (922 F.2d 1210, 1213).

Regarding the Peyote Church of God's Establishment Clause claim, the court was a bit evasive. It recognized that "the establishment clause exists to ensure governmental neutrality toward religion," and that "the [Native American Church] exemption facially singles out one religion," while holding that "the federal NAC [Native American Church] exemption represents the government's protection of the culture of quasi-sovereign Native American tribes and as such, does not represent an establishment of religion in contravention of the First Amendment" (922 F.2d 1210, 1217). Although the Supreme Court has not addressed the dual issues presented by peyote, several lower federal courts have reached conclusions different from *Peyote Way Church of God v. Thornburgh*.[6]

The American Indian Religious Freedom Act of 1978[7]

Whereas the freedom of religion for all people is an inherent right, fundamental to the democratic structure of the United States and is guaranteed by the First Amendment of the United States Constitution;

Whereas the United States has traditionally rejected the concept of a government denying individuals the right to practice their religion and, as a result, has benefited from a rich variety of religious heritages in this country;

Whereas the religious practices of the American Indian (as well as Native Alaskan and Hawaiian) are an integral part of their cultures, tradition and heritage, such practices forming the basis of Indian identity and value systems;

Whereas the traditional American Indian religions, as an integral part of Indian life, are indispensable and irreplaceable;

Whereas the lack of a clear, comprehensive, and consistent Federal policy has often resulted in the abridgment of religious freedom for traditional American Indians;

Whereas such religious infringements result from the lack of knowledge or the insensitive and inflexible enforcement of Federal policies and regulations premised on a variety of laws;

Whereas such laws were designed for such worthwhile purposes as conservation and preservation of natural species and resources but were never intended to relate to Indian religious practices and, therefore, were passed without consideration of their effect on traditional American Indian religions;

Whereas such laws and policies often deny American Indians access to sacred sites required in their religions, including cemeteries;

Whereas such laws at times prohibit the use and possession of sacred objects necessary to the exercise of religious rites and ceremonies;

Whereas traditional American Indian ceremonies have been intruded upon, interfered with, and in a few instances banned: Now, therefore, be it

Resolved by the Senate and House of Representatives of the United States of America in Congress assembled. That henceforth it shall be the policy of the United States to protect and preserve for American Indians their inherent right of freedom to believe, express, and exercise the traditional religions of the American Indian, Eskimo, Aleut, and Native Hawaiians, including but not limited to access to sites, use and possession of sacred objects, and the freedom to worship through ceremonial and traditional rites.

Approved August 11, 1978.

The American Indian Religious Freedom Act Amendment of 1994[8]

Be it enacted by the Senate and House of Representatives of the United States of America in Congress assembled,

SECTION 2. TRADITIONAL INDIAN RELIGIOUS USE OF THE PEYOTE SACRAMENT.

The Act of August 11, 1978 (42 U.S.C. 1996), commonly referred to as the "American Indian Religious Freedom Act," is amended by adding at the end thereof the following new section:

SECTION 3.

The Congress finds and declares that for many Indian people, the traditional ceremonial use of the peyote cactus as a religious sacrament has for centuries been integral to a way of life, and significant in perpetuating Indian tribes and cultures; since 1965, this ceremonial use of peyote by Indians has been protected by Federal regulation; while at least 28 States have enacted laws which are similar to, or are in conformance with, the Federal regulation which protects the ceremonial use of peyote by Indian religious practitioners, 22 States have not done so, and this lack of uniformity has created hardship for Indian people who participate in such religious ceremonies; the Supreme Court of the United States, in the case of Employment Division v. Smith, 494 U.S. 872 (1990), held that the First Amendment does not protect Indian practitioners who use peyote in Indian religious ceremonies, and also raised uncertainty whether this religious practice would be protected under the compelling State interest standard; and the lack of adequate and clear legal protection for the religious use of peyote by Indians may serve to stigmatize and marginalize Indian tribes and cultures, and increase the risk that they will be exposed to discriminatory treatment. Notwithstanding any other provision of law, the use, possession, or transportation of peyote by an Indian for bona fide traditional ceremonial purposes in connection with the practice of a traditional Indian religion is lawful, and shall not be prohibited by the United States or any State. No Indian shall be penalized or discriminated against on the basis of such use, possession or transportation, including, but not limited to, denial of otherwise applicable benefits under public assistance programs. This section does not prohibit such reasonable regulation and registration by the Drug Enforcement Administration of those persons who cultivate, harvest, or distribute peyote as may be consistent with the purposes of this Act.

This section does not prohibit application of the provisions of section 481.111 of Vernon's Texas Health and Safety Code Annotated, in effect on the date of enactment of this section, insofar as those provisions pertain to the cultivation, harvest, and distribution of peyote.

Nothing in this section shall prohibit any Federal department or agency, in carrying out its statutory responsibilities and functions, from promulgating regulations establishing reasonable limitations on the use or ingestion of peyote prior to or during the performance of duties by sworn law enforcement officers or personnel directly involved in public transportation or any other safety-sensitive positions where the performance of such duties may be adversely affected by such use or ingestion. Such regulations shall be adopted only after consultation with representatives of traditional Indian religions for which the sacramental use of peyote is integral to their practice. Any regulation promulgated pursuant to this section shall be subject to the balancing test set forth in section 3 of the Religious Freedom Restoration Act (Public Law 103–141; 42 U.S.C. 2000bb-1).

This section shall not be construed as requiring prison authorities to permit, nor shall it be construed to prohibit prison authorities from permitting, access to peyote by Indians while incarcerated within Federal or State prison facilities.

Subject to the provisions of the Religious Freedom Restoration Act (Public Law 103–141; 42 U.S.C. 2000bb-1), this section shall not be construed to prohibit States from enacting or enforcing reasonable traffic safety laws or regulations.

Subject to the provisions of the Religious Freedom Restoration Act (Public Law 103–141; 42 U.S.C. 2000bb-1), this section does not prohibit the Secretary of Defense from promulgating regulations establishing reasonable limitations on the use, possession, transportation, or distribution of peyote to promote military readiness, safety, or compliance with international law or laws of other countries. Such regulations shall be adopted only after consultation with representatives of traditional Indian religions for which the sacramental use of peyote is integral to their practice.

For purposes of this section—

the term "Indian" means a member of an Indian tribe;

the term "Indian tribe" means any tribe, band, nation, pueblo, or other organized group or community of Indians, including any Alaska Native village (as defined in, or established pursuant to, the Alaska Native Claims Settlement Act (43 U.S.C. 1601 et seq.)), which is recognized as eligible for the special programs and services provide by the United States to Indians because of their status as Indians;

the term "Indian religion" means any religion—which is practiced by Indians; and the origin and interpretation of which is from within a traditional Indian culture or community; and the term "State" means any State of the United States and any political subdivision thereof.

Nothing in this section shall be construed as abrogating, diminishing, or otherwise affecting—the inherent rights of any Indian tribe; the rights, express or implicit, of any Indian tribe which exist under treaties, Executive orders, and laws of the United States; the inherent right of Indians to practice their religions; and the right of Indians to practice their religions under any Federal or State law.

Approved October 6, 1994.

NOTES

1. See H. R. Rep. No. 103–675, 103rd Cong., 2nd Sess. (Aug. 5, 1994).

2. Schedule I drugs are described by statute as narcotic substances that have a high potential for abuse, have no currently acceptable medical use in treatment, and lack any accepted safe use under medical supervision. For further information, see the Controlled Substances Act (CSA) of 1970, Title II of the Comprehensive Drug Abuse Prevention and Control Act of 1970, 21 U.S.C. § 812.

3. See 11 Cong. Rec. 14608, 15977 (1965), and H. R. Rep. No. 103–675, 103rd Cong., 2nd Sess. (Aug. 5. 1994).

4. 21 C.F.R. § 1307.31 (1990).

5. In 1978 Congress enacted the American Indian Religious Freedom Act (AIRFA), which was essentially a congressional policy statement regarding the government's relationship with Native Americans. After an extensive statement of congressional findings, Congress declared that "on and after August 11, 1978, it shall be the policy of the United States to protect and preserve for American Indians their inherent right of freedom to believe, express, and exercise the traditional religions of the American Indian, Eskimo, Aleut, and Native Hawaiians, including but not limited to access to sites, use and possession of sacred objects, and the freedom to worship through ceremonials and traditional rites."

6. For example, see *United States v. Boyll* (1991), which dismissed a May 10, 1990, federal grand jury indictment of Robert Lawrence Boyll, a non–Native American, for unlawfully importing peyote through the United States mail and possessing peyote with the intent to distribute it, in violation of 21 U.S.C. §§ 952(a), 960(b)(3), 843(b) & (c), & 841(a)(1) (1981) on the grounds that it violated Boyll's rights under the Free Exercise Clause; *Kennedy v. Bureau of Narcotics and Dangerous Drugs* (1972), which—without addressing First Amendment issues—refused to accept the distinction between the members of the Native American Church and the members of another church, the Church of the Awakening, which is largely composed of Native Americans but admits as members all persons who are willing to subscribe to the church's tenets.

7. Legislative History—S. J. Res. 102. H. R. Rep. No. 95–1308 (H. J. Res. 738, Comm. on Interior and Insular Affairs). S. Rep. No. 95–709 (Comm. on Indian

Affairs). Cong. Rec. Vol. 124 (1978), Apr. 3, considered and passed Senate; July 18, H. J. Res. considered and passed House; proceedings vacated and S. J. Res., amended, passed in lieu; July 27, Senate concurred in House amendment.

8. Legislative History—H. R. 4230. H. R. Rep. No. 103–675 (Comm. on Natural Resources); Cong. Rec. Vol. 140 (1994): Aug. 8, considered and passed the House; Sept. 26, considered and passed the Senate.

THE EQUAL ACCESS ACT OF 1984

The idea of Congress enacting legislation forcing local high school officials to recognize certain student groups may be a "somewhat surprising notion," as one judge recently put it, but that is precisely what Congress did when it enacted the Equal Access Act of 1984 as part of the Education for Economic Security Act.[1] The act also illustrates the uneasy relationship between the Free Exercise Clause and the Establishment Clause. The notion of an equal access requirement for all groups in a high school setting began with *Widmar v. Vincent* (1981), which invalidated a state university regulation that prohibited students from using the school's facilities for religious purposes. Congress extended the *Widmar* rationale to high schools three years later with the passage of the Equal Access Act.

Under the Equal Access Act, if a school that accepts federal funds allows some "noncurricular" student groups to exist and use school property, it cannot deny other "noncurricular" groups the same facilities and opportunities due to the religious, political, philosophical, or other content of their speech. The act, which was passed with broad support from members of Congress in both houses, was intended to address a perceived widespread discrimination against religious speech in public high schools.[2] Committee reports show that the act was also in part a reaction to two federal appellate court decisions that had recently held that student religious groups could not meet on school premises during noninstructional time without violating the Establishment Clause.[3] According to one of the act's proponents, Senator Carl Levin (D-MI), the legislation "will allow students equal access to secondary schools' student-initiated religious meetings before and after school where the school generally allows groups of secondary school students to meet during those times."[4]

The Equal Access Act was upheld by the U.S. Supreme Court against an Establishment Clause challenge in *Board of Education of the Westside Community Schools v. Mergens* (1990). The *Mergens* case began when Westside High School in Omaha, Nebraska, denied students the right to form a Christian club and use the school's facilities on the same basis as other Westside student groups. The aggrieved students sued in federal court, seeking a court order requiring the school board to comply with the Equal Access Act. Although members of the Supreme Court could not agree as to the specific reasons that the Equal Access Act did not violate the Establishment Clause, there was broad agreement that the act was constitutional because it was neutral, namely by giving equal access to both secular and religious speech.

Although Congress may have enacted the Equal Access Act "to end [religious] discrimination by allowing students to meet and discuss religion before and after classes," Congress had to use neutral, inclusive language that embraces all types of student groups, including religious and philosophical groups, that may make First Amendment claims under the act.[5] This inclusiveness has enabled other student groups to use the act as a tool in achieving their free exercise rights. For example, many high school students are using the Equal Access Act as leverage with school administrators to organize student clubs that school officials might otherwise disfavor. A recent example is the effort of students at El Modena High School in Orange County, California, to organize a Gay-Straight Alliance to promote the acceptance of different sexual preferences among their peers.

The impetus for the origin of the Gay-Straight Alliance at El Modena was the death of Matthew Shepard, a young man in Laramie, Wyoming, who died on October 12, 1998, after being brutally assaulted because he was gay.[6] The students' club, the Gay-Straight Alliance, has a stated goal "to raise public awareness and promote tolerance by providing a safe forum for discussion of issues related to sexual orientation and homophobia." The Orange County school board assumed jurisdiction over the students' application and rejected it on three grounds: (1) that the club has a "subject matter related to sexual conduct and sexuality," (2) that the school offers "courses that address sex" and related matters, and (3) that an "unrestricted, unsupervised student-led discussion of sexual topics is age-inappropriate and is likely to interfere with legitimate educational concerns of the [school] District in this sensitive area of sex education."[7]

Several El Modena students sued in federal court under the Equal Access Act to obtain an injunction prohibiting the school board from continuing to deny them the same access to school facilities that the school accords to other student groups. The Equal Access Act provides that if a school has a "limited open forum" for "noncurricular" student organizations, it must offer the same forum to all noncurricular students. A school has a "limited open forum" whenever it "grants an offering to or opportunity for one or more noncurriculum related student groups to meet on school premises during non-instructional time" (20 U.S.C. § 4071(b)).

Upon a finding by Judge David Carter that El Modena High School had created a "limited open forum" for "noncurricular" student clubs, he issued a preliminary injunction against the Orange County school officials, pending a full trial on the merits to decide if school officials had violated the students' free speech rights under the Equal Access Act. Regarding the controversial nature of the Gay-Straight Alliance, Judge Carter stated that "Congress passed an 'Equal Access Act' when it wanted to permit speech on school campuses. It did not pass a 'Religious Speech Access Act,' or an 'Access for All Students Except Gay Students Act' because to do so would be unconstitutional" (83 F. Supp. 2d 1135, 1142).[8]

Afterwards, Orange County's school district agreed to comply with the statutory mandate by permitting the Gay-Straight Alliance to participate alongside all noncurriculum student groups in the "limited open forum." There are, however, other ways of complying with the act. The Salt Lake City, Utah, school board chose to comply with it by ending its "limited open forum" altogether to prevent the establishment of a student club that would express "gay-positive" viewpoints.[9] Although ending the "limited open forum" for all noncurriculum-related clubs maintained neutrality, it shut down forty-six student clubs, including many traditional clubs such as Students Against Drunk Driving, the Young Republicans Club, and the Young Democrats Club. A group of students sued the Salt Lake City school board, seeking a declaration that the policy—mainly in the manner they carried it out—violated the Equal Access Act. U.S. District Judge Bruce Jenkins, though declaring that the "First Amendment protects the expression of all viewpoints, despite either their popularity or lack of general acceptance, or even the fears that particular opinions may engender," nonetheless upheld the school board's policy of excluding all but curriculum-related clubs. Judge Jenkins held that the school's policy was a "clear, express and unequivocal statement of policy" that prohibited all viewpoints that were not within the existing curriculum-related forum.[10]

The Equal Access Act of 1984[11]

Section 407. Denial of equal access prohibited

(a) Restriction of limited open forum on basis of religious, political, philosophical, or other speech content prohibited—

It shall be unlawful for any public secondary school which receives Federal financial assistance and which has a limited open forum to deny equal access or a fair opportunity to, or discriminate against, any students who wish to conduct a meeting within that limited open forum on the basis of the religious, political, philosophical, or other content of the speech at such meetings.

(b) "Limited open forum" defined—

A public secondary school has a limited open forum whenever such school grants an offering to or opportunity for one or more noncurriculum related student groups to meet on school premises during noninstructional time.

(c) Fair opportunity criteria—

Schools shall be deemed to offer a fair opportunity to students who wish to conduct a meeting within its limited open forum if such school uniformly provides that—

(1) the meeting is voluntary and student-initiated;

(2) there is no sponsorship of the meeting by the school, the government, or its agents or employees;

(3) employees or agents of the school or government are present at religious meetings only in a nonparticipatory capacity;

(4) the meeting does not materially and substantially interfere with the orderly conduct of educational activities within the school; and

(5) nonschool persons may not direct, conduct, control, or regularly attend activities of student groups.

(d) Construction of subchapter with respect to certain rights—

Nothing in this subchapter shall be construed to authorize the United States or any State or political subdivision thereof—

(1) to influence the form or content of any prayer or other religious activity;

(2) to require any person to participate in prayer or other religious activity;

(3) to expend public funds beyond the incidental cost of providing the space for student-initiated meetings;

(4) to compel any school agent or employee to attend a school meet-

ing if the content of the speech at the meeting is contrary to the beliefs of the agent or employee;

(5) to sanction meetings that are otherwise unlawful;

(6) to limit the rights of groups of students which are not of a specified numerical size; or

(7) to abridge the constitutional rights of any person.

(e) Federal financial assistance to schools unaffected—

Notwithstanding the availability of any other remedy under the Constitution or the laws of the United States, nothing in this subchapter shall be construed to authorize the United States to deny or withhold Federal financial assistance to any school.

(f) Authority of schools with respect to order, discipline, well-being, and attendance concerns—Nothing in this subchapter shall be construed to limit the authority of the school, its agents or employees, to maintain order and discipline on school premises, to protect the well-being of students and faculty, and to assure that attendance of students at meetings is voluntary.

Approved August 11, 1984.

NOTES

1. The quotation is from the opinion of Judge David O. Carter in *Colin v. Orange United School District*, 83 F. Supp. 3d 1135 (C.D. Cal. 2000).

2. See H. R. Rep. No. 98–710, p. 4 (1984), and S. Rep. No. 98–357, pp. 10–11 (1984).

3. See H. R. Rep. No. 98–710, at 3–6, and S. Rep. No. 98–357, supra, at 6–9, 11–14, which discuss *Lubbock Civil Liberties Union v. Lubbock Independent School District* (1982), and *Brandon v. Guilderland Bd. of Ed.* (1980).

4. See 130 Cong. Rec. 19236 (1984).

5. The quotation is from *Board of Education of the Westside Community Schools v. Mergens*, 1991, p. 239.

6. See "The New Gay Struggle in the Nation," *Time* 152, no. 17 (October 26, 1998).

7. *Colin v. Orange Unified School District*, 83 F. Supp. 2d 1135 (C.D. California 2000).

8. The Gay-Straight Alliance is currently one of the noncurriculum clubs at El Modena High School. See El Modena's "Clubs & Organizations" World Wide Web page (http://www.orangeusd.k12.ca.us/emhs/) [accessed March 9, 2001].

9. The policy states that "the Board of Education of Salt Lake City School District desires to promote and advance curriculum-related student clubs. However, the Board does not allow or permit student groups or organizations not directly related to the curriculum to organize or meet on school property. It is the express decision of the Board of Education of Salt Lake City School District not to allow a 'limited open forum' as that is defined by the Federal Equal Access Act, 20 U.S.C. § 4701."

10. The court did find that the school violated the Equal Access Act during the 1997–98 school year by allowing at least one noncurricular club to meet then. See the court's later memorandum opinion at *East High Gay-Straight Alliance v. Board of Education of Salt Lake City School District* (1999), which contains the orders implementing its earlier decision. Another federal district judge in Utah, in a more recent decision, found that the Salt Lake City school board violated its curriculum-related requirement by denying a student club application for PRISM (People Recognizing Important Social Movements). PRISM sought to "serve as a prism through which historical and current events, institutions and culture can be viewed in terms of the impact, experience and contributions of gays and lesbians." *East High School PRISM Club v. Cynthia Seidel* (2000).

11. Legislative History—H. R. 1310 (S. 1285). H. R. Rep. No. 98–6, Pt. 1 (Comm. on Education and Labor) and Pt. 2 (Comm. on Science and Technology); S. Rep. No. 98–151 accompanying S. 1285 (Comm. on Labor and Human Resources). Cong. Rec. Vol 129 (1983), Mar. 2, considered and passed House; Vol. 130 (1984), June 6, 26, s. 1285 considered in Senate, June 27, considered and passed Senate, amended, in lieu of S. 1285; July 25, House concurred in Senate amendment. Weekly Compilation of Presidential Documents, Vol. 20, No. 33 (1984), Aug. 11, Presidential statement.

THE NATIONAL MOTTO

JOINT RESOLUTION OF JULY 30, 1956

Finally, we take a look at the national motto that appears on coins, on treasury notes issued by the United States Mint and the Bureau of Engraving and Printing, and on many official government documents.[1] The motto "In God We Trust" was not used in any capacity by the government until an act of Congress on April 22, 1864, permitted the mint to inscribe the phrase on one-cent and two-cent coins. Although not a national motto until 1956, use of the phrase began in the early 1860s, when the secretary of the U.S. Treasury Department, Salmon P. Chase (1808–1873), later chief justice of the U.S. Supreme Court, responded to a campaign by many religious people in the country who wanted the United States to recognize God on U.S. coins. Salmon wrote the director of the mint, stating that "the trust of our people in God should be declared on our national coins. You will cause a device to be prepared . . . expressing in the fewest words and tersest words possible this national recognition."[2]

Through the years, Congress has enacted various pieces of legislation requiring other coins to bear the inscription "In God We Trust," and in 1956 it adopted the phrase as the national motto.[3] The new motto replaced *E Pluribus Unum* (out of many, one) that had been adopted by the revolutionary Congress on June 10, 1782. In rejecting *E Pluribus Unum* for "In God We Trust," Congress stated through a committee report that "it will be of great spiritual and psychological value to our country to have a clearly designated national motto of inspirational quality in plain, popularly accepted English."[4]

The designation and use of "In God We Trust" has been unsuccessfully challenged in several cases that alleged that establishing the national motto and requiring its inscription to appear on coins and currency violated the Establishment Clause.[5] In *Aronow v. United States*, the court, holding that the uses made of the motto were "secular," declared that "it is quite obvious that the national motto and the slogan on coinage and currency . . . has nothing whatsoever to do with the establishment of religion." In short, according to *Aronow*, use of the motto is "excluded from First Amendment significance because [it] has no theological or ritualistic impact" (432 F.2d 242, 243). In *Gaylor v. United States*, the court declared that the motto is "a form of 'ceremonial deism' which through historical usage and ubiquity cannot be reasonably understood to convey governmental approval of religious belief" (74 F.3d 214, 216).[6] Although the U.S. Supreme Court has not made a direct ruling on the matter, it has refused to hear any appeals in the cases.

While Congress and the courts have rallied around the flag, so to speak, when it involves the national motto, they will no doubt continue their struggle with each other and with the dual aspects of the First Amendment's freedom of religion provision as well. The battle between the two branches of government has already prompted the Subcommittee on the Constitution of the Committee on the Judiciary in the House of Representatives to conduct extensive and provocative hearings on the relationship between Congress and the courts regarding the issue of which branch of government should the ultimate authority on constitutional interpretation.[7] As Congress and the courts continue this exchange, we may have to be content with a comment by Chief Justice Warren Burger that the "course of constitutional neutrality in this area cannot be an absolutely straight line; rigidity could well defeat the basic purpose of these provisions, which is to insure that no religion be sponsored or favored, none commanded, and none inhibited. The [only] general principle deducible from the First Amendment and all that has been said by the Court is this: that we will not tolerate either governmentally established religion or governmental interference with religion. Short of those expressly proscribed governmental acts there is room for play in the joints productive of a benevolent neutrality which will permit religious exercise to exist without sponsorship and without interference" (*Waltz v. Tax Commissioner of City of New York*, 1970, p. 669).

Joint Resolution of July 30, 1956

Resolved by the Senate and House of Representatives of the United States of America in Congress assembled, *That the national motto of the United States is hereby declared to be* "In God we trust."
Approved July 30, 1956.

NOTES

1. The United States Mint and the Bureau of Engraving and Printing are part of the Department of Treasury. The Mint issues coins and the Bureau issues treasury notes.

2. "History of the Motto, 'In God We Trust,' " Fact Sheet OPC-11, U.S. Department of the Treasury, (http://www.treas.gov/opc/opc0011.html#mint) [accessed March 6, 2001].

3. Two years earlier, Congress enacted a provision that inserted "under God" in the pledge of allegiance to the national flag.

4. H. R. Rep. No. 1959, 1956 U.S. Code Cong. and Adm. News, p. 3720.

5. See *O'Hair v. Blumenthal* (1978); *Aronow v. United States* (1970); and *Gaylor v. United States* (1996).

6. The *American Heritage Dictionary* defines deism as "the belief, based solely on reason, in a God who created the universe and then abandoned it, assuming no control over life, exerting no influence on natural phenomena, and giving no supernatural revelation."

7. See "Congress, the Court, and the Constitution," Serial No. 124. Hearing before the Subcommittee on the Constitution of the Committee on the Judiciary. House of Representatives, 105th Cong., 2nd Sess., January 29, 1998.

Appendix A

List of Cited Statutes

Act for Reform in Emerging New Democracies and Support and Help for Improved Partnership with Russia, Ukraine, and the Other New Independent States, (Pub. L. 103–199, Title VIII, § 803, 107 Stat. 2329, Dec. 17, 1993

Act for the Encouragement of Learning, by Securing the Copies of Maps, Charts and Books, to the Authors and Proprietors of Such Copies, 1 Stat. 124, May 31, 1790

Act of July 4, 1840, c. 45, 6 Stat. 802

Act of Oct. 1, 1888, 25 Stat. 501

Act to Regulate the Immigration of Aliens into the United States, 32 Stat. 1213, chap. 1012, Mar. 3, 1903

Adamson Law of Sept. 3, 1916, 39 Stat. 721, chap. 436

Adolescent Family Life Act of 1981, Pub. L. 97–35, Title XX, § 955(a), 95 Stat. 578, Aug. 13, 1981

Alien Act, 1 Stat. 570, June 25, 1798

Alien Enemies Act, 1 Stat. 577, July 6, 1798

Alien Registration (Smith) Act of 1940, Pub. L. 76–670, ch. 439, 54 Stat. 670, June 28, 1940

American Indian Religious Freedom Act (AIRFA) of 1978, Pub. L. 95–341, S.J. Res. 102, 92 Stat. 469, 102, Aug. 11, 1978

American Indian Religious Freedom Act of 1978, Amendment of 1994, Pub. L. 103–344, 108 Stat. 3125, Oct. 6, 1994

Anti-Dial-a-Porn Act of 1989 (the Helms Amendment to the 1935 Communications Act), Pub. L. 101–166, Title V, § 521(1), 103 Stat. 92 1192, Nov. 21, 1989

Child Online Protection Act of 1998, Pub. L. 105–277, Div. C, Title XIV, 112 Stat. 2681–736, Oct. 21, 1998

Civil Rights Act of 1964, Pub. L. 88–352, Title VII, § 702, 78 Stat. 255, July 2, 1964

Civil Service Act of 1883, 22 Stat. 403, § 2, Jan. 16, 1883

Clayton Antitrust Act of 1914, 38 Stat. 730, chap. 323, Oct. 15, 1914

Communications Act of 1935, Amendment of 1983, Pub. L. 98–214, 97 Stat. 1470, Dec. 8, 1983

Communications Act of 1935, Amendment of 1988, Pub. L. 100–297, 102 Stat. 424, Apr. 28, 1988

Communications Act of 1935, Helms Anti-Dial-a-Porn Amendment of 1989 (*see* Anti-Dial-a-Porn Act of 1989)

Communications Decency Act of 1996, Pub. L. 104–104, Title V, 110 Stat. 133, Feb. 8, 1996

Communist Control Act of 1954, Pub. L. 83–637, ch. 886, § 2, 68 Stat. 775, Aug. 24, 1954

Community Services Block Grant Act, Pub. L. 105–285, Title II, § 201, 112 Stat. 2728, Oct. 27, 1998

Comstock Act of 1873, ch. 258, 17 Stat. 598, Mar. 3, 1873

Copyright Act of 1790, 1 Stat. 14, May 31, 1790

Copyright Act of 1976, Pub. L. 94–553, 90 Stat. 2541, Oct. 19, 1976

Corrupt Practices Act of 1925, 43 Stat. 1070, Title III, chap. 368, Feb. 28, 1925

Customs Law of 1842, 5 Stat. 566 § 28, Aug. 30, 1842

Department of the Interior and Related Agencies Appropriation Act of 1990, Pub. L. 101–121, § 304, 103 Stat. 741, Oct. 23, 1989

Draft Card Mutilation Act of 1965, Pub. L. 89–152, 79 Stat. 586, Aug. 30, 1965

Drug Abuse Control Act Amendments of 1965, Pub. L. 89–74, 79 Stat. 226, July 15, 1975

Education Consolidation and Improvement Act of 1981, Pub. L. 97–35, ch. 2, 95 Stat. 469, Aug. 13, 1981

Elementary and Secondary Education Act (ESEA) of 1965, Pub. L. 89–10, Title I, 79 Stat. 27, Apr. 11, 1965

Elementary and Secondary Education Act (ESEA) of 1965, Amendment of 1994, Pub. L. 103–382, Title I, § 101, 108 Stat. 3519, Oct. 20, 1994

Emergency Detention Act of 1950, Title II of the Internal Security (McCarran) Act of 1950, chap. 1024, Pub. L. 81–831, 64 Stat. 1019, Sept. 23, 1950

Equal Access Act of 1984, Pub. L. 98–377, Title VIII, § 801, 98 Stat. 1302, Aug. 11, 1984

Erdman Act of 1898, 30 Stat. 424, chap. 370, June 1, 1898

Espionage Act of 1917, Pub. L. 65–24, ch. 30, 40 Stat. 217, June 15, 1917

Family Planning Services and Population Research Act of 1970, Pub. L. 91–572, 84 Stat. 1506, Dec. 24, 1970

Federal Election Campaign Act, Amendments of 1974, Pub. L. 93–443, § 1, 88 Stat. 1263, Oct. 15, 1974

Federal Election Campaign Act, Amendments of 1976, Pub. L. 94–283, § 1, 90 Stat. 475, May 11, 1976

Federal Election Campaign Act, Amendments of 1980, Pub. L. 96–187, Title I, 93 Stat. 1339, Jan. 8, 1980

Flag, Pledge Amendment, 68 Stat. 249, ch. 297, June 14, 1954

Flag Protection Act of 1968, Pub. L. No. 90–381, § 1, 82 Stat. 291, July 5, 1968

Flag Protection Act, Amendment of 1989, Pub. L. 101–131, 103 Stat. 777, Oct. 28, 1989

Foundation on the Arts and Humanities Act of 1965, Pub. L. 89–209, 79 Stat. 845, Sec. 2, Sept. 29, 1965

Hatch Act of 1939, 53 Stat. 1147, August 2, 1939, amended by 54 Stat. 767, July 19, 1940

Hatch Act, Amendments of 1993, Pub. L. 103–94, Sec. 2(a), 107 Stat. 1001, Oct. 6, 1993

Improving America's Schools Act of 1994, Pub. L. 103–382, 108 Stat. 3518, Oct. 20, 1994

Income Tax Act of 1894, ch. 349, 28 Stat. 509, Aug. 27, 1894

Indian Appropriations Act of 1895, ch. 188, 28 Stat. 876, Mar. 2, 1885

Indian Appropriations Act of 1896, 29 Stat. 345, ch. 398

Internal Security (McCarran) Act of 1950, Pub. L. 81–831, ch. 1024, 64 Stat. 987, Sept. 23, 1950

Labor Management Relations (Taft-Hartley) Act, 61 Stat. 136, ch. 120, Title I, § 101, June 23, 1947

Labor-Management Reporting and Disclosure Act (Landrum-Griffin Act) of 1959, Pub. L. 86–257, Title I, 73 Stat. 519, Sept. 14, 1959

Legal Services Corporation Act, Pub. L. 93–355, 88 Stat. 378 (1974), July 25, 1974

Morrill Anti-Bigamy Law of 1862, Section 5352 of the Revised Statutes

National Defense Authorization Act for Fiscal Years 1988 and 1989, Pub. L. 100–180, § 508, 101 Stat. 1019, 1086–87, Dec. 4, 1987

National Foundation on the Arts and Humanities Act of 1990, Amendment of 1990, Pub. L. 101–512, § 103(b), 104 Stat. 1963, Nov. 5, 1990

National Labor Relations (Wagner) Act of 1935, 49 Stat. 449, ch. 372, July 5, 1935

National Motto, Joint Resolution, H.J. Res. 396, Pub. L. 84–140, ch. 795, 70 Stat. 732, July 30, 1956

Naval Appropriations Act (1867), 14 Stat. 492, ch. 173, § 3, March 2, 1867.

Newlands Act of 1913, 38 Stat. 103, chap. 323, July 15, 1913

Norris-LaGuardia Act of 1932, 47 Stat. 70, ch. 90, Mar. 23, 1932

Omnibus Consolidated Rescissions and Appropriations Act of 1996, Title V, § 504, 110 Stat. 1321–53, Apr. 26, 1996

Pendleton Act, 1883, 22 Stat. 403, ch. 27, Jan. 16, 1883

Personal Responsibility and Work Opportunity Reconciliation Act (PRWORA) of 1996, Pub. L. 104–193, Title I, § 104, 110 Stat. 2105, Aug. 22, 1996

Publicity Act of 1910, ch. 392, 36 Stat. 822, June 25, 1910, amended by ch. 33, 37 Stat. 360, August 23, 1912.

Railway Labor Act of 1926, 44 Stat. 577, ch. 347, May 20, 1926

Railway Labor Act of 1926, Amendment of 1934, 48 Stat. 1185, ch. 691, June 21, 1934

Railway Labor Act of 1926, Amendment of 1951, 64 Stat. 1238, ch. 1220, Jan. 10, 1951

Religious Freedom Restoration Act (RFRA) of 1993, Pub. L. 103–141, 107 Stat. 1488, Nov. 16, 1993

Religious Land Use and Institutionalized Persons Act (RLUIPA) of 2000, Pub. L. 106–274, 114 Stat. 803, Sept. 22, 2000

Revenue Act of 1971, Pub. L. 92–178, Title VII, § 701, Title VIII, § 801, 85 Stat. 560, Dec. 10, 1971

Sedition Act of 1798, ch. 74, 1 Stat. 596, July 14, 1798.

Sedition Act of 1918, Pub. L. 65–150, ch. 75, 40 Stat. 553, May 16, 1918

Selective Draft Law of 1917, 40 Stat. 76, ch. 15, May 18, 1917

Sherman Antitrust Act of 1890, 26 Stat. at L. 209, chap. 647, July 2, 1890

Subversive Activities Control Act of 1950, Title I of the Internal Security (McCarran) Act of 1950, Pub. L. 81–831, chap. 1024, 64 Stat. 987, Sept. 23, 1950

Tax Reform Act of 1976, Pub. L. 94–455, 90 Stat. 1520, Oct. 4, 1976

Tillman Act of 1907, ch. 420, 34 Stat. 864, Jan. 26, 1907

Transportation Act of 1920, Title III, chap. 91, 41 Stat. 456, 469, Feb. 28, 1920

Universal Military Training and Service Act of 1948, as amended by the Draft Card Mutilation Act of 1965, Pub. L. 89–152, 79 Stat. 586, Aug. 30, 1965

War Labor Disputes (Smith-Connally) Act of 1943, 57 Stat. 163, chap. 144, June 25, 1943

Appendix B

List of Cited Cases

Abrams v. United States, 250 U.S. 616 (1919)

A.C.L.U. v. Reno (*Reno I*), 521 U.S. 844 (1997)

A.C.L.U. v. Reno (*Reno II*), 31 F. Supp. 2d 473, 476 (USDC ED Penn. 1999)

A.C.L.U. v. Reno (*Reno III*), 217 F.3d 162 (3rd Cir. 2000), cert. granted, Ashcroft v. A.C.L.U., 532 U.S. 1037 (2001)

Agostini v. Felton, 521 U.S. 203 (1997)

Aguilar v. Felton, 473 U.S. 402 (1985)

Albertson v. Subversive Activities Control Board, 382 U.S. 70 (1965)

Aptheker v. Secretary of State, 378 U.S. 500 (1964)

Aronow v. United States, 432 F.2d 242 (9th Cir. 1970)

Arver et al. v. United States, 245 U.S. 366 (1918)

Bella Lewitzsky Dance Foundation v. Frohnmayer, 754 F. Supp. 774 (C.D. Cal. 1991)

Berger et al. v. United States, 255 U.S. 22 (1921)

Blawis v. Bolin, 358 F. Supp. 349 (U.S.D.C. Arizona 1973)

Board of Education of the Westside Community Schools et al v. Mergens, 496 U.S. 226 (1990)

Boerne, City of v. Flores, 521 U.S. 507 (1997)

Bowen v. Kendrick, 487 U.S. 589 (1988)

Brandon v. Guilderland Board of Education, 635 F.2d 971 (2nd Cir. 1980), cert. denied, 454 U.S. 1123 (1981)

Buckley v. Valeo, 424 U.S. 1 (1976)

Buckley v. Valeo, 519 F.2d 821 (D.C. Cir. 1975), rev'd, 424 U.S. 1 (1976)

Bullock v. Carter, 405 U.S. 134 (1972)

Burroughs v. United States, 290 U.S. 534 (1934)

Burrow-Giles Lithographic Co. v. Sarony, 111 U.S. 53 (1884)

Cantwell v. State of Connecticut, 310 U.S. 296 (1940)

Carlin Communications, Inc. v. FCC (Carlin I), 749 F.2d 113 (2d Cir. 1984)

Carlin Communications, Inc. v. FCC (Carlin II), 787 F.2d 846 (2d Cir. 1986)

Carlin Communications, Inc. v. FCC (Carlin III), 837 F.2d 546 (2d. Cir. 1988), cert. denied, 488 U.S. 924 (1988)

Charles Wolff Packing Co. v. Court of Industrial Relations, 262 U.S. 522 (1923)

Common Cause et al. v. Democratic National Committee et al, 333 F. Supp. 803 (D.D.C. 1971)

Communist Party v. Subversive Activities Control Board, 367 U.S. 1 (1961)

CSC v. Letter Carriers, 413 U.S. 548 (1973)

Debs, In re, 158 U.S. 564 (1895)

Debs v. United States, 249 U.S. 211 (1919)

Dennis v. United States, 341 U.S. 494 (1951)

Dial Information Services Corp. v. Thornburgh, 938 F.2d 1535 (2d Cir. 1991), cert. denied, 502 U.S. 1072 (1992)

Duplex Printing Press Co. v. Deering, 254 U.S. 443 (1921)

East High Gay-Straight Alliance v. Board of Education of Salt Lake City School District, 81 F. Supp. 2d 1166, 1170 (C.D. Utah, October 6, 1999)

East High Gay-Straight Alliance v. Board of Education of Salt Lake City School District, 1999 U.S. Dist. LEXIS 20254 (C.D. Utah November 30, 1999)

East High School PRISM Club v. Cynthia Seidel, 95 F. Supp.2d 1239 (C.D. Utah April 26, 2000)

Employment Division (Oregon) v. Smith, 494 U.S. 872 (1990)

Euclid v. Ambler Realty Co., 272 U.S. 365 (1926)

Everson v. Board of Education of Ewing et al, 330 U.S. 1 (1947)

Ex parte Yarbrough, 110 U.S. 651 (1884)

Flores v. Boerne, 877 F. Supp. 355, 358 (WD Tex., Mar. 1995)

Gaylor v. United States, 74 F.3d 214 (10th Cir. 1996), cert. denied, 517 U.S. 1211 (1996)

Gertz v. Robert Welch, Inc., 418 U.S. 323 (1974)

Gitlow v. New York, 268 U.S. 652 (1925)

Goldman v. Weinberger, 475 U.S. 503 (1986)

Gompers v. Buck's Stove & Range Co., 221 U.S. 418 (1911)

Griswold v. Connecticut, 381 U.S. 479 (1965)

Harmon v. Dreher, 2 Speer's Equity Reports 87 (S.C. 1843)

Harper v. Virginia State Board of Elections, 383 U.S. 663 (1966)

Harper & Row, Publishers, Inc. v. Nation Enterprises, 471 U.S. 539 (1985)

Hoffman v. United States, 445 F.2d 226 (D.C. Cir. 1971).

Johnson v. Eisentranger, 339 U.S. 763 (1950)

Joyce v. United States, 454 F.2d 971 (D.C. Cir. 1971), cert. denied, 405 U.S. 969 (1972)

Kennedy v. Bureau of Narcotics and Dangerous Drugs, 459 F.2d 415, (9th Cir. 1972), cert. denied, 409 U.S. 1115 (1973)

Larkin v. Grendel's Den, Inc., 459 U.S. 116 (1982)

Lee v. Runge, 404 U.S. 887 (1971)

Legal Services Corporation v. Velazquez, 531 U.S. 533 (2001)

Lemon v. Kurtzman, 403 U.S. 602 (1971)

Loewe v. Lawlor, 208 U.S. 274 (1908)

Lubbock Civil Liberties Union v. Lubbock Independent School District, 669 F.2d 1038, (5th Cir. 1982), cert. denied, 459 U.S. 1155 (1983)

Lubin v. Panish, 415 U.S. 709 (1974)

Mammoth Oil Co. et al. v. United States, 275 U.S. 13 (1927)

Marbury v. Madison, 5 U.S. 137 (1803)

Mather v. Roe, 432 U.S. 464 (1977)

Mazer v. Stein, 347 U.S. 201 (1954)

Mills v. Alabama, 384 U.S. 214 (1966)

Mitchell v. Helms, 530 U.S. 793 (2000)

Monitor Patriot Co. v. Roy, 401 U.S. 265, 272 (1971)

National Association for the Advancement of Colored People v. Alabama, 357 U.S. 449 (1958)

National Broadcasting Co. v. United States, 319 U.S. 190 (1943)

National Endowment for the Arts v. Finley, 524 U.S. 569 (1998)

National Labor Relations Board. v. Gissel Packing Co., 395 U.S. 575 (1969)

Near v. Minnesota, 283 U.S. 697 (1931)

Newberry v. United States, 256 U.S. 232 (1921)

Nichols v. Universal Pictures Corporation, 45 F.2d 119, 121 (2nd Cir. 1930)

Noto v. United States, 367 U.S. 290 (1961)

O'Hair v. Blumenthal, 462 F.Supp. 19 (W.D. Tex. 1978), aff'd sub nom, O'Hair v. Murray, 588 F.2d 1144 (5th Cir. 1978), cert. denied, 442 U.S. 930 (1979)

Pan American Petroleum & Transp. Co. v. United States, 273 U.S. 456 (1927)

Perry v. Sindermann, 408 U.S. 593 (1972)

Peyote Way Church of God v. Thornburgh, 922 F.2d 1210 (5th Cir. 1991)

Phoenix v. Kolodziejski, 399 U.S. 204 (1970)

Railway Employees' Dept. v. Hanson, 351 U.S. 225 (1956), rehearing denied, 352 U.S. 859 (1956)

Regan v. Taxation With Representation of Washington, 461 U.S. 540 (1983)

Reuben Quick Bear v. Leupp, 210 U.S. 50 (1908)

Reynolds v. United States, 98 U.S. 145 (1879)

Roe v. Wade, 410 U.S. 113 (1973)

Rosenberg v. United States, 346 U.S. 273 (1953)

Roth v. United States, 354 U.S. 476 (1957)

Rust v. Sullivan, 500 U.S. 173 (1991)

Sable Communications of California, Inc. v. FCC, 492 U.S. 115 (1989)

Scales v. United States, 367 U.S. 203 (1961)

Schenck v. United States, 249 U.S. 47 (1919)

Sherbert v. Verner, 374 U.S. 398 (1963)

Simon v. Eastern Kentucky Welfare Rights Organization, 426 U.S. 26 (1976)

Smiley v. Holmes, 285 U.S. 355 (1932)

Smith v. Goguen, 415 U.S. 566 (1974)

Spence v. Washington, 418 U.S. 405 (1974)

Street v. New York, 394 U.S. 576 (1969)

Stromberg v. California, 283 U.S. 359 (1931)

Texas v. Johnson, 491 U.S. 397 (1989)

Thomas v. Collins, 323 U.S. 516 (1945)

Tilton v. Richardson, 403 U.S. 672 (1971)

Tinker v. Des Moines Independent Community School District, 393 U.S. 503 (1969)

United Federal Workers of America (C.I.O.) et al. v. Mitchell et al., 56 F.Supp. 621 (D.D.C., Aug. 3, 1944)

United Public Workers of America (C.I.O.) et al v. Mitchell et al, 330 U.S. 75 (1947)

United States v. Boyll, 774 F.Supp. 1333, D.C. N.M. (1991), appeal dismissed, 1992 U.S. App. LEXIS 14537, No. 91–2235, (10th Cir. 1992)

United States v. Classic, 313 U.S. 299 (1941)

United States v. Dennis, 183 F.2d 201, 212 (2nd Cir. 1950), aff'd 341 U.S. 494 (1951)

United States v. Eichman, 496 U.S. 310 (1990)

United States v. Ferguson, 302 F.Supp. 1111, (N.D. Calif. August 8, 1969)

United States v. Hall, 248 F.150 (D. Mont. January 27, 1918)

United States v. O'Brien, 391 U.S. 367 (1968)

United States v. Robel, 389 U.S. 258 (1967)

United States v. Schutte, 252 F.212, 213 (D. N.D. 1918)

United States v. Skinner, 25 F.3d 1314 (6th Cir. 1994)

United States v. Three Cases of Toys, 28 F.Cas. 112, U.S.D.C. S.D. New York (1843)

United States v. Wurzbach, 31 F.2d 774 (W.D. Texas, April 3, 1929)

United States ex Rel. Turner v. Williams, 194 U.S. 279 (1904)

Walz v. Tax Commission of the City of New York, 397 U.S. 664 (1970)

Watson v. Jones, 13 Wall. (U.S.) 679 (1871)

Watts v. United States, 394 U.S. 705 (1969)

Wheaton v. Peters, 33 U.S. 591 (1834)

Widmar v. Vincent, 454 U.S. 263 (1981)

Wisconsin v. Yoder, 406 U.S. 205 (1972)

Yates v. United States, 354 U.S. 298 (1957)

Zacchini v. Scripps-Howard Broadcasting Co., 433 U.S. 562 (1977)

Index

About the Author

CLYDE E. WILLIS is Associate Professor of Political Science at Middle Tennessee State University.